FIERCE

HOW COMPETING FOR
MYSELF CHANGED EVERYTHING

ALY RAISMAN

WITH BLYTHE LAWRENCE

LITTLE, BROWN AND COMPANY
New York   Boston

To my parents, whose love and support
have made all the difference

Dear Reader,

The year since *Fierce* first came out has been one of the most eventful of my life, full of challenging, empowering, and illuminating moments. I had always envisioned writing a book one day, as I kept a journal as a young girl. But sharing thoughts and feelings in a journal is one thing, taking the step forward to write my first book was a whole different experience for me. So the book you're holding is very personal and came from my heart. And while it was a step outside my comfort zone, something amazing happened once I started sharing my life experiences and meeting readers: You started sharing your stories with me. From preschoolers who came to book events in leotards to older kids who asked intelligent and hopeful questions to people of all ages who said that hearing my voice encouraged them to raise their own—I see you. And you inspire me.

Turn the page to see how and why I fell in love with gymnastics, how I mastered skills I once thought were beyond my reach, and what it was like to train intensely while trying to balance school and a social life. Join me on the floor of major competitions—including two Olympic Games—and behind the scenes of my life. Along the way, I reveal the joys of my happiest triumphs and the struggles of my toughest moments, as well as the life lessons that helped get me through. Thanks to supportive people and my belief that staying kind and working hard would lead to success, I stayed positive and kept reaching for my goals.

All these experiences helped shape who I am today, even as I continue to grow and become ever more comfortable in my own skin. And support from people like you, who care enough to discover my story and even to share your own stories with me, has helped strengthen and sustain me as I continue to share my story.

Thank you so much for reading *Fierce*. I hope you enjoy it and are able to take away something for yourself, too.

Love,

Aly Raisman

November 2018

PROLOGUE

Rio de Janeiro, Brazil
August 2016

I'm sitting on the floor of the airy warm-up gym in the Rio
Olympic Arena and fiddling with the fraying white rug beneath
my feet, grateful for a distraction. The countdown to the 2016
Olympic Games is officially over, but these final minutes of
waiting before the women's gymnastics competition begins are
killing me.

Out of the corner of my eye, I cast a glance at my teammates. Like me, they're staring off into space, each in her own
little world. Every now and then we come back to earth for a
second, make eye contact, and give one another a little smile of
encouragement. We don't exchange words. After weeks of sharing arduous training sessions, ice-cold recovery sessions, and

laughter-filled leotard fittings, we've become so close that we don't have to.

The sounds of coaches giving last-minute corrections and advice in several languages float across the gym. I couldn't help thinking that our own warm-up could have gone better. Despite all our careful preparation, there had been errors on bars, falls off the beam, and out-of-bounds landings on floor—all the classic pre-competition jitters. Even national team coordinator Martha Karolyi, usually so full of energy, had seemed a little quiet.

The announcer's booming voice breaks into my reverie. "Attention, gymnasts: Please make your way to the hallway to prepare for competition." We've heard these words at practically every meet since we were children, but this time they convey a reality that is thrilling and utterly terrifying at the same time. This is it. All the work I've put in all those years, all those repetitions, all those sit-ups and pull-ups, all that chalk and tape—all that will be tested for the next several days, starting right now.

As usual, Martha wastes no time. "Okay, girls, let's do this!" she says, her voice brisk and commanding. "We are prepared. Just like practice." We stand up and fall into line, just like at the beginning and end of each training session. One by one, she gives each of us a nod of approval, projecting reassurance and calm. Watching her, I feel my breathing start to return to normal. If Martha believes we can do it, we can do it. We are ready.

It's cold in the dimly lit hallway that connects the warm-up gym to the arena. We line up shortest to tallest: Simone Biles. Laurie Hernandez. Madison Kocian. Gabby Douglas. Me. Barefoot in our patriotic leotards, we wait for our cue. Some of the gymnasts from other countries have cupped their hands to their mouths and are blowing warm air into the palms of their hands. The minutes pass slowly, each one like an hour. I feel like I need to keep moving, do anything to make the time go by more quickly, so I run in place.

Without warning, the wave of confidence I've been riding evaporates and the nerves come rushing back in. My stomach turns and I begin to gag, struggling to regain my calm. I focus on taking deep, slow breaths, even though my heart is pounding and my throat feels like it's closing up. I can't believe this moment is finally here. All my hard work will be put to the test.

Pull yourself together, I tell myself. *Remember that you've worked so, so hard—you deserve to compete well.* I close my eyes and repeat this over and over in my head as I breathe in slow, deep breaths.

I peer around the dark tunnel in search of Mihai, my coach since I was ten. One of the advantages of having known each other so long is that we can communicate without using words. In this moment, my face tells him I need to see reassurance in his eyes, I need his confidence. Mihai smiles at me. I exhale.

Next, I look to Martha. She catches my eye and nods her

head. Right now, her eyes say, *You can do it, Aly. Everything will be okay.*

In the arena, the announcer is talking. Suddenly, like a fuzzy radio signal coming sharply into focus, we hear:

"The United States of America!"

As we begin moving forward, there's a loud roar from the thousands of fans in the stands as they anticipate the entrance of the reigning Olympic team champions. It's real now. The last thing that registers as we walk out of the darkness is Martha's voice. She's yelling in her strong Romanian accent, "Let's go, girls. It will be a good one!"

Yes, it will. As I step into the cheerful green arena with its shiny new equipment and white Olympic rings everywhere, I hide my nerves. With my head held high and a genuine smile spreading from ear to ear, I give myself a moment to take it all in. To savor the feeling of a dream as it comes true. I did it. I am one of the five: The Final Five, representing the United States of America on the Olympic stage.

As we make our way toward the floor exercise, I allow myself to embrace the journey I've taken. I picture another Aly, age eight, sitting on my living room floor a foot away from the TV, watching a different team enter a different arena for their own Olympic moment. Seeing the US women's team march in to compete at the 1996 Olympic Games in Atlanta filled me with a passion for gymnastics that would never fade. My smile grows wider, thinking of some eight-year-old out there, who might be watching us right now with a dream growing in their mind. Maybe that kid will *know*, just like I did, that they will be out here someday.

From eight years old on, I had dreamed of nothing but this. Of course, I had no idea how improbable that dream was. I had no idea how many years of my life I would dedicate to it, or how hard it would be to get there—and then to get there a second time.

In those days, the only thing on my mind was how much I loved gymnastics and how badly I wanted to be one of those women, marching into the arena in an American flag leotard, radiating confidence and ready to compete for Team USA.

The best thing about being a kid with a dream is that it never occurs to you that it might not be possible. As I walk into the Rio Olympic Arena fourteen years later, just for a second, I become that eight-year-old again.

In this moment, no dream is too big.

CHAPTER 1

SUPERGIRLS

Newton, Massachusetts
Summer 2002

Chills of anticipation raced up my spine. Staring at the TV, I bounced up and down on the couch, so excited I could hardly sit still. No matter how many times I watched the tape, it felt like I was seeing it for the first time.

The crowd inside the Georgia Dome was on their feet and already making a deafening amount of noise as the seven American women filed into the arena to begin the 1996 Olympic gymnastics women's team final.

The excitement that greeted the US women's gymnastics team as they marched briskly toward the uneven bars was the most captivating thing I had ever seen. The air in the arena was so supercharged with electricity that I could feel it in my own living room, through the screen, six years after the fact.

My journey to Rio really began with those Olympic Games. I was only two years old on that warm July evening in 1996 when the Magnificent Seven (as they came to be known) kicked off a competition that concluded with one of the most dramatic endings in sports history.

I wasn't watching that night, but my grandfather was. He knew that my mom, a former high school gymnast, would be interested in seeing the event, so he taped it for her. When he gave her the tape a few days later, my busy mom thanked him, then laid the tape aside and promptly forgot about it.

She unearthed it on a quiet afternoon at home six years later. I can still see her standing by the VCR in our living room in Newton, Massachusetts, with its dark green leather couch and green and gold carpet.

The smell of chicken roasting in the kitchen wafted into the room. I was attempting to keep an eye on my two-year-old sister, Chloe, who toddled around while my two-month-old sister, Madison, slept in her portable crib nearby.

As we waited for my dad to get home from picking up my brother, Brett, from hockey practice, Mom popped the tape into the VCR and stood back with an air of satisfaction.

"I was going through some old tapes and came across this. I think you'll like it, Aly," she said with a knowing smile as she fiddled with the remote.

Watching TV with my mom was our special time together, and I cherished it. Raising four young children didn't leave a lot of time for kicking back, but whenever she wasn't too busy, we would sit down on the couch and pick out a tape to watch.

Our choice usually involved our favorite sport—you guessed it: gymnastics. Gymnastics wasn't broadcast as often as the endless stream of football and basketball games, but on the rare occasions gymnastics competitions were televised, we made sure to tape them. I would watch those tapes over and over until I knew all the routines by heart.

My mom would eventually get tired of yet another screening of a US Championships or an invitational, but I couldn't get enough. When I wasn't doing homework or at gymnastics practice, I was parked in front of the TV, watching one of those tapes.

One day I want to be just like them, I thought, enchanted by the figures flying across the screen. I had already decided that I would be a gymnast when I grew up. Well, either that or a pop star, like Britney Spears, my favorite singer. That sounded good, too.

As they lined up, the faces of the seven US team members—Amanda Borden, Amy Chow, Dominique Dawes, Shannon Miller, Dominique Moceanu, Jaycie Phelps, and Kerri Strug—projected concentration, confidence, and strength. In their American flag leotards, they were my Supergirls. All they were missing were capes.

The American women had never won an Olympic team gold medal, and in Atlanta, they were considered underdogs to the powerhouse Russian and Romanian teams, who were expected to battle it out for gold. Though the United States managed to finish second in the qualifying rounds, Russia and Romania were still favored to finish ahead of the United States in the final. But on that magical night, lifted by the support of the home crowd and their belief in themselves, their sterling performances surpassed all expectations.

On the unpredictable uneven bars and precarious balance beam, they were confident and flying high. One near perfect routine followed the next. It seemed like nothing could stop them.

By the time the final event rolled around, the Olympic team gold medal was within reach. It all came down to Kerri Strug— if she landed one of her two vaults, the Americans would be the Olympic champions for the first time ever.

On her first attempt, the unthinkable happened: Kerri landed short, and fell to the ground. When she stood up and walked back down the runway, she was limping badly. But she had to do one good vault to clinch gold for the team (at the time, gymnasts were allowed to count the best score out of two vaults. Today, in elite competition, gymnasts only perform one vault).

Her coach, Bela Karolyi, urged her on from the sidelines. "You can do it, Kerri!" he cried.

Blocking out the pain, she raced down the vault runway and launched herself into the air. She landed well this time, but immediately raised her left leg in pain. She had to hop sideways to salute the judges, signaling the end of her routine. Then she collapsed onto the mat.

It could not have been more dramatic. Seeing them standing on that medal podium, hands over their hearts as the US flag was raised over the arena, filled me with eagerness. I was certain I wanted to be standing in their shoes—or more accurately, their leotards—one day.

The US team's victory wasn't the only moment that had me mesmerized. Of all the events—vault, uneven bars, balance beam, and floor exercise—floor was the one that captivated me the most. It was the only event where gymnasts got to perform to music, allowing spectators a glimpse of their different personalities and styles.

One gymnast stood out from all the others. Her name was Liliya Podkopaeva, and at first glance you would have thought she was a ballerina. In her dark green velvet leotard with its delicate row of rhinestones edging the neckline and with her brown hair swept into a neat bun, the seventeen-year-old Ukrainian carried herself like she was taking the stage in a grand theater.

She flew across the equipment, flipping, leaping, twirling, and making it all look effortless. Her floor routine was sheer magic. Heels tucked squarely into a corner of the mat, she began by sweeping her arms over her head in a graceful arc before rising high up on her toes and taking off. Liliya's masterful performances on all events in Atlanta earned her the Olympic all-around gold medal, given to the gymnast with the highest total score for all four events. In addition to all-around, Liliya won floor gold. I was in awe of her tumbling passes, which were unique and very difficult.

From my tapes and lessons at Exxcel Gymnastics in Newton, Massachusetts, I already knew a few things about the sport. I knew, for example, that there were different kinds of competitions at the Olympics and other major meets, including a team competition, the individual all-around (which determined the best overall gymnast), and individual event finals (won by the best on each event). I didn't yet have a complete grasp of how a gymnast wound up at the Olympics, but I knew that was where I dreamed of being.

As I watched the Magnificent Seven stand atop the Olympic medal podium and listened to the national anthem, I felt pride well up inside of me.

The 1996 tape was my favorite. I'd watch it over and over, taking in every little detail. I was studying it, trying to soak up the gymnasts' confidence, their attitudes, and the way they moved. No matter how many times I watched it, my heart pounded like I was seeing everything for the first time.

When short "fluff" segments showed the top gymnasts training in their own countries, I discovered that there was more to admire about them than their gymnastics. Liliya, for instance, was shown to spend her only day off going to watch ballet with her coaches to study new techniques—she lived and breathed gymnastics. Some of the best gymnasts had overcome great hardships to realize their Olympic dreams. Some trained in poor conditions, with little medical support if they got sick or hurt. Some were already helping to support their families, even though they were still teenagers. Their stories inspired me, but I didn't yet truly understand how much work and how many tough days were behind those medals and smiles. What I saw were strong, confident young women—and I wanted to be just like them.

From that day on I was absolutely convinced that I would one day go to the Olympics, too. I had it all planned out: My teammates and I would win the team gold, like the Magnificent Seven had, and then I would win the floor gold, like Liliya.

What would it be like, I wondered, to compete at the Olympics in a beautiful red, white, and blue leotard, to wave victoriously to the cheering crowd with my teammates? What would it be like to stand on a medal podium, feeling the weight of a gold medal around my neck and knowing that I was the best in the world at something? These thoughts would propel me to my feet, and I would dance around the living room on my toes, imitating Liliya's floor choreography.

"Aly, dinner's ready!" my mom would call from the kitchen.

"I'm practicing, Mom, just a few more minutes!" I'd plead, my eyes glued to the screen.

Soon I realized that if I grew up to be an Olympic gymnast, I might become famous! That meant people would want my autograph. I had better practice my signature, I figured. Soon I was signing my name to everything I could get my hands on... including the living room wall with a permanent marker.

For some reason my parents were less than thrilled—even after I explained that I had just been practicing.

CHAPTER 2

CARTWHEELS

Newton, Massachusetts
1994–2002

The name on my birth certificate, issued May 25, 1994, reads Alexandra Rose Raisman, but for the first few years of my life everyone called me Lexie. Until I was five, I thought my given name actually *was* Lexie. When I learned the truth, I was indignant that people had been calling me the wrong name all those years. "Please call me Alexandra. It's my real name!" I begged my parents, my grandparents, and everyone else.

Though I've always adored my regal first name, I can admit now that "Alexandra" was a mouthful for other five-year-olds. In first grade, I met a girl named Allison, whom everyone called Ali. We became inseparable and wanted to match in every way, right down to our first names. Since she was "Ali with an *i*," I became "Aly with a *y*."

It was as "Aly Raisman" that I trained at Exxcel Gymnastics in Newton, Massachusetts.

It's hard to say exactly where I got my Olympic athletic genes. My dad, Rick, a former hockey and baseball player, likes to joke that it's all him. There's no doubt where I got my love for the sport, though: That comes from my mom, Lynn, who did gymnastics as a child and later competed on her high school team.

It was Mom's idea to enroll in a "Mommy and Me" class at a local gymnastics club near our house in Newton when I was just eighteen months old.

In the beginning, it was just a fun activity for my mom to do with an energetic toddler who loved playing in the gym. My parents also thought I was quite muscular for a two-year-old. After the Mommy and Me class ended, Mom signed me up for a toddlers-only class, then a thirty-minute beginner class.

For an on-the-go kid like me, a gymnastics gym was a paradise. With its colorful blocks to climb on, springy trampolines to bounce on, and a pit filled with soft foam blocks to dive into, a gym is the coolest playhouse any young child can imagine.

When I was five, an instructor approached my mom about having me do a pre-team tryout. Mom was hesitant at first. It seemed strange to her, bringing such a young child to a tryout for a team. She worried that I was too young for the stress of competition, but the instructor talked her into it. They explained the tryout would be with a different coach, one who would be able to measure my potential.

When we arrived on the day of the tryout, I was the youngest child there—all the other kids were seven or eight. Mom told me it was just another lesson. She didn't want me to know that it was a tryout so that I wouldn't be disappointed if things didn't work out. Since even then I couldn't get enough of the gym, I galloped off happily and tried to do whatever they asked.

At the end of the tryout, the coach came over to my mother. "I'm sorry," she said apologetically. "But Aly's not physically strong enough to be on the pre-team."

Mom hadn't felt confident about bringing me in the first place, and she was embarrassed that this coach might have thought she was a pushy stage mother for bringing her five-year-old to a tryout, but she shrugged it off. Climbing some sort of team ladder didn't matter in the least to her. I obviously adored gymnastics and was happy at the gym, and that was the most important thing.

As for me, I remained oblivious that there had been a tryout and that I'd been rejected. I continued with a weekly hour-long class, happily swinging on the bars, picking my way across the balance beam, and zooming around on the bouncy floor mat.

And that, Mom figured, would be that.

On weekends, my family would often get together at my mother's parents' house. My grandfather Richard's bulky desktop Apple computer was an object of fascination to me and my younger brother, Brett. (My first word, "apple," was apparently a reference to the computer, not the fruit.) At each visit, Brett and I would run through the house, or head next door to greet Grandma and Grandpa's neighbor, who we called the "Cookie Lady" because she always had delicious cookies for us each time we rang the bell, just as she had for our mother when she was our age.

Dad often brought his video camera on family outings. It was clear to everyone when he would begin to film; as soon as the camera turned on, I perked up. I loved being the center of attention. Somehow I got the idea that if I stated the date that I would be the first to be filmed each time the recorder came on. Usually after that I'd belt out a song, most often by Britney Spears or Christina Aguilera. Brett, meanwhile, would execute his Power Rangers dance and then take a break to search for his favorite snack, a bagel with cream cheese.

I was always in motion. Whatever surface there was, I was jumping on it! One of my favorite places to jump was on my parents' bed. Their mattress was so bouncy, it was almost as good as the trampoline at the gym. I vividly remember hopping up and down on it excitedly one day in May 2000 as we waited for my mom to arrive home from a special Florida trip. I was getting a new sister!

Mom and Dad always wanted a big family, but after Brett was born in 1996, Mom was advised against another pregnancy. My parents had room in their hearts for more children, so they decided to adopt. One day my parents got a call and left for Florida for Chloe's birth. I was so excited to have another girl in the family. I was already planning how I'd teach her to sing and dance and do gymnastics with me.

My mom woke me up in the middle of the night to introduce me to my baby sister, Chloe Elizabeth Raisman, a little bundle with a full head of dark hair who had been born only a few weeks before. After a while, Mom laid her carefully on the bed, and I resumed my jumping exercises.

"Aly, stop jumping on the bed!" cried my dad's mother, whom we all called Bubbie and who lived a few miles away. "You're going to squish the baby!" I hadn't thought of that.

Horrified, I stopped. Grandma and Bubbie frantically gestured for me to come down.

Chloe was a little over a year old when my parents got a call from the adoption agency, who informed them that Chloe had a sibling on the way. Might our family want to adopt a second child? My parents immediately said yes, and Brett and I were so excited when they told us that we broke out into our Power Rangers singing and dancing routine. That's how Madison, born in March 2002, completed our family. This time, I knew better than to jump on the bed when Mom laid her down.

I adored being a big sister. My siblings and I would spend hours playing together. Since I was the oldest, I would pretend to be their mom, mimicking the things my mom would do for us. I took immense pride in "cooking" imaginary meals for them and taking them places in our little motorized play car that could actually be driven around the driveway. When Chloe and Madison were little, they had trouble pronouncing my nickname. When they tried to say "Aly," it came out "Lala." My family still calls me that today.

When friends came over, we would play school, pretending to sit in a classroom and learn things. When it was my turn to be the teacher, I relished standing at the center of the "classroom," writing importantly on our kid-sized whiteboard, or play-grading papers. I'll admit it: I loved being in charge.

Bubbie would take her six oldest grandkids out every Friday. Brooke, Mikayla, Tyler, Brett, Drew, and myself would all pile into the back of her minivan, which she had bought because it was the only thing you could fit so many grandchildren into. As she drove, Bubbie would quiz us: "If I have five apples, and I get two more apples, how many apples do I have?" "Seven!" we'd chorus in unison.

"All right, if I have eight bananas and three pineapples, how many bananas do I have?" she'd ask. "Eight!" we'd cry, delighted not to have fallen for the trick. "You can't fool us!"

Bubbie was a lady with very good taste. She worked several years in retail and had a great eye for clothes. Her signature item was a golden Burberry raincoat, which she wore everywhere. One of our favorite games was to stealthily hide crackers and pretzels in the hood of the coat. Inevitably, the next time it rained, Bubbie would flip her hood up and the pretzels and crackers would fall everywhere as we shrieked with laughter. Bubbie would be annoyed, but she got over it quickly when she saw us giggling uncontrollably. She loved us unconditionally.

At night, my sisters would come into my room and cuddle up in my bed. We'd pull the covers up over our heads and pretend the bed was a boat and that we were adrift on a stormy sea. Every now and then I would cautiously stick my head out from under the covers, scanning for a lighthouse as we plotted ways to survive. Eventually, we'd fall asleep, and our parents would find us all cuddled up together the next morning.

In my waking hours, I was a little tornado of energy,

careening here and there, cartwheeling through the kitchen while my mom was trying to cook, kicking into handstands against the living room wall, and being an all-around nuisance. Several jars from Mom's collection of antique spice jars fell victim to my flying feet.

I may have been a pro at doing cartwheels, but I was not so graceful at ordinary things, like walking. Going from one room to another, it seemed like I would knock over anything in my path. I tripped over everything, especially my own feet. At restaurants with my family or at the local temple's monthly Friday night dinners with my aunts and uncles and cousins, I would invariably spill soda as I was pouring it—on myself, on the table, on the floor, everywhere, it seemed, but into the cup it was destined for.

I was less accident-prone when there was nothing around for me to knock into. Maybe that's why I spent so much time playing sports in wide open spaces. Besides gymnastics, I took ice skating lessons at the local rink, and played softball, basketball, and soccer, which my dad coached.

Through it all, gymnastics remained my favorite activity. The subject of pre-team came up again when I was six, and this time I was invited to join without trying out. Being on the preteam involved longer hours at the gym, so I had to give up some of my other activities, though I stuck with soccer.

I absolutely loved pre-team. There were no competitions,

but I got to go to the gym more often. Pre-team classes were held later in the afternoon, so practice times overlapped with those of older girls who were skilled enough to be members of the gym's team.

Gymnasts who are just beginning to compete start at the beginner team level. If they do well, they usually advance through the years with the goal of progressing up to level 10. A small handful of gymnasts qualify to go beyond level 10, to what is referred to as elite. This is the path I would ultimately choose. Many of my club teammates continued working at level 10 and a number were able to get college scholarships.

The team girls—who participated in Saturday competitions in shiny red leotards—became my idols. I thought they were amazing. Someday being as good as they were became my not-so-secret goal.

At the end of the year, most of the girls in my pre-team class moved up to the team level, with the goal of competing that season. But my coaches felt I wasn't ready, and decided it was best to have me repeat pre-team.

The problem was floor. I was having a hard time with my roundoff back handspring. Without mastering it, I wouldn't be able to move forward.

Having a strong roundoff back handspring is extremely important for all gymnasts. A roundoff is a cartwheel where both feet land at the same time, while a back handspring is a backflip where your hands touch the floor. With these two skills as a base, the gymnast can punch into more difficult flips and twists. That goes for Olympic gymnasts as well as pre-teamers.

Skills didn't come easy to me. In those early years I was so excited to be at gymnastics class that it didn't even occur to me that I was supposed to be making small modifications to improve my technique.

As a result, every turn looked exactly like the last one: I would canter happily into my roundoff, throw myself backward, and immediately bend my arms, causing my head to touch the floor before my feet hit the ground and killing any backward momentum. No matter how often the coach would gently remind me to straighten my arms, I did not seem to hear it. As a result, my back handspring was more like a back headspring. And it stayed that way for some time.

Fortunately, at my age, no one was in a rush for me to advance to the next level. Making sure their gymnasts had a good foundation was the most important thing to my coaches, Rett, Pete, Alex, Gary, Melissa, and Tatiana. None of this registered with me. I still zipped around having a blast, oblivious to things like levels.

The following year, I was finally ready to move up to the team, which meant practicing a few more hours each week. I kept playing soccer on the weekends, but was starting to miss out on some playdates with friends.

A few weeks into the season, we were all measured for our

competition leotards and warm-up suits. I was so excited to be getting a real competition leotard, like the team girls I admired. But I was still behind my teammates skills-wise, and it was privately suggested to my mother that we wait to order anything. My coaches weren't sure I'd be ready to compete that year, and they didn't want my mom paying for a leotard and warm-up suit if they weren't going to be used.

Mom never told me I was behind. When I found out that a few of the girls on my team had competed in a meet, my mom said they were staggering the gymnasts and that some girls would compete before others. I still didn't think anything of it. I kept going to practice and counting down the days before I could put on that red team leotard and show off my skills for the judges. All day at school, I daydreamed about practice. At practice, I fantasized about competing.

When I would talk to my parents about how excited I was to compete, my dad would say, "Just keep working hard. Hard work always pays off."

It finally clicked that practice wasn't only about trying things out and having fun, but actually making improvements in order to be the best I could be.

Once I realized that, I improved so rapidly that I was cleared to participate in my first competition. I actually had to borrow a competition leotard from my friend Abbey, because mine was ordered so late, it wouldn't arrive in time.

I was so excited and felt ready and happy, no pressure. *Today is the first meet of my life*, I thought, *and I'm going to make it a good one.*

And I did. I enjoyed competing and I won the all-around.

"I'm so proud of you," Mom said in the car that night as we drove home. "But let me tell you something: It's the person you are who matters, not how high you place. Remember that when you're out there."

Back at the gym, I continued to admire the older team girls. The best group were the level 10s. I watched in awe as they did double backflips on floor, marveling at the power and coordination that went into that skill. When they were in the gym, I would stare, fascinated. Sometimes I even forgot what I was doing because I was so focused on watching them.

"Aly! Anybody home?" Pete would tease. "You need to concentrate on what we're learning here and not looking around so much, okay?"

I might not have been focusing on what my coaches were saying, but I was concentrating, hard, on what I wanted to achieve. *One day*, I vowed as I watched the level 10s, *I will be as good as they are.*

There was always something about gymnastics that made me feel unstoppable. While I was never the most talented one on the team, I had the most important component for success: a love for what you do. If you love something and work hard at it, nothing can stop you from achieving spectacular results.

As I got older and chose to dedicate myself more and more to the sport, I made the decision to miss out on parties and family vacations—even my high school graduation ceremony!—because I had to train.

But the downsides always paled in comparison to the high I got from flipping across the floor or nailing a tumbling series on the balance beam. Despite the challenges, I always gladly came back for more.

The story of my life in gymnastics is an underdog one. From pre-team right up to making the Olympic team, people doubted whether I'd be successful. But that year and all the rest that followed, I was never made to feel like I was any less talented than the other girls. Mom never made comparisons. Dad kept repeating that the hardest worker always finds their way.

Even the Magnificent Seven faced their moments of adversity, I'd remind myself. If they had found ways to work through them, so would I.

My parents focused on being parents and left the coaching to the professionals. They never pushed me, but they saw the value of being part of something that made me leap out of bed, excited for the day.

I would never wake up one day to find I was the best on the

team. Quite the opposite: I was often the one who struggled the most to keep up with my teammates. But I worked ferociously, pushing myself so hard that I would eventually catch up. Struggling, falling behind, and climbing my way back became my normal.

CHAPTER 3

THE A TEAM

Newton, Massachusetts

2004

Life at Exxcel was bliss. There was always something new to try, and the coaches were all so kind. Alex in particular took real joy in seeing his students grow and learn new skills. He was also very patient, no matter how silly my teammates and I occasionally got.

Rett could always make us laugh. She called me "Alberto," and when I did something she liked she would put her fingers to her lips the way you do after a good meal and say "Alberto, *bravissima!*" in an Italian accent. She emphasized the importance of flexibility and artistry in gymnastics. Having straight legs and good toe point was an important part of achieving good scores in competition, she explained.

My teammates and I loved coming to the gym. Only one

thing could have made it better: being allowed to spend more time there.

"Just one more turn, Alex," I begged. "Pleeease?"

"No," Alex said, firmly but kindly. "Practice is over, Aly. It's time to go home."

"But why?" I asked, jumping up and down. I was so close to mastering a new skill on beam, and I was itching to try it a few more times. "I'm not tired at all!" I added brightly, hoping that would convince him.

Alex looked at me and smiled. I was nine, and he and I had been having this conversation on a weekly basis. I was inexhaustible in the gym, always wanting to take a thousand turns and never wanting to leave. Alex had been an elite gymnast in the USSR, a world medalist, and a two-time Olympic team member, although boycott and injury would prevent him from participating both times.

"Do you know what burnout is, Aly?" he asked one day. I shook my head. "It's when you do too much, and then you risk getting hurt, or just getting tired of it," he explained. "I don't want that to happen to you. A big part of being a high-level athlete is knowing when to practice and when to rest. I'll see you next time, all right?"

Perplexed, I went to meet my dad, who was waiting for me in the parents' viewing area as usual. I could understand burnout when it came to something like homework. But gymnastics? I couldn't imagine ever getting tired of that.

To complement our training, Rett started preparing us to test for a special program called TOPs. This stood for "Talent Opportunity Program," and it was a way of measuring the potential of young gymnasts all across the nation.

We would practice in the gym, and then travel all the way to Binghamton, New York, for a day of physical testing, Rett explained. We would be asked to demonstrate twenty chin-ups, twenty leg lifts, ten press handstands (where you start from a sitting position and use your upper body strength to "press" yourself into a handstand), ten cast handstands (done on the bar), a timed fifty-yard dash, a vertical jump, sixty-five push-ups in one minute, and various markers of our flexibility. It wasn't just about the numbers. We also had to show proper form.

The gymnasts with the best TOPs test scores from every region of the country were invited to the National Team Training Center at the Karolyi Ranch in Texas for another round of testing. The top twenty there made the TOPs A team, while the next twenty made the TOPs B team. Both TOPs teams were also invited back to the ranch for a brief training camp during the year.

I had heard about the Karolyis, but I learned about their ranch through TOPs. Martha Karolyi and her husband Bela had coached the great Nadia Comaneci in Romania before coming to the United States. They settled on a ranch in Texas and

opened a gym on the property, and they had been very successful. Martha Karolyi was now the US national team coordinator.
I didn't know *exactly* what that meant, but I understood it was
important. The national teams often went to train at the Karolyi
Ranch, where Martha personally monitored everyone's progress. If you wanted to go to the Olympics, you had to impress
Martha.

I gave my all during the TOPs tests, and hoped for a good
outcome. Some time later, I was at Bubbie's house when my parents got a call that I had made the B team. I was most excited that
my teammates Stephanie and Petra and I all made TOPs together.

At the ranch, we slept in cabins and explored the property,
which housed Bela's collection of exotic animals. Before we left,
we all signed our names in Sharpie on the cabin wall.

It was a huge treat to travel to Texas and work out in the
same gym where the national team prepared for big competitions. But the B team trained separately from the A team. Before
long, I wanted more.

I returned from TOPs camp invigorated, determined to work
harder than ever. The competitive season flew by happily until a
rumor circulated that Rett and Pete had accepted jobs at different gyms. My teammates whispered about it as we chalked our
hands for bars and waited to take our turns on beam.

Petra, Stephanie, and I were heartbroken when we found out the rumor was true. I loved the team coaches at Exxcel, and formed a wonderful bond with them over the years. It was under their direction that my friends and I had begun the long climb toward the elite level, and our eyes were constantly looking upward.

Rett managed the TOPs program. Without her guidance, I worried I might never make the TOPs A team and get a chance to show Martha Karolyi what I could do.

Petra, Stephanie, and I held an emergency conference as we sat stretching one day.

"What are you going to do?" Petra asked. "Do you think you might try another gym?"

I was taken aback. Exxcel felt like my second home. I had never considered leaving.

Petra had other ideas. "I might go to Brestyan's," she said thoughtfully. "Their team is really good. And everyone says Mihai Brestyan is a really good coach!"

Stephanie and I got kind of quiet at the mention of Brestyan's. We already knew all about the gym.

Brestyan's had a reputation for excellence. The best gymnast in the northeast, Alicia Sacramone, trained there. Alicia was just fifteen, and she was already one of the strongest tumblers and vaulters on the national team.

But there were other things to consider. The gymnasts who trained at Brestyan's were expected to work very, very hard.

Maybe a little too hard. As much as I desired to be an elite gymnast, I was hesitant to make the move.

"I don't know," I said doubtfully. But Petra had already made up her mind. She cleaned out her locker and left the next day.

When I told my parents about Petra, they asked if I might like to try Brestyan's, too. I said I wasn't sure. They told me it was my decision, even though Brestyan's was farther away from our house, which would mean more time driving me to and from practice.

I spent the next few months wavering. I even visited Brestyan's but left undecided. I loved Exxcel and was happy working with Alex, who wanted us all to have a great experience in the sport, no matter what.

But with Rett and Pete gone, Alex was busier than ever, and our team didn't get to work with him as much as we would have liked to. And I missed Petra, who could always make me laugh.

That September I made the TOPs B team again. My mom and I flew to Houston for the second round of testing, even though parents weren't allowed to accompany their children in the gym. On the plane ride, we weighed my options. If I went to Brestyan's, I would be at a gym that had proven success, and could help guide me down the elite level path. If I stayed at Exxcel, the future seemed less clear.

"Take your time and think about it," Mom said. "It's your decision if you want to try to go down the elite road, and your father and I will support you no matter what. But are you sure that this is the life you want, all this training and traveling and competing? Are you sure you might not be just as happy if you stay on the path you're on, and maybe try for a college scholarship later on?"

My parents surely would have preferred that I stay at Exxcel. The gym was just ten minutes from our house. Changing gyms meant my parents would have to alter their schedules, which wasn't easy with four kids.

I loved Exxcel and its coaches. At the same time, I wanted to train more hours and move up. The training camps in Texas had opened a window into the world of elite gymnastics, and I very much wanted to be a part of it. Training with coaches like Mihai and Silvie Brestyan, who already had an elite gymnast, made sense.

As our plane touched down in Boston, I turned to my mother. "I want to be an elite gymnast," I said firmly. "Let's give Brestyan's a try."

A few months earlier, I was glued to the television as Carly Patterson became the first American woman since Mary Lou Retton in 1984 to win the Olympic all-around title.

Just as I had so many times before, I sat down to watch gymnastics with my mother. Only this time we were watching Carly Patterson live as she battled for the all-around gold.

The all-around final was a tight battle between Carly and Russia's Svetlana Khorkina. They had both been preparing for this moment their whole lives. As a child, coach after coach told Svetlana she was too tall for gymnastics. Nevertheless, she persisted. She found a coach who believed in her potential, and together they created innovative routines full of original skills that played to her strengths and her height. The quality Svetlana was told was her biggest disadvantage wound up being her biggest asset.

The all-around final began as a close battle, but Carly pulled away after hitting a stellar beam routine. It ended with a dismount where she did a roundoff back handspring, followed by a half turn and two front flips. She was the first person to do that, and the skill was called The Patterson in her honor. She stuck the landing perfectly and a huge grin spread over her face.

My mom let out a sigh as Carly stuck the dismount. "I'm so nervous and I don't even know her. Her mom must be a wreck." Mom laughed. "Thank goodness I'll never have to go through that."

"What?" I cried, scandalized. "How can you say that? I'll be at the Olympics someday. Don't you think I can do it?"

"Of course I do," she said quickly, a surprised look crossing her face. "Of course," she repeated. "I just never realized you wanted to go."

Years later when we recalled this conversation she said she thought I was delusional but didn't want to hurt my feelings and decided to encourage me. I tease her now that the video of her being nervous at the Olympics went viral as payback for thinking I was deluded!

Summer for my family meant a few weekends in Maine crabbing, burying one another in the sand on the beach, and ordering nonalcoholic chocolate mudslides practically by the dozen at the hotel pool. When I was younger, I went to my Uncle Michael and Auntie Lauren's Camp Wicosuta in Hebron, New Hampshire, along with my cousins Mikayla and Brooke, where we swam in the local lake, did arts and crafts, and went canoeing, hiking, and horseback riding. There was even a gymnastics class—where I loved showing off my skills! At night, we sat around a bonfire and everyone roasted marshmallows and sang camp songs while my uncle played guitar. I missed those moments, but my commitments to gymnastics meant I could no longer attend camp as a camper, though I did go for occasional weekend visits.

Even over summer break, gymnastics was never far from my mind. During the relaxing times, I longed to get back into the gym and work on new skills. In 2003, when we wrote about the things we hoped to accomplish one day in our camp yearbook, I put that I hoped to go to the Olympics.

It was with that Olympic dream in the back of my mind that I walked into Brestyan's American Gymnastics Club in fall 2004. Stephanie made the switch as well. When I went into the locker room, Petra and Stephanie were already there. They ran up and hugged me as the other girls looked on. I looked around shyly, feeling like the new girl in school.

During my first practice, as we worked on beam, I tried to impress my new coaches, Mihai and Silvie Brestyan, by launching into a huge switch leap. But I lost my footing and the beam rose up to meet me. I wound up with one foot off each side of the beam, which we call splitting the beam. It happens to every gymnast many times in their careers, though it's never a nice feeling! But I popped right back on and kept going, mentally shaking my head. I had wanted to stand out, but not like *that*.

I caught Mihai Brestyan's attention anyway. As usual, I was not the best on my new team, but as Silvie told me years later, they noticed a sparkle in my eye. Mihai used to say that he'd rather train a hard worker than an effortlessly talented gymnast, because he believes that hard work can often beat out talent. That was ideal for someone like me, who had struggled early on. I loved gymnastics, and I was willing and eager to work hard.

I had been training at Brestyan's for less than three months when my dad and Mihai started talking at pickup.

"Okay, Mihai, give her a hug good-bye," Dad said jokingly as I came up to join them. "We're off to Florida to see her grandparents over the school holidays," he explained. "She'll be back in ten days."

Mihai's eyes widened and his eyebrows raised. "Aly told me

she wanted to be a world and Olympic champion. Is that right, Aly?" I nodded. "Okay, let me tell you this. Being number one in the world at the top level is very, very hard; however, staying there is even harder. The best athletes don't take vacations. The best athletes are the smartest: They know when to work hard, they know how to eat healthy, they know how to sleep well each night, they know how to rest when they need rest. The best athletes are professionals. If you want to be there someday, that starts now."

Mihai looked at my dad and continued. "It's all right this time, because you didn't know. But this will be the last time Aly ever gets to go on vacation, aside from when we close the gym for one week in the summer."

At first my dad thought he was kidding. But when he asked some of the other parents, they assured him Mihai had not been joking at all.

I had wanted serious gymnastics. It appeared I was going to get it.

CHAPTER 4

GETTING SERIOUS

Needham, Massachusetts
2005–2009

"Fifty push-ups," Mihai ordered.

Everyone in my training group dropped to the floor without a word. Mihai circled around us, making minor corrections as we strained and groaned. "Cheat and you'll start over again," he warned.

Forty-five minutes of every workout was devoted to serious conditioning, which meant I was doing dozens and dozens of push-ups, squats, press handstands, rope climbs, and more—in addition to the countless repetitions and routines that make up a training session—every single day.

Sometimes we would race each other through the conditioning. Other times Mihai would invent games involving conditioning skills. April, Julohn, Michelle, Petra, Stephanie, Talia, and I would be laughing and having so much fun that we wouldn't realize how hard we'd been working until we woke up sore the next morning. Once, Petra did forty press handstands in a row. I tried to match her, but I collapsed on the mat after twenty, completely exhausted. Doing five press handstands was hard; most gymnasts couldn't even do one! Forty in a row was just unheard of. "That must be a world record," I told her.

Needless to say, after several months of this, I was in fantastic shape, with muscles in places I didn't know it was possible to have them.

Around this time, my family moved from Newton to Needham, the next town over. After having the same classmates for years, I was suddenly the new girl at Newman Elementary School.

My muscles must have intimidated some of the boys at Newman, because they began paying a lot of attention to them.

"Look at her arms," one of the boys said one day, pointing at my biceps. "They're huge!"

"Disgusting," said another, scrunching up his face. "She must be taking steroids!" At that, they all roared with laughter. Soon they were calling me Roids. "Hey, Roids!" they'd yell as they whizzed by on the playground.

I would bite my lip, fighting back tears. It hurt a lot to be made fun of for something I worked hard for and needed for my sport. I had been proud of my muscles, and then these boys came along and tried to make me ashamed of them. I looked around at the other girls in my class. Since they didn't have big muscles, I assumed the problem must be with me. Having muscles wasn't girly, I concluded.

The solution seemed obvious: cover myself up. The next time I went clothes shopping, I avoided tank tops and stocked up on short- and long-sleeved shirts so I wouldn't be flashing my muscles at everyone.

On days when people called me Roids, Brestyan's became my sanctuary. Inside the gym, my muscles were admired, and when I was out there all alone on the floor or up on the balance beam, I felt confident and strong.

I may not have liked being called Roids, but I was never truly ashamed of my muscles. Somewhere deep down I must have realized that without them I wouldn't be able to flip and tumble the way I was learning to. And there couldn't be anything freakish about having a six pack, since all my teammates had one, too. It was reassuring to go to the gym every day after school and see people whose bodies looked like mine and be reminded of what they could do.

It was a good thing I felt so at home in the gym, because I was spending a lot of time there. I was doing four-hour workouts every weeknight from 5:00 to 9:00 PM, as well as three hours on Saturday mornings. Unless I was really sick, there were no good excuses for missing practice.

"Gymnastics first, school second," Silvie would joke. Some

coaches at other gyms really felt that way. They liked their gymnasts to be homeschooled or take online courses whenever possible, which opened up more hours for them to practice during the day. Mihai and Silvie didn't advocate homeschooling, since they believed school provided a key source of balance in a gymnast's life. Both they and my parents were clear that school was very important. "You must put the same effort into both," Mihai insisted.

With gymnastics taking up so much of my time, I had to learn how to manage my schoolwork so that I wouldn't have to stay up doing homework and then be tired at the next day's practice. Every minute became important. My mom would quiz me on the drive to and from the gym, and I often did schoolwork in the car, trying not to let the bumpiness of the road mess up my handwriting. Immediately after dropping me off, my mother would turn the car around and return home to spend the evening with my dad and siblings. After dinner, she would frequently set a plate aside for me that my dad would reheat a few hours later. I would eat the dinner in the car ride home. Dad would often arrive early for pickup so he could watch the end of my practice. When I was training a new skill, I would be so excited to show him my progress. My siblings were young at this point, so having everyone travel to a gymnastics competition was too difficult. In those days, Mom would take me to meets (borrowing Dad's video camera, so he and the family could watch the competition upon our return). Because he missed those early competitions, he loved catching the end of practice—and I loved having him there.

My days became school, practice, homework, sleep, repeat. That probably sounds like a lot for a ten-year-old, and it must have seemed a little crazy for my parents. They wanted me to have a normal life: trick-or-treating, hanging out with my friends, and certainly going on family vacations.

But I couldn't have been happier. I loved gymnastics and was glad my coaches saw something in me that made them want to push me to be better. My parents, for their part, trusted me and my coaches. Now when vacation time came around, my dad would take my sisters to Florida to visit Bubbie and Papa and Grandma and Grandpa, who spent winters there, and my mom would stay home to shuttle me back and forth to practice.

Mom never complained, even though this arrangement meant she was giving up her vacation, too. She just drove the car back and forth, twice a day sometimes, and always made sure there was a hot healthy plate of food waiting for me as soon as practice was over, experimenting with different ways of keeping the dish warm.

When I didn't have double sessions (morning and evening practices) during a school vacation, we would do something fun together, like going to the movies or shopping. Most of the time we just ended up at home on the couch as it snowed outside, picking out a tape to watch and ordering Chinese takeout, which we both loved. After dinner, we would make chocolate chip cookies for dessert. Spending this time together brought us closer than ever.

Things got even more complicated for her the year Brett started skipping family vacations to attend hockey practice. Mom recalls one vacation in which both of us had practices, each in the opposite direction from the other. She literally spent every single day of that break on the road, driving from the ice arena to the gym or vice versa, to pick one of us up or drop the other off!

Mom could have put her foot down and insisted that kids should be kids and we were all going on vacation, period. But she trusted us to decide what was best for ourselves, and supported our choices. I had no idea how lucky I was. It might sound crazy, but I really believe that if my mom had said that I had to go on vacation with the family, and she hadn't been willing to stay home with me so I could train, I wouldn't have been as successful as I ended up being.

I took those school vacations and used them to cultivate new skills in the gym. That following year, I finally made the TOPs A team and got to partake in the A-team camp at the Karolyi Ranch. The hard work seemed to be paying off.

That was the first time I saw national team coordinator Martha Karolyi in person. I was wearing the white GK TOPs national team leotard that we received when we arrived at camp, practicing my front tuck on the mats by the beam. We always practiced skills on a line on the floor to start building the muscle memory so we could one day do them on the low beam, then the high beam. I caught a glimpse of Martha peering out at us through the glass window of her office just off the gym. There was no mistaking the sharp brown eyes, close-cropped hair, and tawny skin.

The atmosphere always changed a little when Martha walked into a room. As national team coordinator, Martha was the main force in deciding who made the Olympic team, and who didn't. A faint air of power and command always radiated from her. All heads would snap toward her. She walked proudly with her head held high, commanding everyone's attention. It was very clear who was in charge. You just wanted to impress her. When Martha was in the room, everyone stood up a little straighter, and tried a little harder.

That day, as she was talking to someone, I saw Martha point at me. I looked away quickly, pretending not to see, as my heart leapt with delight. Of all the girls in the gym, Martha Karolyi had noticed *me*, though I had no idea why. Even better, I was one of the few girls invited back for a special pre-elite camp that winter. I returned to Boston flying high and determined to work even harder than I already was.

Though I was progressing rapidly, Petra was the first to

qualify to compete at the elite level. Her talent was getting her noticed, drawing speculation from gymnastics pundits that she would be the next big thing from Brestyan's, maybe one day joining Alicia on the senior national team.

Stephanie excelled as well. She was a natural athlete and already demonstrated the speed and coordination that would one day earn her a place on the Dartmouth College track team. Stephanie was fearless when it came to learning new skills. She shone on floor and vault.

As for me, I was behind, as usual. I was especially behind on floor exercise. We were now learning to do flips with twisting elements. Learning to do a back somersault with a full twist in the air proved tricky. One day when we were tumbling, I punched into the skill, twisted too early, and came down on my head. Mihai didn't let me do it again until he had broken down the components of the skill one by one and taught me the correct technique. The process took months, but Mihai was a patient and good teacher. "You're not going to do this until you're ready," he said firmly. I sighed in relief. Mihai had me skip the skill entirely for months, replacing it with a back layout with no twists so that I could figure out the timing. I was the only one in my group that wasn't able to twist their layout, but Mihai never made me feel as behind as I was and always had faith in me.

When the state meet came around months later, I was prepared. I understood what I needed to do so well that the full twist was no problem in competition. I was even able to add an extra half twist in for the regional meet a few weeks later, and began working even harder on twisting skills after that. It may have taken me longer to learn certain skills, but once they clicked, there was no stopping me.

Finding doctors who understood the sport and my desire to train—even if things hurt—proved difficult. At one point early on, I had a small wound on my foot. I went to the doctor expecting to receive an antibiotic and be on my way.

"You should take two weeks off," the doctor announced after examining the cut.

"Two weeks?" I exclaimed, incredulous. "No way! I have a meet tomorrow. I'm going to practice as soon as we leave here." The doctor cast a horrified look at my mom, no doubt concerned about my willingness to put health on hold for the sake of a gymnastics competition. "I can't possibly skip a meet," I continued, oblivious. I went on and on, trying to make him understand how important this meet was. Finally, when I saw that I was getting nowhere, I pretended to agree to take time off. We left the office and went straight to the gym, me fuming about being late for practice all the way there. Of course I competed the next day. No way was a little cut on my foot going to prevent me from doing gymnastics. I competed, but the cut did get infected. It eventually healed, though it left a scar.

That summer my back was hurting a lot. When I was twelve and thirteen, I downplayed or ignored the issue for as long as I could. I wanted badly to qualify to compete at the elite level, and I was worried that a lot of time off, even to let an injury heal, would make it impossible to catch up. The summer of 2007, I delayed mentioning my back pain to anyone so I could compete in an important meet in Battle Creek, Michigan. The Classic had different divisions, one for the elite gymnasts and one for the up-and-coming hopefuls. Stephanie and I competed in the junior pre-elite division. The next day, I took a seat in the stands to watch the elite session.

After the competition, dressed in my maroon Brestyan's tracksuit, I ran around filling the pages of my program book with autographs of every elite competitor I could find. Years later, I realized that one of the people who signed my book—a girl from Michigan with a shiny brown ponytail—was Jordyn Wieber.

As hard as I tried to ignore it, the pain was so intense that eventually I had to seek medical attention and take six months off from competition. I continued going to workout, but I could only do conditioning. I was worried about falling further behind. Plus, I didn't want Mihai to forget about me.

The first back doctor we saw had a reputation for being one of the best in the Boston area. I sat in his waiting room for two hours before being called back to the examination room. He looked me over for three minutes and announced I needed a back brace to heal my spine. I wore it twenty-three hours a day for six weeks and went back for a checkup. After another long wait and brief appointment, the doctor prescribed another six weeks in the brace.

When I told Mihai, he cocked his head to the side. "You got an MRI, right?" he said. "Is there a fracture?" No fracture, I told him. "If there's no fracture, you don't need to be in a brace," he said, pulling on his schooling in Romania. "I'd get another opinion if I were you."

I wound up seeing two more doctors. Both of them agreed with Mihai: Since there was no fracture, I didn't need to be in a brace. Later, I heard that the doctor was paid a fee for each brace he prescribed. Even though I didn't need the back brace I still had to allow my back to heal. I was given strict instructions: no activity that aggravated my back. I spent the next several months building my core and easing back into additional conditioning and gymnastics. My back still hurts me to this day, requiring intermittent physical therapy and treatment.

By the time I was ready to compete again, I had missed most of the season. As always, if you look hard enough you can find a silver lining. The time I had to take away from competition gave me a much-needed mental break, and when I returned I was more determined. I spent the next several months regaining my skills as well as conquering some fears that were holding me back. I had struggled for several seasons to master a full twist on vault. As Mihai would tell me, I was physically strong enough to do it, but my mind was preventing me. A year later I would qualify elite having mastered the full twist on vault.

The 2008 National Championships was held in Boston. My teammates and I all went to watch. While the elites were warming up, the emcee found my friends and I in the crowd during a trivia game. He asked us where the 2008 Beijing Olympics would be held. I was so nervous that I looked to Petra for help, and she stared back, shocked by my cluelessness. "Aly, it's Beijing!" The whole audience laughed as I repeated, "Beijing!" The emcee handed me my prize of a hat and a T-shirt that read "Future Olympian" and said maybe I'd be at the Olympics someday. *I will be*, I thought to myself.

That was the last season Petra, Stephanie, and I did gymnastics together. Petra quit first. She had been having a hard time adhering to the rigorous training schedule, and I think it ate away at her love of the sport. Stephanie left several months later. As we moved into high school, she decided she wanted to devote more time to other activities and have more of a social life, as well as pursue track.

I was sad to see my friends step away from the sport we'd loved so fiercely as children, though I also understood. With every year that passed, the skills got more difficult, and the training and sacrifices more intense. But it was the world I had chosen for myself.

All the hours we put in were paying off. Our team won and

won and won. State and regional titles flowed in one after the other, though Mihai didn't let us get cocky. "There is always more work to do," he would tell us. "Remember what your goals are."

I hadn't forgotten. And by early 2009, I was finally ready to take the next step.

CHAPTER 5

MEET THE ELITE

Dallas, Texas
2009

Qualifying to become an elite gymnast is kind of like passing a driver's test. If you can demonstrate that you've mastered certain basic skills, you get a kind of license: not to drive, but to compete at the international, or Olympic, level. But if you get too many points off, you have to try again another time.

The standard is so high that in the United States, usually less than fifty girls compete at the elite level at any given time. In order to "go elite," as we say, you have to prove yourself at a designated qualifying meet.

At elite qualifiers, gymnasts are asked to show two different routines on each apparatus. The first routine is called a compulsory. Compulsories are routines where gymnasts demonstrate that they can perform basic skills with good form. While the skills may be "basic" (or, some may say, easier), they are critical for success and the judges are looking for these routines to be performed properly. If you don't have a good foundation for your sport, it is harder to improve and get better. Every gymnast at the qualifier performs an identical required routine composed of these easier skills, making it a long day for everyone. I suspect even the judges can get bored after seeing the exact same routine fifty times in a row!

If compulsories are meant to ensure that a prospective elite has good basics and form, the second routines, known as optionals, showcase her most difficult skills. The more difficulty in your exercise, the higher you have the potential to score. At the elite level, gymnasts earn two scores for every routine—one for the difficulty and the other for execution. These scores are added together, giving you your total score for every event.

The harder your skills are, however, the harder they are to perform with good execution. The ideal is to have it all: difficulty and power, as well as flexibility, control, and artistry. The most successful elites are those whose routines have a lot of risk, which gives them a high difficulty score, but who also have excellent execution, meaning they come within a point or so of the maximum execution score of ten.

In February 2009, Mom and I flew to Texas with Mihai for the first elite qualifier of the year. I was nervous and excited, because I knew the judges at the qualifier would be elite level judges. I had been dreaming of becoming an elite for years, and I was finally healthy and ready to show what I was capable of.

Leading up to the meet, Mihai had me work mostly on my optional routines. While we didn't ignore the preparation necessary to do good compulsories, once you met the elite qualifying compulsory score, you never did those routines again. Since optionals would be more important for the future, most of our time was spent refining those.

That was fine with me. Thanks to a combination of Mihai's teaching and conditioning and my willingness to push myself, I was gaining the capability to do a high degree of difficulty everywhere, especially on floor. Despite my earlier struggles on the event, once I mastered the basics, I was able to build on them. Within a few months, it went from being my biggest weakness to my biggest strength—not to mention my favorite to perform. Out on that forty-by-forty-foot stage, I felt powerful.

The judges were picky, and eager to take deductions for imperfect form. My first event in the compulsory round was on floor. Silvie reminded me to always keep my head high. I kept my chin up and took it one skill at a time to emphasize every move and present it as well as I could. I performed the routine, saluted the judges, and walked off the mat. I was satisfied with how I'd done as I walked over to join Mihai, knowing I had performed the required moves well. I was already thinking about the next event when my score flashed on the electronic scoreboard: 8.35 out of 10.

8.35? Mihai and I exchanged confused looks. We both thought I had done well, without any obvious mistakes. Certainly the routine deserved better than that?

Mihai walked over to the judges table and inquired about my score. One of the officials bent toward him to say something, and suddenly I saw Mihai's face clear. He nodded and walked away.

"Aly," he said when he was within earshot, "you forgot the straddle jump." The straddle jump was one of the requirements in the routine, and leaving it out (or in my case, simply forgetting to do it) cost me half of a point.

Uh-oh. I stared at Mihai, waiting for his reaction. To my surprise, a grin spread across his face. It got bigger and bigger, until he was practically doubled over with laughter.

"All the things you can do," he guffawed, "and you forget the straddle jump!"

I was having a harder time seeing the humor in the situation. That stupid straddle jump had just made it harder for me to get the overall score I needed.

Upset at myself for having made such an obvious mistake, I was too distracted to do proper math. In reality, I now needed to average about 9.0 on the other three events in order to hit the qualifying score of 35. But in my confusion, I somehow convinced myself that I only needed an 8.3 average. Since that was what I had gotten on floor even with an error, I figured that I'd be okay if I didn't make any more big mistakes. I never heard the end of it from Mom, who has a master's degree from Harvard. "Are you really my daughter?" she teased.

The mistake on floor might have hurt my math brain, but the gymnastics part of my mind locked into the competition. As I worked my way around the gym for the next two hours, I was focused and deliberate. On every skill I did, I fought not to give away any deductions.

Vault: 9.7.

Bars: 9.1.

Beam: 8.725.

When it was all over, I had totaled 35.875, almost a point more than the score needed to meet the compulsory benchmark. The next day I competed in the optional portion, tallying 54.55. I fell once, on beam. Mihai was pleased with my results overall, but reminded me that Martha doesn't like it when girls fall on beam.

I had accomplished my goal: I was now an elite gymnast. I breathed an enormous sigh of relief.

At home, Dad was not faring so well. Chloe and Madison kept up their tradition of wandering into my room on a Saturday night. My room was just far enough down the hall that Dad did not realize the two were jumping on my bed so late at night. A short time later, he was awoken by Madison's suggestion that Chloe needed to be taken to the hospital. Sure enough, Chloe had broken her elbow.

We flew back to Boston the next day, and the morning after, I was back in the gym, a newly minted elite. With both Petra and Stephanie no longer around, Mihai worked closely with my friend Talia Chiarelli and me to increase our difficulty. I had come a long way in my five years at Brestyan's.

"Survival of the fittest," Mihai pronounced at practice that morning. "It's hard getting to this level, and very few people make it. Here you are. You have the potential, I think, to go far. Who knows? Maybe the World Championships. Maybe more. Your job—and it's going to be a hard one—is to maintain this level. When you compete and you do well, everyone is going to be trying to beat you. To stay ahead, you have to want it more than you want anything else. Everyone gets twenty-four hours to prepare. The smartest and most successful athletes are the ones who make those twenty-four hours count. For you, that begins now."

If I thought I'd worked hard before, I now began to learn what real work was. Mihai and Silvie gave me a list of harder skills to work into my routines to boost my difficulty, and a few more on top of them months later. They were creative in thinking of sequences that would allow me adequate time to rest and recharge before launching into the next set of skills. I quickly discovered that elite gymnastics is about pushing your limits—physically and mentally. No matter how much you do and how well you do it, you can always do more. You can always do better. Sometimes it drove me crazy.

The repetitions were endless. I did series after series of skills, and routine after routine, sometimes for hours at a time. If I missed one skill or connection a few times, Mihai would make me repeat it again and again until it wasn't a problem anymore. I conditioned more than I ever had, doing more box jumps, levers, rope climbs, press handstands, and cardio exercises than anyone else in the gym. I always left the gym tired. Always.

Bigger skills, more repetitions—and a smaller tolerance for mistakes from Mihai and Silvie. "No, no, no, no!" Mihai would say if I had a hard time picking up a skill or didn't do something well enough.

"The tough days are the days that make you stronger," Mihai said. "Everything counts now. If you don't always do your absolute best, it isn't worth it. And if you're not going to be one of the best, you might as well not even try. Do you think the judges will care if you're sick or tired?"

During the next few years, a level 8 or 9 gymnast who was considering moving to Brestyan's would occasionally come and observe one of my workouts. After seeing firsthand the numbers I did in a single workout, most of them didn't come back.

I quickly learned that doing elite gymnastics meant taking care of my body outside the gym as well. If I didn't eat healthy and get a good night's sleep, my workouts suffered. Meanwhile, a lot of my school friends were drinking on the weekends and smoking weed. When I was in ninth grade, Mihai pulled me aside for a talk on, as he put it, "the importance of being healthy and being smart." Smoking and drinking are incredibly dangerous, he reiterated, not to mention illegal, and he assured me I would regret it deeply if I fell into either habit. "If you're the only one at a party who isn't drinking, it puts you in a different category, and everyone will respect you," he'd say. "And if they don't respect you, you need new friends." He was right—I was worried people would make fun of me if I was the only one not drinking or smoking, but it turned out that they respected my decision, and even told me that they believed my dedication would get me to the Olympics.

"Trust me, Aly," Mihai said. "Be smart, make good choices, and I promise you they'll pay off."

I stood just off the floor at the 2009 US Junior National Championships that August, scanning the arena and trying to play it cool, even though my heart was hammering away in my chest.

The marathon two-day meet was nearly at an end—and if things continued as they had been going so far, by the end of my ninety-second floor routine, I would be the junior national champion.

Floor had definitely become my best event. I was even training two tumbling passes that ranked among the most difficult being done by anyone, anywhere. I knew it, and felt very proud of it.

Silvie urged confidence. "Walk into every gym with your chin high and a smile on your face," she said. "Never let Martha or the judges see fear in your eyes. Fake it until you make it."

For my first Junior National Championships, my goal was just to hit all of my routines. And on the first day, I did! Mihai always taught me not to look at the scoreboard until I was finished with all my routines, so as not to get overconfident—or dejected. When I finally looked at the scoreboard at the end of the first day of the meet, I was shocked to see my name near the top. I was in second place, behind Kyla Ross.

At the biggest meets, gymnasts perform on a podium, meaning the apparatuses are raised up about three feet above the arena floor. A little flight of stairs is placed to one side of the podium for access. Most of the time, being on a podium makes the equipment feel bouncier, which makes a big difference. You're also performing under bright arena lighting and in the presence of TV cameras.

It was a lot to get used to, which was why the "podium

training" day, where everyone trains in the arena on the same equipment they'll compete on, was especially important. Podium training allowed us all to get a feel for the equipment and what it was like performing in that particular arena before the competition began.

When you're standing on the podium, you're actually above your coaches and the judges, who sit to the side of each apparatus. While you're waiting, it's easy to see everything that's going on around you.

So on day two, I had a clear view of Kyla as she fell from the uneven bars. Then, as I turned my gaze to the other side of the gym in order to distract myself, I saw Bridgette Caquatto, who was also in third the day before, overrotate her beam dismount and land on her seat.

Meanwhile, I had done my first three routines without any major errors.

I began to picture the medal ceremony unfolding, my name being called in first place, stepping up to receive the gold medal, and waving to the crowd. I'd played this scene in my head so many times. Maybe this was the day it would become real.

The green light came on. I saluted the judges and stepped onto the mat. As my music came on, I took a deep breath and launched into my first tumbling run, a series of five complex elements ending with an Arabian double front, a half twist in the air followed by two front flips. I nailed it, sticking the landing cold!

I could already hear my name being called: *Aly Raisman, national champion.* Could this be happening?

I stepped back into the corner and prepared for my second tumbling pass, a triple twist. I was excited to do this pass and get through the rest of the routine—too excited, with too much energy as I punched off the floor.

I had too much height, and when I reached the point when my feet usually landed on the floor, I was still a foot and a half in the air. The momentum had me flying backward, out of control. I wiped out straight on my back, mortified.

The rest of the routine was a blur. But when I came down off the podium, Mihai said, "You must learn to be in the moment and take one skill at a time. Don't watch what everyone else is doing next time! Be smart."

I finished third, behind Kyla and Bridgette. I was a little disappointed with the mistake on floor, which had left me with a headache, but still elated to have earned a bronze medal at my very first National Championships. My mind was already skipping ahead to the next competition.

Mihai had also been thinking ahead. Before Nationals, I had started working on a brand-new pass on floor, combining a few different skills I had mastered together to form a unique tumbling run. It was so original—and so complicated—that nobody else had ever done it. Difficulty sets you apart from the rest of the pack, but difficulty *and* originality is even better.

Mihai was so confident that he sought out Martha in the hotel after the meet. As they were chatting, he described the pass and casually mentioned that his gymnast could do it.

"Impossible!" Martha said.

Mihai smirked. "Wait and see."

CHAPTER 6

THE RANCH

New Waverly, Texas

2009

"Fishbowl" was the word Silvie used to describe the national team camps when I asked what they were like.

"Remember, when you're there, Martha will always be watching," she said firmly. "Never show her that you are tired, scared, injured, sick, or afraid. You must not show any weakness. Smile and show her that you're working hard and pleased to be there."

My third place finish at Nationals meant I was officially a member of the junior national team, which Mihai and Silvie saw as a stepping stone to greater things. Being on the national team meant that I was now in the pool of gymnasts who had a shot at making the teams that traveled to international competitions, like the World Championships.

And, eventually, the Olympic Games.

Being on the national team meant I would now travel to Texas for monthly training camps at the Karolyi Ranch, where my progress could be monitored by the national team staff, including Martha.

Especially Martha.

And as Mihai and Silvie's gymnast, I already knew one of the most important rules: Always be early for practice; if you show up on time, you are late!

With all of their advice in mind, I boarded a plane for Houston and a place that would become like a second home during the next several years. I was so excited to train on the same equipment as so many of my idols had before me.

After emigrating from Romania in the early 1980s, Martha and Bela Karolyi bought a forty-acre property outside a town called New Waverly, about an hour north of Houston. Using corrugated tin, Bela built several gyms on their property for training their own athletes.

Bela was appointed national team coordinator. Then, when the US women finished without a medal in Sydney, Martha took over. The Karolyi gyms deep in the forest became the official national team base. Nobody trained there full-time, but every four to six weeks, twenty to thirty national team members descended for an intense five-day training camp.

At the ranch, we would be up at 7:00 AM, go to breakfast in

the dining hall, then walk over a wide expanse of field where chickens roamed freely for the first of two daily workouts in the gym.

Practice began at 8:30 AM sharp, but we all arrived by 8:00. We would line up on the floor, shortest to tallest, and stand at attention while Martha talked about the goals for the day and the things she wanted to see emphasized during the workout. We would then be split into groups with our coaches and rotate through each of the four events, as well as a rotation focused on dance, presentation, and choreography.

Martha watched everything. Mistakes, even in training, made her frown. I got the impression that she kept a tally of errors in her head. Practice was just as important as a competition where Martha was concerned. Martha never forgot a performance and had a knack for predicting who would go far. We used to joke that she was psychic.

Practice ended around noon, at which point we would troop back to the dining hall for lunch. Depending on the day, we had the option of a soup and salad bar, and either salmon, chicken, steak, or pork.

After lunch, we would head back to our cabins. I would nap before the afternoon training session. At 3:30, we'd be back in the gym to stretch for half an hour before the second workout began. Mihai was right: Martha was always in the gym twenty minutes before the workout was scheduled to begin, looking around to see who was there and who wasn't. If you weren't early, you would be scolded for being late. So no one was ever late!

After the second workout, we would head to dinner. Before bed, I would often eat some candy or chocolate that I'd brought from home. The lights would go out between 9:30 and 10:00 PM.

Five days after it began, camp would end. Each of us would get into a car with our coach, drive to Houston, then fly home.

Camp wasn't easy, and it wasn't supposed to be. Since becoming part of the semi-centralized training system Bela and Martha set up in 2000, the national team camps had been honed and refined. The method had produced the best results in American gymnastics history: The 2004 and 2008 Olympic teams had won the team silver medal, and the 2003 and 2007 world teams had taken gold. A host of the best individual gymnasts had won the world all-around title. In addition, the program had produced two Olympic all-around champions.

The coaches liked camp because it was secluded. The gym was impeccably clean, and the equipment top of the line. There were few distractions from training—unless you counted the camels, peacocks, and dogs that Bela kept on the property.

The gymnasts had mixed feelings. Most of us thought the food was bad and everyone agreed the internet and cell phone service were horrible. We slept in run-down wooden cabins on uncomfortable wooden bunk beds. The shower smelled like eggs, and we didn't always have hot water. There was not enough medical staff and no sports dietitian to help us on-site, and not enough equipment for recovery after workouts, even though our bodies demanded it.

Personally, I thought the food we were served was subpar: the eggs were powdered, the coffee tasteless, and the meat dry and coated with cooking spray. To cover the bland taste of the meat, a lot of people coated it with ketchup. But we made sure to eat it anyway—we needed fuel for our workouts! "Your body is your tool," Mihai would say. "The better shape you're in, the better you'll compete."

We were all together as we sweated and strained through the demanding hours of practice. The challenging circumstances of our sport and the expectations of our coaches meant that we bonded quickly. And because we were all in this together, we grew to understand one another in a way that only people dealing with the same challenges can.

We did everything we could to help each other out. If one girl's coach was tough on her, another girl was there with a hug and consoling words. If someone had a bad workout, we'd tell jokes until she cheered up.

At the ranch, I was able to connect with girls I had seen and occasionally gone up against at competitions throughout my childhood. In addition to being competitors, we became friends.

I clicked instantly with McKayla Maroney, the reigning junior national champion on vault. McKayla had a special gift for vault. She had already mastered the Amanar, an incredibly difficult vault that I was also working on. McKayla made it look downright easy. She got so much height it made my jaw drop. Even Martha, who demanded absolute perfection, couldn't find anything wrong with it. I would watch McKayla, and she would give me advice on how to approach my own Amanar.

Like we all did, McKayla kept her eyes down and followed her coach's instructions to the letter inside the gym. Outside of it, she was hilarious. She had a confidence about her that I admired. McKayla didn't seem to worry about what other people thought of her. In the dance classes, held in one of the ranch's older gyms, our instructor Antonia would sometimes put a piece of music on and make us step up one by one and improvise while everyone looked on. McKayla was the best at it. She would let loose, pretending to be a model strutting down a runway or channeling her inner pop star. Her impressions would leave us on the floor, howling with laughter. Even Antonia wouldn't be able to keep it together.

McKayla brought me out of my shell and helped me enjoy myself. She and I quickly discovered that we had the same tastes in clothes and music. We would dance wildly around the cabin, singing "The Climb" by Miley Cyrus and "Leave (Get Out)" by JoJo, while Kyla put her hands over her ears and begged us to stop.

Our love of clothes evolved into us pretending we were on photo shoots, strutting around outside and striking silly poses for the camera between workouts. If we had finished our school-work, we would shop online.

"Go on, buy it," she'd say whenever I pointed out something cute. "You totally deserve it."

"I don't have anywhere to wear this," I'd protest.

"Who cares?" she'd return. "One day we'll have other things to do besides rolling around in chalk. And then you can wear it!"

"You're a horrible influence on my shopping habits," I said as I clicked the BUY button. "And I love it!"

My mother was not so pleased when one too many packages showed up at our doorstep. "Where are you going to wear these?" Mom would question.

I also became close with Jordyn Wieber, the sleek brown-haired girl whose autograph I had gotten at the Classic years before and who was now one of the top juniors in the country. Jordyn and I would try to go to sleep at lights-out, but an hour later, we'd often still be talking and giggling about our lives outside of the gym. We'd spend hours imagining what our lives would look like a few years in the future.

We also joined forces in battle against the many varieties of bugs found in Texas. Flies and beetles flocked to our sleeping quarters. One day, we returned to find that someone had accidentally left the outside light on, and every bug within a five-mile radius seemed to be hovering right in front of the door.

We swatted our way through, but as soon as we opened the door, all the bugs swarmed right inside with us! While Jordyn hurriedly built a towel fortress around her bed, the rest of us dove shrieking under the covers, hysterically arguing over who would get rid of the bugs and swearing we'd come loaded down with bug spray next time.

Eventually we kind of got used to the bugs. We grew so fond of them that we would give them names, take photos of them, and post them to Facebook.

No doubt about it: Camp could make you a little stir-crazy.

After a few days without good cell service, we would all get a little silly. *I swear this camp does weird things to people*, I thought as I watched Alicia drumming on her schoolbook one afternoon, wielding her pink highlighter like a microphone and singing into it. "This place makes me feel like I'm thirteen again," she confessed with a grin when she saw me watching her.

In the evenings, the coaches were expected to eat and play canasta at the big ranch house where Bela and Martha lived. While they were there, we would giggle, gossip, and play cards. The girls who went to regular school filled the girls who were homeschooled in on things that went down in public high schools. We painted pictures of crazy teachers, couples making out in the hallways, and weekend parties with underage drinking.

The homeschoolers were horrified at our description of the real world. I was surprised to learn how sheltered some of my teammates seemed. I realized that I was sheltered, too, but not quite to that extent—I had been overhearing stories about drinking and sex from the older girls since I was ten, and going to a regular high school made a difference, too. Eventually, tired out from workouts and whispering in the dark, we'd fall asleep.

The national team camps were not official competitions, but we were always tested. Throughout each camp, we would have to "verify" our routines, usually on a different event at each workout, performing a routine as though we were in competition. On the last day of camp, medals for the winners on each event were bestowed by Martha. The best at the conditioning tests from the beginning of the week received medals as well.

Sometimes there were bigger things at stake—like being selected for a team that would travel to an international competition. At a camp a few months after the 2009 Nationals, several of the top juniors were verifying for a selection to determine who would travel to the Junior Pan American Championships in Aracaju, Brazil.

Mihai and I arrived in Texas for the selection camp after a four-hour flight from Boston. After the hour-long drive to the ranch, we went straight to the gym for the "accommodation workout." It was supposed to be a light practice to get you moving after hours of sitting on an airplane, though as the years went on those workouts became just as demanding as the ones we were expected to do once we'd had a rest. The expectation was that we would always be prepared to do anything. They wanted us to be prepared, no matter what.

I came off the bumpy plane ride feeling sick from the turbulence. Once in the gym, with Martha looking on, I kept "sitting down" my first tumbling pass—under rotating it and falling backward onto the floor. I bit my lip and bit back tears. I had wanted so badly to do everything perfectly and make a good impression in front of Martha. Instead I just kept messing up. Mihai looked more exasperated with every turn I took.

When we had our mock competition, I didn't fall on my first pass, though I landed out of bounds doing it, a deduction. Only four girls would be selected to go to Brazil. The competition was tight. I had messed up, so I assumed I was out.

I was in the bathroom, sobbing, when Silvie came in. "Stop crying. They're taking you," she announced. "They decided not to count your out of bounds on floor. Consider yourself lucky, and toughen up." And she walked out.

I tried to hide my tear-stained face when Martha walked over to us a few minutes later. Of course, she wasn't fooled. She patted me on the head and looked me in the eyes.

"If you want to be a successful gymnast, Aly," she said, "you must learn to handle your nerves. You must learn to control your emotions, even when you're practicing. You have a lot of potential," she continued, looking at me brightly. "You know, you could be a gold medalist at the World Championships or

Olympic Games if you continue to work hard. But that does not come like *that*. You must earn it all."

We traveled for thirty-two hours to get to Brazil, missing a connecting flight. Martha, never one to be deterred from training by something as trivial as not being in a gym, instructed us to stretch while we waited, then do some kicks, squat jumps, and walkovers as the other people waiting for the flight stared at us, no doubt surprised by this unexpected show of agility from their fellow passengers.

We had a lot of fun in Brazil. I had never traveled out of the country before, and Brazil was an eye-opening experience in more ways than one. The training gym, for example, was outdoors, with fencing instead of walls. Tumbling and doing release skills on bars in direct sunlight and covered in sweat (no air-conditioning!) was a dangerous challenge.

At night, Kyla, Bridgette, Sabrina Vega, and I would have dance parties on the hotel balcony. One night, there was a party outside of our rooms. The music was so loud that it was like we had a DJ right on our balcony!

The Brazilian crowd loved us. Warm and supportive, they applauded wildly at each of our routines. Smiling fans wanted our autographs, to touch us, to shake our hands.

I was buying chocolate at the duty-free shop in the airport three days later when a lady shyly came up and asked if we could take a photo together. "I saw the competition on television," she said, "and you were fantastic." We snapped a picture, and when she left, I dropped all of my belongings and ran to tell Mihai I was officially famous.

He laughed and said, "That's great." He looked down at my empty hands. "But where did you put your passport?"

Brazil, I decided as I ran back to get my things, was a pretty cool place. I would definitely have to come back someday....

CHAPTER 7

AMERICAN DREAMER

Worcester, Massachusetts
Spring 2010

I had become a senior elite at the beginning of the year, and went to the American Cup selection training camp with the expectation that I'd be showing Martha my Amanar. But after watching me struggle so much in practice, Martha told Mihai it was enough, I was too nervous, that there was always next time. Mihai and Silvie pulled me aside and said, "You're stressing yourself out way too much. The American Cup is too hard to make; only two girls are selected. Let's focus on getting ready for the next training camp so you can verify for Italy."

A few days later, all eyes were on Martha when she announced the American Cup selection—except for Mihai and Silvie's. They were having a quiet conversation, but their ears perked up when my name was announced after Rebecca Bross's. Silvie quietly said, "Oh, wow," and we all looked at one another, surprised. I had surpassed everyone's expectations, including our own.

The American Cup is a very important competition. Not only is it the biggest international competition held in the United States each year, but its list of past winners also reads like a who's who of US gymnastics, some of whom went on to win Olympic gold medals.

The American Cup was being held in Worcester, Massachusetts, barely an hour away from my house. Word had gotten around that I would be making my senior international debut there, and a lot of girls from my gym were planning to come cheer me on.

Tape recorders in hand, a group of journalists navigated their way around the apparatus podiums of the Worcester arena the day before the meet. They came to a halt at the edge of the floor podium, where I sat in my black USA tracksuit, and formed a semicircle around me.

"This is a big meet for you, your first senior competition, first American Cup, and in front of your home crowd," one said. "Are you feeling the pressure?"

"No, I feel very confident," I assured him. I thought that's what I was supposed to say to the media, but when the journalists left, I began to ponder the question further. Suddenly the enormity of what I was about to do came down on me like a load of bricks. *Maybe I do feel the pressure now*, I thought. When I was done with the pre-competition interviews, I was very quiet. Mihai noticed my stricken face. "What's the matter?" he asked.

"What if I don't do well?" I burst out. "I just told everyone how confident I was, and now I don't feel confident at all. What if I mess up?"

Mihai put his hands on my shoulders. "The best thing to do when talking to the media is to stay humble," he remarked. "Never say that you're expecting anything. All that you can do is what you've done in practice. And you've practiced a lot. You're ready."

That night, I recalled the interaction with the media to my dad. He gave me a piece of advice he would continue to repeat throughout my career: "Just relax; do your talking on the floor."

We got to the arena early the next day for a two-hour warm-up before the competition began. The American Cup is one of the few big competitions where men and women compete at the same time, and the men, who have six events to do, are up first. The women don't make their appearance until about an hour later.

There was nothing to do but wait. I sat in the darkness just off the arena, listening to the sounds of the crowd and the announcers, and the hushed silences when someone was performing. Soon I'd be out there, and everyone would be watching me. I gulped and tried to stay calm.

As I stood at the end of the vault runway half an hour later, I thought I was going to throw up from the nerves. I had never been more scared of anything. I could hear the voices of little girls calling my name as I stood at the foot of the vault runway. It wasn't so long ago that I had been just like them, sitting in the stands, cheering for the girl on the floor, and wanting to be just like her. I wanted to make them proud. But was I ready? When the judge lifted the green flag in her hand above her head, I tried to calm my breathing as I raised my hand to salute her. My nerves made me feel like my throat was closing. It's just one vault, I told myself. I lowered my arms, took my mark, and began to run.

The vault was very good: high and controlled, and I stuck the landing.

One down, three to go.

Bars was next, then balance beam. I tried my best to convince myself I was at practice, going over the numbers I had practiced with Mihai. I turned in an especially clean routine on beam, the highlight of my day. And when I did my new dismount—the same one Carly Patterson had used when she won the Olympics in 2004—I stuck it cold.

The crowd erupted in cheers, but best of all was Martha's reaction when I came down from the podium. "The beamer!" she exclaimed with a big smile, taking my face in her hands and giving me a hug. You know you've done well when Martha gives you a hug.

The meet ended on floor and my scores were good enough

for second in the all-around, just behind Rebecca. It was a good debut, and I was delighted—not to mention very relieved.

But in this sport, there are no guarantees—you're only as good as your last performance.

I was home for a few days and then went back to camp. This time, a trip to Italy was at stake to compete at the annual City of Jesolo Trophy, an experience-building competition. Even though I had done well at the American Cup, I knew that I'd always have to prove that I was ready to go again. Once again, I made the cut.

Jesolo, Italy, an Italian beach town just an hour north of Venice, is also the site of one of my biggest firsts in gymnastics: the first time I won a major all-around title. It was very exciting to compete among some of the best gymnasts not only from the United States but from Russia, Italy, and Great Britain, three top countries. It felt great that all my hard work was paying off.

Usually after competitions, there was a banquet. Along with the other girls, I helped myself to a small slice of pizza, and had just bitten into the cheesiness when I felt a tap on my shoulder. It was one of the national staff members.

"I need to talk to you for a minute," they said. I put my slice down and followed the person out the door.

"You were eating pizza in there," they said accusingly as soon as we got outside.

I didn't understand. The competition was over. I'd won. And everyone else had taken a slice. What was the big deal?

"Do you know how disappointed we are to see you eating pizza? Aly, you are *never* allowed to do that again, as long as you're competing," the person continued, genuinely angry. "Don't you see that there's always the next competition, and the one after that? What were you doing? Were you using your head at all?" With that, they stormed off.

I called my mom in tears. "I'm so embarrassed," I told her, sobbing. "USA Gymnastics will probably never like me again. I'll never get picked to be on another team." I thought my life was over.

"All this because you ate a slice of pizza?" Mom asked.

I sniffled. "Yeah."

"I'm sure they're not mad at you," she reassured me. "You just won the meet. I'm sure they're okay with you having one slice of pizza. You're a kid—go ahead and eat. You need your energy."

I went back inside, but I didn't have any more pizza. As the banquet went on around me, I sat feeling sick with embarrassment and shame. I had gotten the message: I could not slack off, even for a minute. I was determined to prove that I deserved to be among the best.

Even years later, I feel sad when I look back on that moment. What the coach wanted me to understand was that as an elite athlete, everything you put into your body contributes to your performance. Staying disciplined and making sure that *most* of what you eat is good for you is part of training. What a shame this excellent message was so poorly delivered.

What I know now is that it's also important to live your life, be happy, and treat yourself. Sure, splurging should be done in moderation. But nobody should ever encourage you to deprive yourself of food.

However, at the time, I didn't think that. At the time, I thought if achieving my goals means giving up pizza and depriving myself sometimes, so be it.

Once again, I was home for a few days, then repacked my bag for camp. A third big competition was looming—the Pacific Rim Championships in Melbourne, Australia.

If I had been a little tired before Italy, I was now approaching exhaustion. I had competed twice in a month, sandwiching camps in between meets, and I was ready for a rest—or as much of a rest as training with Mihai would permit. The schoolwork was piling up, too. My teachers were slowly becoming accustomed to me coming to them and asking for two or three weeks of work to do on the road. Most of my teachers were accommodating about my increasing number of absences, but some were not. None of my teachers cut me any slack when it came to turning in projects and assignments, though. I became a pro at managing time. Which meant schoolwork and sleeping whenever I could. Sleep was important, and I learned quickly that international flights presented a great opportunity to catch up on sleep. The only way to survive the intense training, traveling, and pressure of meets was to get lots of rest.

My body may have been telling me to rest, but a little voice in my head was reminding me how lucky I was. *You're on the national team*, it said. *You're getting to travel the world and compete. Just because you've done well the last few times doesn't mean you're a safe bet. You still have to prove yourself. You don't want them to stop picking you, do you?*

So I went back to camp, gritted my way through tough workout after tough workout, hoping to be selected for the next competition. During practice at the ranch, it was hot and windy outside, and the doors of the gym were wide open. When I went for my triple twist on floor exercise, a bug flew right in front of my face! I still went for the twist, because I didn't dare stop and offer "Sorry, a bug flew in front of my face" as an excuse. Martha would not have gone for that! You were expected to show her that you were prepared for absolutely anything—even bugs in the face.

I was named to the Pac Rim team. Gymnasts from Russia,

China, Australia, and Canada would be meeting in Melbourne to compete. It was another chance to build my reputation.

The American squad for this meet consisted of seniors Rebecca, Bridget Sloan, and myself, as well as three of the top juniors: Jordyn, Kyla, and Sabrina. A day after the team was selected, we headed to the airport.

Mihai and I were put in a car with Sabrina and her coach, Teodora (who had been Nadia Comaneci's teammate!), who teamed up with Mihai to tease us that Australia was down under at the end of the world. "Did you remember to pack your bathing suits?" Teodora teased us. "Because we'll be jumping off the plane into the water!" We giggled as they teased us. The coaches were serious inside the gym, but they made us laugh when we weren't at practice.

We were standing by the luggage carousel in the Melbourne airport when a security guard came around with a pair of drug-sniffing dogs on a leash. Their noses moved cautiously over the ground, and as I watched them, I felt a chill of terror skate up my spine. We all snuck snacks into our luggage for Australia. Mine included oatmeal, energy bars, trail mix, chocolate, and watermelon Sour Patch Kids. I never went anywhere without watermelon Sour Patch Kids, which I considered good luck.

I was afraid the dog would smell my food and somehow alert the coaches. I pictured their reactions when they discovered the contraband in my bag. Then everyone else's bags would be searched, and their snacks (including the jars of Nutella and peanut butter I knew were in someone else's bag) would be confiscated. And it would all be my fault.

I even worked out a defense. I'd say that I had just packed the snacks in case of a low blood sugar crash. Then I was going to eat one—just one, I swear—of the Sour Patch Kids to revive myself. They were like medicine. Really. I let out a deep breath of relief when the dogs didn't show any interest in my bag, but I didn't fully relax until we had left the airport.

Other high schoolers I knew were sneaking out at night or drinking on the weekends. Our form of civil disobedience was to pool our desserts in someone's hotel room and have an impromptu picnic.

In Australia, I struggled with the thirteen-hour time difference, sheer exhaustion from back-to-back-to-back meets, and the pressure of proving myself yet again. *How many times was it going to take?* I wondered.

To make matters worse, my right hamstring had been acting up. My heels were also hurting from landing front flips on the beams in Italy, and my quads were so sore that I couldn't even touch my heel to my bottom. Worst of all was my back, which hurt no matter what I did. On top of the pressure, I had to work through pain.

A national team staff member noticed me wincing through the workout. I was jet-lagged and looking forward to passing out as soon as we got back to the hotel when the woman came up to me.

"Dr. Nassar is here in Australia," she said. "I'll get him to come see you."

"Thanks," I said, "but I'm really tired. I think I just want to go to sleep."

"You have to see him," she insisted. "He's the best there is, and it's a huge honor that he agrees to work with the team. Seriously—you won't regret it." I didn't want to be labeled as uncooperative, so finally I said okay.

Larry Nassar came to my hotel room. At first, I didn't think too much of the massage. There were two other people in the room, and I was wearing leggings. There was something about the massage that made me uncomfortable, but the staff member's words stuck in my head.

The quicker he worked on me, the quicker I could go to bed. I was desperate to feel better so I would compete well. No one really wanted to say they felt injured. Being injured meant potentially missing out on assignments, which would give other athletes a chance to take your spot. If they did well, you risked being forgotten.

Larry also proved to be very understanding. "USA Gymnastics sometimes goes overboard with their expectations," Larry said as he massaged me. "They shouldn't push you as hard as they do."

I remember feeling grateful that he understood me.

All through practice, I kept crash-landing. We had gotten off a fourteen-hour flight days before, it was 4:00 AM in Boston, and here we were working out. Throughout the day, I felt dizzy and a bit lightheaded. We had been warned that the third day in Australia was the worst for jet lag.

When I unintentionally did a vault straight to my back without even flipping off the table, Mihai said, "You get back down that runway and do that vault again." Bending toward me, he added in a whisper, "Do you want Martha to be mad and think you can't handle the pressure? Because that's what you're showing her right now."

I hated it when I messed up on vault, because it had come to be the event that scared me the most. But Mihai liked me to end each event on a good note, and he didn't want me to go to sleep stressed out about my wipeout on vault.

I wanted to ask to do an easier vault to clear my head, but there was only time for one more vault. I had convinced myself that if I made even one mistake in competition, I'd never be selected for another team. I shook myself and began to run. I did manage to do the vault, but it was under rotated and I was lucky not to hurt myself.

Spooked, I was putting my grips on to begin the bars workout when Martha came over and squatted down beside me. She looked deep into my eyes and said simply, "You have to turn the page." I swallowed and nodded, trying to let it all go. It didn't sink in at the moment, but over the years it has been invaluable advice—and not just in competition, but in life.

I told the female trainer who had come with us that my heel was bothering me, but asked her not to repeat that to Mihai and certainly not to Martha. I had been doing so well, I didn't want them to pull me from the meet. I wanted to keep proving myself.

"Even if it's bruised, I'll still be able to compete," I assured the trainer. I hadn't come halfway around the world to sit out.

The next day, I learned the trainer had told Martha and Mihai about my heel anyway. They were nervous about the potential injury—and upset that I hadn't told them how I was feeling. "You need to communicate with your coach," Martha told me sharply.

Mihai wasn't pleased, either. "Why didn't you tell me first?" he asked, looking hurt.

On the morning of the competition, Mihai said that I

seemed completely ready. I felt wiped out from all the meets, so I was glad to hear it. Mihai is a tough coach, but inside he's a softy. His training was rigorous because he saw my potential.

Running on fumes, I made it through the competition. Once again, the results were very good: gold with the team and three individual silver medals for beam, floor, and in the all-around.

I even made bar finals, which must have made Mihai wonder if the end of the world was near! Mihai had been known to say that never in a million years would I make bar finals at a major competition, and the Chinese team was favored to win. "Who knows, maybe you'll even medal!" he said cheerfully. "We'll just have to ask the Chinese team to skip the final!" Everyone laughed.

In the final, I was transitioning from the low bar to the high bar when one of my hands slipped off and I fell flat on my face. Mihai hugged me when the routine was over. He was just glad I made the final.

Everyone was in a good mood, happy the competition was over and elated with our results, which included bunches of medals from both the seniors and juniors. Before we left the next morning, I glanced around to make sure no one was watching, then took a big red strawberry and dipped it into the chocolate fountain at the buffet. *I deserve this*, I reminded myself right before biting into it. It tasted like heaven.

CHAPTER 8

WORLDS AWAY

Rotterdam, the Netherlands
October 2010

When I was younger and Alicia went to the World Championships, we would gather around her in a circle on the floor and have story time for a whole hour when she came back. We'd sit wide-eyed while she described the arena, the training gyms, the crowds, and the funny things that happened to the team. She would always bring in her medals, too, and pass them around. I remember reverently weighing one of her golds, holding it lightly as though it were a sacred object that might disintegrate in my hands.

So it meant a lot when I was selected to be part of the team that traveled to the World Championships in Rotterdam, the Netherlands, in October 2010.

Worlds. I could hardly believe it. Next to the Olympics, Worlds is the most important gymnastics competition there is, and it's very special to be able to compete there. And if ever there is a stage to prove yourself as an Olympic contender, Worlds is it.

I now had five senior meets under my belt, having finished third at 2010 Nationals to Rebecca and Mattie Larson after my run of success in the spring. I wasn't the only Raisman who got attention at Nationals—the family sitting behind mine was so sure that I would make the Olympic team that they asked for photos and autographs with Brett! Sure enough, they found my mom in 2013, and showed her that they kept the picture on their phone.

Earlier that summer, I had received a sharp reminder of just how precarious a place on the team could be. It happened after the US Classic. I had been working hard on the Amanar vault in the gym, and it was starting to come together. Some days I would land several on my feet. Other days I wouldn't land any. Mihai suggested that I give it a try at the Classic anyway. Even though it wasn't consistent, he wanted to see whether the adrenaline of competition would help push me through it.

In the weeks before the Classic, my back pain was the worst it had ever been. I could barely arch or twist my back, since most movement sent blinding pains all down my legs. I again tried to work through it since I knew now was not the time to ease up. World Championships were just around the corner.

The pain limited my ability to practice, and that caught up to me in competition on the vault. I didn't even get close to landing it. It was a nasty fall, one that could have easily damaged my knee, and I was lucky to have walked away from it with my cartilage intact.

After we were done competing, Martha approached me. "You've had such a good year," she began. "You've really built a name for yourself in the sport. But when you come here unprepared and you fall, you tear your name down." I was heartbroken. More than ever, it was clear that no matter how many routines I hit, even one fall could damage my standing in Martha's eyes.

That fall, the cabins at the ranch hummed with college talk. Mackenzie Caquatto and Kytra Hunter were set to attend the University of Florida that winter. Bridgette Caquatto announced plans to go as well.

The college question weighed on me. I felt a lot of pressure to choose a school and make a commitment, even though I was only sixteen. For the moment, though, I pushed it out of my head.

Ahead of the final selection camp at the ranch before Worlds, Mihai told me he wasn't nervous. "I know you're going to do well," he said. "Go out there and be confident." His kind words gave me the extra boost I needed to make the team.

The day before the second selection camp ended, the list of the seven athletes who would travel to Rotterdam was announced: Alicia, Rebecca, Mackenzie, Mattie, Bridget Sloan,

Chelsea Davis, and me. There could only be six gymnasts on the final team, but as always when it comes to World Championships, Martha would wait until the very last minute to decide who would be the alternate.

If things weren't consistent, especially in front of Martha, Mihai would get stressed out. But after one tough practice, he hugged me. "I only push you because you work so hard at the gym, and I just want to see the same thing here," he said.

We arrived in the Netherlands expected to make the podium, though not to win. There were four big contenders: Russia, China, Romania, and the United States. Russia was especially strong and heavily favored to win gold. There was a lot of buzz about Russia's Aliya Mustafina. Rotterdam was the first time we competed against each other, and it would not be the last.

It seemed like things were really coming together. My tumbling on floor was getting better and better. One coach had even begun calling me "Radar" because of how often I stuck my tumbling lines.

"Nice job, Radar!" he'd say, offering a high five. Martha had a nickname for me, too. When she was pleased, she called me Miss Consistency. I liked that.

"I just hope everyone has a positive attitude and enjoys the experience because this is a once-in-a-lifetime opportunity," I confided to my journal. "I am going to remember this for the rest of my life and I want to think fondly of it." I understood that making one world team didn't necessarily mean you'd ever make another, so the experience was to be savored.

In Rotterdam, Martha liked to duplicate competition scenarios as much as possible. Since the United States had drawn a start time of 8:00 AM, we got up early every morning and boarded a shuttle to the practice gym near the arena. "This way, your bodies will know what to expect in the competition," she told us.

It was cold and rainy in Rotterdam. The gym was freezing because we arrived so early that the heat hadn't had time to warm the area yet. During one of our first sessions in the training gym, we had just finished on uneven bars when a volunteer dashed up to Martha. "I just wanted to let you know that the bars haven't been set up all the way yet," he said, out of breath. "We're still getting them completely anchored to the ground." When Martha informed him that we had just finished our workout on bars, his eyes widened in shock and he looked aghast. She was in a bad mood for the rest of the morning, probably thinking about how we could have all been injured.

At eight o'clock that night, I was alone in my hotel room when there was a tap on the door. I opened it to find Larry Nassar standing in the hall. "I thought you could use a massage," he said.

Things went well for me in the first round of competition. Not only did I make the all-around final, but I was also in the top eight on floor, making that final as well. These results were way beyond anyone's expectations. I had a great day, and one of the best moments came when it was over, when Mihai told me he was proud of me. My family was so excited about my showing that my dad booked a ticket to Rotterdam (my mom was already there) so he could cheer for me in person.

A few days later, my teammates and I were stuffed into an elevator descending to the ground floor of the hotel and belting out one of our go-to workout songs, on our way down to lunch right before the team final. We were mid-rap and laughing hysterically when the doors opened and we practically fell out onto the coaches, who were waiting for us in the lobby. Mihai's eyebrows shot up as he looked at me busting out Soulja Boy's rhymes, and he broke out laughing, too!

We had qualified in third place, behind Russia and China, and we had had the highest team scores for both vault and beam.

The team started the competition on bars, though beam was the first event I performed on in the team final. It's not easy performing on beam at any competition, but knowing a World title was on the line made it even more difficult. We knew Martha wanted to win. Although we all did our best to block out the pressure, Alicia, Rebecca, and I each nearly fell once during our beam routines. We were eager to make up those deductions on floor.

Mattie fell on floor. She looked so sad as she came down from the podium. Rebecca was next, then I took a deep breath and walked up the steps to begin my routine.

When the music came on, all the hours of training came out. I hit my routine, with clean landings on the tumbling passes and what I hoped was expressive dance. Because I was shy on the competition floor, showmanship was an area I had been working hard to improve.

We closed out the final on vault, which is always the quickest event at a competition. Although we all did clean vaults, we knew it would be close with Russia. China, having counted too many falls, was out of the gold medal race. But we had a shot at it, depending on how the Russians responded. They had an excellent vaulting team, with higher difficulty scores than ours. But, like China, Russia had come apart, counting three falls on bars and opening the door for another team to get past them. It was going to be very close.

As Aliya, Russia's last competitor, stepped onto the floor, we all huddled to watch, clutching one another's hands and holding our breath as one. The routine was enchanting and beautifully performed. But on her very last tumbling pass, she landed her triple twist off-kilter and took a big step backward—and out of bounds. That would cost her, we knew. On opposite sides of the arena, our two teams waited anxiously for the score to flash. Would it be us with the gold, or would it be them?

It was them. In spite of the deduction for going out of bounds, Aliya's routine was enough to put Russia over the top for the gold by only two-tenths of a point.

My first World Championship medal! I quickly got the sense, though, that silver was a huge disappointment. Even though we entered the meet in third place (at the qualifying meet two days before), finishing second when we had been so close to gold was hard for the staff. There were a lot of little things that could have tipped the scales the other way, especially avoiding some of the mistakes that we had all made on beam.

However, Mattie was blamed. Some people looked past her like she didn't exist. She sat quietly at dinner that night and picked at her food. I could see she was trying hard not to cry. Mattie continued to get the cold shoulder from many until our plane touched down in Houston several days later. She never competed at the elite level again.

I'd qualified to the all-around in third place, and I couldn't wait to compete. As I pulled on my maroon USA leotard with white ribbon detail that afternoon, I remembered all the times I'd snuggled in bed with my mom watching Worlds when I was a kid. It felt so amazing to be competing in one myself.

The only thing that could make it better would be leaving Rotterdam with an individual medal of my own.

In all-around finals, we began on vault, then went to bars. My bar routine started well. I got through my two big release moves on the high bar before a successful transition to the low bar. *So far, so good*, I thought. I tried to extend every skill and hit vertical handstands, which is important for the execution score.

Things were going well until my second-to-last skill, called a toe shoot stalder, where the gymnast puts her feet on the bar as she swings backward. As you swing through the bottom, you're supposed to shoot your feet toward the ceiling. If it goes right, you end in a handstand on top of the bar. The timing is critical: If you shoot your toes too early or too late, you'll fall or miss the handstand, either of which results in a big deduction.

I shot my toes to the sky a fraction of a second too early. That caused me to have to arch my back a little in the handstand, and the next thing I knew I had to do a quick half pirouette to keep from falling. Frantically, I did a handstand pirouette and then another, trying to cover up for the mistake, but it didn't work. I turned over the bar and wound up on the ground, knowing I had likely blown any chance of an all-around medal. I could hear the whole crowd gasp. I felt so embarrassed for falling. I felt defeated and numb. I felt like I didn't deserve to be there, that I wasn't good enough. I don't remember the rest of the meet because I blocked out everything. I finished in thirteenth place, a disappointment since I'd qualified in third.

At least Mihai was happy. Talking to a reporter afterward, he dismissed my mistakes. "Oh, she is so young," he commented. "She came from nowhere in the last year, and she did very well this year. She did well with her team, out there with her friends, but alone not so well. But she is too young just yet. I was so proud of her, for coming back after a mistake, for doing good on her last events. Aly had hopes, though. But her dream was too big, and when she woke up—bang—it frightened her!"

Privately, Mihai joked that maybe my dad flying out at the last minute was the bad luck charm, and that maybe he should stay home next time. Mihai and Silvie were often superstitious when it came to competitions. Silvie always needs to sit in her ticketed seat, for example, so in Rotterdam she sat where she was assigned even though she could have moved to an empty seat closer to the floor!

But bad luck and superstition had nothing to do with it. I had put too much pressure on myself to be perfect. I had been too worried about what others would think of me, and now I was worried that since I didn't medal, people wouldn't like me.

"You still have floor. You can end Worlds on a good note," Mihai said encouragingly. I put everything into my floor routine, and it was the best I had ever done. I hoped it would be enough for a medal. Up until the last competitor, I was in third place, and I was beginning to picture myself on the podium.

When the final gymnast's score came through and bumped me to fourth by a mere .05 points, I was crushed. I felt tears welling up. "Don't cry," Mihai said. "And don't be so hard on yourself. This was your first Worlds. You did great. There's always next year."

Being ranked fourth in the world at anything should have felt great, but it felt horrible to be so close to a medal and have it be just out of reach by an extremely small margin. I hoped to never finish fourth again. I took Mihai's words to heart: I was still young and still had a lot to look forward to.

After more than a month away, I was so glad to see my family. To sleep in my big, comfy bed. Best of all, when I proudly walked into the gym the next day, with the World silver medal in my bag, the little girls of Brestyan's flocked around me, all excitedly asking questions at the same time. I settled down in a corner of the floor mat, my heart bursting with pride as they arranged themselves in a circle around me, and gathered myself for story time.

CHAPTER 9

PRESSURE COOKER

Saint Paul, Minnesota
August 2011

The injuries began at the 2011 National Championships in Saint Paul, Minnesota.

To mark my second year on the senior national circuit, Silvie had choreographed a cool new floor routine to music from "Hava Nagila" for me, and I was looking forward to showing it off in competition. The folk song was a fun departure from the more modern pieces many other gymnasts were using, and I liked it because it was something the crowd could clap along to.

Even better, that unique tumbling pass that Mihai had hinted to Martha about—six big skills connected together and packed into a supercharged line—had really come together.

With Bubbie and half of her retirement community in the

stands cheering me on, I won the bronze medal at the American Cup in Jacksonville, Florida, that spring, behind Jordyn and Aliya. I was especially glad to be able to perform in front of Bubbie, who was undergoing treatment for lung cancer. She was still the same Bubbie, though, proudly bragging about her grandkid; she'd already told all her friends I was going to the Olympics.

On my second trip to represent the United States in Jesolo, McKayla, Jordyn, newcomer Gabby Douglas, and I had grabbed the top four spots in the all-around, ahead of some of the best from Russia and Italy. I followed up with a victory at the CoverGirl Classic that July.

With new seniors Jordyn, Gabby, and McKayla all posting impressive results and Rebecca having won two individual medals in Rotterdam, people began talking about the exciting potential of the American team. Even as my coaches and I focused on the big upcoming meets—Nationals and the World Championships in Tokyo—I understood that everyone was already looking ahead to the 2012 Olympic Games in London, now only a year away.

Maybe Olympic fever played with my mind a bit, too. When we arrived in Minnesota for the US Championships, I seemed to have forgotten everything I had worked so hard to finesse in training. The equipment felt strange. The bars and beam podiums seemed bouncier than ever, throwing my timing off and making my skills feel unfamiliar. The pressure was getting to me.

As always, Nationals was a two-day meet, with the senior competition shown live on NBC. The live broadcast led to delays, since the TV crew didn't want top contenders performing on different events at the same time. It was common to wait several minutes on the podium before you got the green light, with long pauses during commercial breaks.

I'm not sure whether it was the slow pace of competition, or just the pressure, but almost everyone fell on something the first day. Several of us wanted to forget the first day as soon as it was over, but things were better on the second day—at least at first.

I was on the podium getting set to mount the beam for my third routine of the day. I had a whole ritual for getting myself collected before beam: First, I made sure the springboard was precisely set for my mount. Then I looked to see that there was enough chalk on my feet and shins (which I grabbed during my dismount). After that, I needed several moments to calm my breathing. I would finish by pacing around a bit trying to keep warm—when you're wearing nothing but a leotard in a chilly arena, you get cold quickly!

I had reached the pacing phase when I saw Rebecca out of the corner of my eye, racing down the vault runway. I turned my head just in time to watch her do a roundoff entry onto the springboard and lift up into her double-twisting Yurchenko. Unfortunately, she didn't finish the twist in time to land safely. As she hit the ground, her body, specifically her right knee, was still twisting. Even before she opened her mouth, I knew something was very wrong.

Her scream of pain echoed throughout the arena as she grabbed her bent right knee and flopped onto her back. Her coach, Valeri, hopped up onto the podium and raised his arm, signaling to the medical staff posted around the arena. The other gymnasts, coaches, and spectators looked on in horror as the medics rushed to her and began stabilizing her leg. It was awful to see her get injured, and her cries of agony scared me.

"Every single person in this arena that is affiliated with gymnastics knows that that can be the deadliest of combinations: an under rotated, still twisting into the floor landing," said NBC commentator Tim Daggett, who was doing the live broadcast from his seat.

I turned back to the beam, but my concentration was absolutely shattered. In the background, I could hear Rebecca crying. My heart broke for her. Few had worked harder than Rebecca to get where she was. Like everyone, she'd prepared for this competition for months. To have it end in a second because of one bad landing seemed monstrously unfair.

Every now and again, you get a reminder of how dangerous gymnastics can be. The fear keeps you up when you're trying to sleep. Or it wakes you up, sweaty and terrified, in the middle of the night. Good training techniques minimize the danger, but there's no way to completely eliminate the risk.

Mihai recovered from the shock quicker than I did. "Stay in the zone," he said, placing himself between me and the scene unfolding on vault. He looked into my eyes and nodded encouragingly. I looked across the arena to where Martha was sitting. She was looking straight at me, the light glinting off the lenses of her glasses. I felt like the judges took an hour to give me the green light. When they did, I jumped up onto the beam, feeling terrified.

Normally when I'm up on beam, everything else ceases to exist. For ninety seconds, it's me and the beam, alone in the world. This time, however, I couldn't block anything out, and my performance suffered. On a particularly difficult leap, I came so close to falling that I had to grab the beam to stay on—a big deduction. The entire crowd gasped, and I registered their reaction, which just distracted me more. My body mechanically performed the movements as my thoughts went in a thousand different directions: *Is Rebecca all right? What happens now? I just hope I can get through this. What if something happens to me, too? Please just let this be over.*

Somewhere in the middle of the routine, I heard the crowd start applauding, and realized Rebecca was being wheeled out of the arena. A few seconds later, I heard a single beep—the warning that I had ten seconds to do my dismount or I'd incur a time deduction. I was still on the beam ten seconds later when the second beep came, signaling overtime.

I don't remember my dismount or my landing. I just remember thinking I'd never been so happy to be done with anything in my life.

Martha came up to me after my beam routine. "Just this once, you have an excuse," she said. She patted me on the back and walked away.

With the World Championships looming, the US team momentum seemed to have ground to a halt. "Right now, is this a team that could go to the World Championships and perform like they did the last two quads and win a gold medal?" NBC commentator John Roethlisberger asked during the broadcast.

"Well, if they perform like they did tonight, John, absolutely not," Tim Daggett responded.

Only three gymnasts compete on each event in a world or Olympic team final. All three scores count toward the team score, putting an immense amount of pressure on each gymnast to avoid mistakes. We all knew that one mistake in a routine could mean the difference between gold or going home empty-handed.

All this meant that the three gymnasts who performed on

each event had to be stellar. And that was a problem, because there was one event where the United States was not that stellar.

At the time, the United States was considered weak on uneven bars. While there were girls who were really good on bars, most of them were considered weaker on the other events. That left the world team selection committee the choice of: a) taking someone who was just okay on bars but could contribute good scores on the other events or b) turning to a "specialist"— an athlete who was very good on bars, but who would likely not be able to contribute to the team score anywhere else.

Rebecca Bross excelled on bars as well as the other events. With her out of commission, many thought Mackenzie Caquatto would be the one to fill her shoes. But at the selection camp, Mackenzie injured her ankles after landing awkwardly on a beam dismount. Suddenly she was out, too.

In the end, seven women—Jordyn, McKayla, Sabrina, Alicia, Gabby, Anna Li, and me—were chosen to make the trip to Tokyo. Of course, the catch was that only six of us would make up the final team, which would be announced a couple of days before the competition began. Until then, in a sport where nothing is guaranteed, we'd continue to prove ourselves.

CHAPTER 10

FIRST TASTE OF GOLD

Tokyo, Japan
October 2011

Shortly before we left for Japan, we learned an exciting piece of news: The US men's team would be staying in the same hotel in Tokyo as we were. Even better, on the same floor. We had just been cloistered for ten days of camp, and the prospect of socializing with the boys was *very* appealing.

I had developed a little crush on blue-eyed Jake Dalton, a top gymnast from the University of Oklahoma who was also an Olympic prospect. So had Jordyn. Our "rivalry" for Jake's attention became an inside joke.

After several years as the designated "next big thing" in American gymnastics, Jordyn had lived up to her billing by winning the National title in Saint Paul as a first-year senior. A hard worker with clean execution, she was also capable of doing extremely difficult gymnastics with ease. She was strong on all four events and had mastered the Amanar vault when she was a junior. By the time she was a senior, her Amanar vault was precise and powerful.

As we saw firsthand with Russia's success at the 2010 World Championships, the Amanar is a very important skill in gymnastics. It is worth so many difficulty points compared to most other vaults that the team able to show three or even two Amanars had a large advantage over countries lacking that vault. In 2010, two of the three Russians had done Amanars in the team final. The Russians had walked out as world champions. This year, McKayla and Jordyn were both planning to show Amanars, and we hoped that would tip the scales.

It was obvious that the girls who could deliver Amanars stood a better chance of being named to the Olympic team, which was why I was still working feverishly on mine. After my scary crash at the 2010 US Classic, I hadn't tried it in a meet since. I didn't want to compete it if I wasn't 100 percent ready. One reason the vault has such a high difficulty rating is that there's a high risk of a knee injury if something goes wrong. Aliya had found that out the hard way at the European Championships earlier that year. In the all-around final, she landed wrong and tore her ACL. Knowing what happened to Aliya made me even more hesitant to attempt the vault before I really needed to.

Even without Aliya, the Russians were still the team to beat. In Aliya's absence, another formidable rival had presented herself. Like Jordyn, Viktoria Komova was a first-year senior with an impressive junior record. She and Jordyn were expected to battle for the all-around title in Tokyo.

The first night in Japan, I went to see my Brestyan's training buddy, Talia, who was competing with the Canadian team and staying in the same hotel. Talia and her teammates were bouncing around their rooms, refreshed from *a whole day off.* "I don't even know what that is anymore," I said enviously. Martha had made us run up and down, stretch, and do walkovers in the hallways as soon as we arrived.

To distract ourselves from the looming competition, we started a prank war with the boys. When you're not allowed to leave your hotel, you find ways to pass the time! Our favorite game was sneaking out, tiptoeing down the hall, ringing the bells to their rooms, and bolting back into ours, slamming the door and collapsing into fits of laughter.

Every day, I Skyped with my family to catch up on what everyone was doing in Needham. My mother would eventually travel to Tokyo with Talia's mom to watch the meet. My dad stayed home with my siblings. "Give Martha a kiss for me," Dad joked at the end of one call.

"Ha, ha, so funny," I shot back sarcastically, but the thought did make me laugh.

Mihai ran me hard during the two-a-day workouts in Tokyo. He took pride in the fact that his gymnasts could handle the most physical work, so I was usually the only one on the team required to do a full floor routine every day, as opposed to the others, who did one every other day.

"How are you not dying?" McKayla asked me incredulously.

"This is what I do at home," I shrugged. "I'm really not exaggerating when I say how hard my program is!" I was terribly jealous that the others only had to do one routine every two days, but I trusted Mihai. "I know it's a lot more than the others," he would say. "But our hard work will pay off one day if you just listen to me." I never doubted it.

On October 6, two days before we were scheduled to compete in prelims, disaster struck. On one of my beam dismounts in the training gym, I didn't get a good takeoff as I punched off the beam. *Pull!* I commanded my body, knowing I hadn't gotten the height I needed to safely complete the dismount. I landed short and felt my ankles give out. The next thing I knew, I was on the mat and Mihai was standing over me, looking frightened. He helped me over to a big yellow block next to the floor while someone else ran for ice.

Cold fear flooded through my mind. *How bad is this? What if I can't train? Will they replace me in the competition? What will Martha think?* Above all, I was wondering what this meant for my chances of making the Olympic team next year.

Not ten minutes later, I watched Alicia tear her Achilles tendon. From the second she punched off the floor into her Arabian double front, I knew something was wrong. Instead of keeping herself tightly tucked as she went up into the air, her leg went limp. She landed sitting down on the mat, her foot splayed awkwardly out to one side. She did not get up. She looked at her leg, banged her hand on the floor in frustration, and lay back.

As the coaches hustled over to Alicia, big heaving sobs welled up in my chest. I felt panicked, like I was going to faint or throw up right there. Stars exploded in front of my eyes, frightening me even further. Two more injuries. Months of careful preparation wiped out in ten minutes. *This can't be happening.*

Mihai and another coach carried Alicia over to the yellow block and sat her down. When we made eye contact, my tears stopped. For some reason, both of us started laughing hysterically. What a pair: me with my swollen ankles covered by bags of ice and Alicia with her Achilles nonexistent. It wasn't funny, of course, but some situations are so uncomfortable and scary that you laugh from sheer awkwardness. "Look at my foot! It's so shriveled up," Alicia said, laughing and crying at the same time.

"What is happening?!" I replied in disbelief.

We sat there for a little while longer, when a voice interrupted my thoughts. "Aly, come on, time for bars."

I looked up at Martha, beckoning me over. "Wait, what?" I asked, confused.

"Tape your foot. You don't use your foot on bars. You can skip the dismount so you don't have to land."

I limped over to the bar, wincing with each step, and started my bar warm-up. Every time my foot moved, I felt pain, and I worried I wouldn't be able to compete. *Why don't they let me rest?* I thought, annoyed. *It hasn't even been an hour since I hurt myself.*

Martha always liked to say that a day with only one practice was like a day off, which drove us crazy. After our practice ended, she gave us "the day off." When we got back to the hotel, Martha told me I could take a nap, but then would have to run up and down the hallway to show her I was okay.

"See? She's fine," Mihai said to Martha as I raced along the hallway. "There's no reason to panic. She'll be good to go on the day."

Martha turned to me. From the look on her face, I could see that she wasn't convinced. "Let me see you run a little bit more," she said. I began skipping, hiding the pain because I wanted to compete.

Alicia was on a plane headed back to the United States for surgery. There was more bad news: Anna wouldn't be competing, either. While other countries would compete with six gymnasts, we'd now have to compete with just five. And should anything else go wrong, their injuries left the United States without a viable alternate.

Our misfortunes had not gone unnoticed. A few journalists had actually been in the training gym observing our practice, and they had seen my rough landing and Alicia's injury. The buzz was that the relatively inexperienced team was headed for a meltdown on the competition floor. The United States had been on every World podium since 2001, but all of a sudden that streak seemed in doubt.

I was determined to do what I could to help keep everyone calm. A strange thing was happening: The other girls started coming to me for advice and encouragement. I was still building my résumé, having done just one World Championships. Still, it was one more than everyone else. Gabby, Jordyn, McKayla, and Sabrina were all first-year seniors.

After my hallway jogging proved to Martha that I could compete, Mihai drew me aside. "Martha needs you to show her and the girls that we can be a team now," he said. "You've all been through a lot during the past few months. You need to pull together now. Can you do that?" I nodded. Oddly enough, the situation reminded me of the childhood game I'd played with my siblings. It was like we were back in our "boat," adrift at sea. As the oldest, it was up to me to see us through.

"Forget what everybody else is saying," I told the others. "We're not going to let anybody tell us what we are or aren't capable of. They don't know us. They don't see how hard we work. We can prove them wrong." And I, for one, fully intended to.

We started on beam in the qualification round, performing right under the noses of the journalists, who were seated just above us. You could hear a pin drop in the arena as Sabrina mounted the beam to lead off Team USA. She was almost flawless: Skill flowed after skill, just like we'd practiced a thousand times.

From then on, everyone was on fire. We delivered routine after hit routine. At the end of the qualification round we were on top, more than three points ahead of Russia. It was a huge accomplishment, especially given the injuries.

In the space of a day, the media went from doubting us to applauding us. "The US kids were more than all right," Nancy Armour of the Associated Press wrote. "They didn't have a single fall, and finished with the highest scores on uneven bars, floor exercise, and vault."

"...with liberty and justice for all."

Anyone passing by backstage before the nations were announced to march in to begin the 2011 Worlds team final would have seen the five of us standing in a circle, hands over our hearts, reciting the Pledge of Allegiance.

We had started it as a joke after a jet-lagged McKayla asked, "Are they going to play the Pledge of Allegiance when we march out?"

"Why would they do that?" Jordyn said.

"You know, to announce every country," McKayla responded, and hummed a few bars of "The Star-Spangled Banner."

"That's not the Pledge of Allegiance," I protested. "That's the national anthem."

"Yeah, yeah, that's what I meant," McKayla said. That had gotten us howling. To tease her, we had gathered in a little circle in the hallway outside the arena before podium training. Hands over our hearts, we solemnly recited the Pledge of Allegiance.

When podium training had gone well that day, we decided to keep it up. It became our thing. Before team finals, we added our own flourish at the end: All of us put our hands together in the middle of our circle, then raised them at the same time, while yelling out "U-S-A!" in unison.

"We were ready to take this on weeks ago. We've all been waiting for this night!" I wrote in my journal just before the team final. "It's going to be good. I can feel it."

The team final went just like prelim: clockwork. By the final rotation, with just McKayla, Jordyn, and me to go on floor, it was clear that if we hit our routines, we'd be world champions.

Even so, I didn't want us to get too ahead of ourselves, so right before the rotation began, I called my teammates over for a last pep talk. Arms around each other's shoulders, we huddled up. "We've done awesome today so far. Let's just hit the rest of our routines perfectly and prove to everyone we are the best team in the world. We can do this. This will be the most special moment of our lives if we can do a good routine. All we've got to do is relax and have fun and enjoy it. Come on!"

McKayla went first. She showed extreme control on her tumbling passes, particularly her challenging second pass, where she came dangerously close to going out of bounds before managing to stay in. (Later, when we watched the video in our rooms, Jordyn and I laughed, and McKayla said, "I'm still not sure how I did that!") Her dance was vintage McKayla, playing to the judges and the audience.

Jordyn followed and hit her new floor routine with all the precision that everyone was coming to expect from her. I floated up the stairs to the podium, feeling light and free, exchanging a hug with Jordyn after she finished her routine. All of the pressure seemed to evaporate as I stepped onto the floor. For the next ninety seconds, with my teammates, Mihai, Martha, and thousands of people looking on, I just did what I had practiced. I'd been working for years to give this performance.

We had developed a huge bond through the training camps and the long, hard days in Tokyo. I had never felt so comfortable and close with another group of girls, and I knew every one of us felt the same way. When one of us stepped up to perform, the rest of us pulled for her. We had been training partners before, but Tokyo made us a team.

In the mixed zone, where reporters mingle with gymnasts, someone asked me if I was surprised by the result. "No," I said honestly. "Even though this is a really young team, we're all so prepared and we have such a close bond. I had a feeling we were going to do really well here."

Standing at the top of the Worlds podium with great friends and a gold medal was only a part of the victory. I felt like we had made our coaches, and Martha, very proud. We had overcome adversity and exceeded expectations—those of everyone else, sure, but more importantly, our own.

Jordyn and I didn't have too much time to celebrate our victory, because we had to prepare for all-around finals. Jordyn had qualified in second place behind Viktoria Komova, while I was in fourth.

I hoped for a medal this time. *I would be happy with a medal of any color*, I told myself as I pulled on the hot pink and black team leotard Martha had chosen for the all-around final. But once again, bars was my undoing. I knew my bars error was costly, but I kept going. All I could give was my best, and over the next two events, I made sure that's exactly what the judges got.

When all was said and done and Jordyn's name flashed at the top of the scoreboard, my normally cool, collected friend began to cry happy tears, overcome with the emotion of becoming a world all-around champion. I gave her a hug, then looked back up to see where I'd placed.

Even with my mistake, I was fourth in the world. I sighed in frustration—I was embarrassed that I didn't compete well when it counted. Fourth again. So close, yet so far away.

Everything happens for a reason, I assured myself. But when I finished fourth again in the beam final two days after that, I couldn't help wondering what that reason was. It seemed like my destiny was to finish just off the podium.

Finally, I broke through on floor, winning the bronze medal. My first individual world medal! I couldn't believe it. I smiled from ear to ear as Mihai swept me up in a hug.

As we were all getting ready to go to the airport in the morning, I asked McKayla where she was keeping her medals.

"Oh, they're in my laptop case," she said.

"No way—mine too!" I said. We reached over to exchange high fives, but I missed her hand and hit her in the head instead. We burst out laughing. World champions or not, we weren't coordinated enough to give each other a proper high five.

CHAPTER 11

GOING PRO

Needham, Massachusetts
2011

A few months before Worlds, I received a letter from the National Jewish Sports Hall of Fame.

"Congratulations, Alexandra," it read. "You've been selected as an Outstanding Female Jewish High School Scholar-Athlete of the year. You're one of three athletes to get the award, and we'd love it if you could participate in a ceremony in New York in March."

As the date of the ceremony approached, it occurred to me that I had been missing an awful lot of school. Writing papers on planes and preparing for tests during downtime at camp allowed me to keep my grades high, and I was as hard on myself over a bad grade as I was over a bad day at the gym. But being away so much was taking a real toll on my social life.

When I was at school, I would sit glumly in the cafeteria at lunch and eat my chicken wrap in silence while my friends excitedly discussed weekend plans. Doing gymnastics was my choice, but it still hurt when they talked about parties I hadn't been invited to, even if it was only because friends assumed that I'd say I couldn't come. Feeling left out of things bothered me a lot.

Since my freshman year, I had followed a program where I took my elective courses online, which allowed me to practice in the mornings once or twice a week before heading to school for the core classes of English, history, math, and science. On those days, I often felt self-conscious because I thought I looked like a slob as I rushed into English or chemistry without even having had time to shower, let alone put on a nice outfit or makeup. *Gymnastics really is a sacrifice*, I thought ruefully one day as I wiped chalk off my neck while sitting in math class. I glanced around to see if anyone had noticed the white line on my neck. Fortunately nobody seemed to. *Phew.*

I felt self-conscious walking through the halls of Needham High School in my sweats from the gym. I watched the students walk past one another in the hallways, and couldn't help wondering if they looked at my body like a gymnastics judge might, noting minor deductions when they saw flaws.

Zit on chin, −0.3. Unkempt hair, −0.5. Big feet for her size, −0.7. Muscled shoulders, −3.0.

I see now that I was being too hard on myself, and that any person who would think of me in those terms must be dealing with their own issues and need support. Over the years, I've gradually realized that confidence must come from within, not from others' opinions, and that it's impossible to feel satisfied with yourself if you're constantly worrying about what other people think. I also learned the importance of surrounding myself with kind, loving people who help make me feel confident and strong. But at the time, the stress of training and balancing school, gymnastics, and friendships was really getting to me. I wasn't able to just be in the moment and appreciate myself.

When you feel most insecure about your body, it can help to take a step back and look at the person you are. Studies show positive reinforcement brightens your mood, so I began talking to myself in the mirror every morning. I would think about the non-physical qualities that were most important—kindness, empathy, and inclusivity, among others—and also repeat three physical traits I liked about myself: my smile, my thick dark hair, and my eyebrows, for example. (Yes, I like my eyebrows—and so should you!)

I also made an effort to carve out moments just for myself. I had very little time to indulge in casual hangouts with friends or afternoons at the mall, but I made the most of every little self-care thing I did, from brushing my teeth to taking a luxurious bath to applying moisturizer (which felt especially great after long days of sweating through training). Having that self-care routine was important to me because it helped me feel comfortable and in control. That sort of daily lift made a difference as I faced yet another intensive training session.

At school, I shrunk away from any recognition that I was somehow different. Every day, some well-meaning classmate would ask me if I was going to the Olympics, not understanding how that question stressed me out. At school, I just wanted to be Aly, the normal student, instead of Aly, the gymnast. I desperately craved the balance. Of course, those who knew me made it clear that they thought what I was doing was pretty cool. The boys on the hockey team seemed to understand what it was like to devote yourself wholeheartedly to a hard training regimen, and they went out of their way to make me feel good about myself.

"Sweet! I get to work with her," my friend Connor would say after pretending to fight with his friends over who got to be my partner for a history project.

"No way," Tommy would chime in, mock-shoving him out of the way while draping an arm around my shoulders. "I'm working with her. I'm her boyfriend."

"She doesn't want to go out with you! You smell bad," Mike retorted. I would just sit there and laugh. Okay, so the attention made me glow a little bit, too. I liked how they truly liked me for me. They didn't make me uncomfortable or comment on my body. I've been called too skinny at school and not skinny enough for a gymnast, and each hurt as much as the other, making me feel judged and uncomfortable.

I can't win, I thought. I had yet to realize that if kids thought of me that way, they weren't my friends anyway.

The boys in my history class were respectful and said they enjoyed hanging out with me because they liked my personality. I liked that.

The 2012 Olympics were now a little more than a year away, and I was beginning to think that if I remained healthy, I had an actual shot at making the team. Martha's directives were clear: "If you want to be on the team, you need to be doing double sessions at least three times a week," she told me firmly at a camp in spring 2011. "You need to improve your form, and you need to have an Amanar vault."

Thinking about the Amanar vault kept me up at night. It was nerve-wracking that my place on the team possibly hinged on mastering that one extremely complicated skill. The vault I was doing had two twists, where the Amanar has two and a half. Between that extra half a twist, and the fact that the skill required a blind landing with precise form, I was terrified about an injury. It didn't help that there were only so many people in the world who even dared to try it, or that I had so many close calls in practice and each one made me more scared to try it again. But I knew I had to bite my lip and push the fear aside. I didn't want to not make the team because I was too afraid I would fail on vault—I wanted to go to the Olympics more than I feared doing the Amanar. Mihai and Silvie believed I could do it before I believed it myself. They tried to be patient and understanding, helping me master the mental and physical aspects of the vault. That's how I finally conquered it, though the fear never fully went away.

My teachers had always been accommodating about how much school I missed, but even they were reaching their limits. Finally, it became clear that the only way I could train the way Martha and Mihai wanted me to was to take all my senior year courses online. Fortunately, almost all the core classes I needed to earn my high school diploma had been completed, leaving only the English and elective credits left to take.

One elective I wasn't worried about was physical education, since in my freshman year, my principal assured me that gymnastics would count toward that requirement. Every other elite gymnast I knew was able to waive physical education on the basis of how many hours she trained, and most used that time as an extra study period. But during my junior year, my school's new principal reversed course and said that even though I was on the US gymnastics team, I needed gym class credit to graduate—no exceptions. The head of the physical education department compared the request to waive PE to someone singing in the shower and asking for chorus credit (ouch!). The principal backed her up.

In the end, I swallowed my frustration and signed up for a physical education independent study in addition to the other classes I was required to take online, freeing myself up to spend mornings and afternoons at Brestyan's. "That's so unfair," Talia said sympathetically when I told her about the situation. "Hey, you should invite your principal to come and watch you work out. Better yet, he could participate," she continued, grinning.

I have to say, I took great satisfaction picturing Mihai forcing the principal to do endless chin-ups and leg lifts. I was pretty sure he had never met a high school gym teacher like Mihai.

I had barely begun my online student career when I had to tackle another big choice: to become a professional gymnast or not? A few agents had approached me, wanting to know if I might be interested in representation. Going pro also would allow me to pursue things I'd hoped would follow the Olympics: endorsement deals, ads in magazines, shows like *Dancing with the Stars*.

There was one major downside: If I became a professional athlete, I would give up my eligibility to compete in gymnastics in college.

College gymnastics coaches had been expressing interest in me since I was in the eighth grade, and their interest ramped up with each passing year. There are strict rules about when a college coach can call an athlete (no phone calls before the junior year of high school). Since athletes were able to call coaches, though, occasionally a coach would call one of my older national teammates and ask them to have me call the coach back!

By the time I turned elite, Brestyan's mailbox was constantly flooded with glossy catalogs and notes from NCAA coaches, inviting me to come to their school for a recruiting visit. Coaches also occasionally visited Brestyan's to watch me work out. One day, the coaches from two major schools appeared at the same time. They looked at each other uncomfortably as they stood in the gym.

I went over and hugged one coach, whom I knew already, and greeted the other coach, whom I didn't know, with a hand-shake. Later on, I found out that that hug had been reported to the NCAA as some sort of recruiting violation! I didn't think I had done anything wrong and felt betrayed that my actions had been twisted. Would I still be able to do NCAA gymnastics, I wondered, or had I thrown it all away by hugging a friend? It made me sad that college coaches seemed to be out to get each other; it seemed to me that they were acting immature. The reporting coach, I thought, was jealous that I'd seemed to like the first coach better. He didn't realize that because he had reported the other coach, I would never consider going to his school afterward. The pressure of the situation, and of the whole recruiting process, weighed heavily on me, and I began to just want it to be over.

Of all the schools, the University of Florida piqued my interest most. Both sets of my grandparents lived in Florida parttime, so it felt like a second home. In addition, the Gators had always had one of the top gymnastics programs, and lately they had ramped up their recruiting, building a team they hoped would dominate NCAA competition for years to come. Florida had won over what seemed like half of the national team, and Gator gymnasts had been more than welcoming when I had gone for a recruiting visit. I had adored their beautiful campus and the sunny weather. Plus, their assistant coaches were Romanian like Mihai, who knew and liked them.

When I was back home, I mentioned that I was close to giving Florida a verbal commitment. To my surprise, both Mihai and my family asked me to wait.

"You'll be able to go to any school you want," Mihai said. "There's time for you to decide. Make sure that you make the choice you want to make. Don't commit just because someone's putting pressure on you."

"Take some time, just to know you're absolutely sure," Dad urged. "Committing to a school is a huge decision, and it will impact your life in a huge way. We just want to make sure you feel good about the situation."

Talia was interested in doing gymnastics for the University of Michigan, and we often talked about it during weekend sleepovers at her house as we munched on her mom's chocolate chip pumpkin bread, which we would heat in the oven and enjoy with a scoop of vanilla ice cream. Talia's talk about Michigan intrigued me, and I knew Mom thought I should visit more schools. "But when would I do that?" I asked her. "I can't take any time off to go spend three days in Michigan or somewhere else."

A few months before 2011 World Championships, I called the University of Florida coach and said I wanted to see how the World Championships went before making a decision about committing. The coach asked me to give a verbal commitment anyway. "And if Worlds go well and I decide to turn pro, you'll understand, right?" I asked anxiously. "You'll be okay if I change my mind?" They promised they would and wished me luck at Worlds. That's when I verbally committed to Florida.

The coach was so excited. I would have the time of my life at Florida, they promised, and they were sure I'd bring a lot to the team.

While I was in Tokyo, Dad spoke with a number of agents over the phone. After we won the team gold, he arranged meetings with three prospective agents for when I came home so I could explore my options and be happy with my ultimate decision.

After I got home, we met with a few agents. Out of them, I chose Peter Carlisle from Octagon. Peter is a Maine-based agent who represents Olympic stars, including Michael Phelps and Apolo Ohno. When we met for the first time at Brestyan's, with Mihai sitting in to make sure the prospective agents understood that training came first, Peter was very confident. When I asked him why I should choose him, he shrugged and said, "In my opinion, I'm the best." I liked his confidence, and that he understood that we might need to say no to some opportunities to prioritize my training—and we knew he meant it since he told us that Michael Phelps took his training very seriously and Peter wouldn't book any media or photo shoots for a few months before the Olympics so Michael could concentrate on his performance. Peter and a few members of his team came to my house soon after with a contract and a press release announcing that I was signing with Octagon.

I kept the press release for a few days before actually signing the contract. I would look at it now and again, thinking about how it could change my life, and getting more and more excited about it. My mom asked me to take a few more days to be sure. "It's a huge decision and I'm worried you will regret giving up your eligibility," she said. "I have every confidence in you, but what if you decide you want to compete for a college?"

But I felt sure. "You need to trust me," I told my parents. "I have a good feeling, trust me to do this." Finally, I took a pen and inked my name. In signing it, a new phase of my life began.

I hoped Florida would take it well. When I called to tell them I was turning pro, most were supportive, but one comment hurt my feelings. That person said that in their opinion, I was making a terrible mistake. "We are concerned about the Amanar vault that you're training, and feel that you are running a large risk of tearing your ACL."

I put down the phone and stared angrily off into space while I absorbed these unkind words. I had dealt with naysayers practically my whole career, and there were others who said I shouldn't go pro. But here was an institution that I respected, that I had been going to entrust with my education and training, that didn't think I had what it takes to compete at the highest level and do well. They expected to see me carted out of an arena in a wheelchair. I was still struggling with the Amanar, and this uncalled-for assessment of my progress did not help me feel better.

I steamed about the call for days. "This person was not my coach, and they had no right to say that about a skill I'd been struggling on," I fumed to my mom. "I trust Mihai and Silvie with my life, and if they believe I can do it, I can do it."

"They're just annoyed," she responded. When I told Mihai and Silvie what had happened, they were upset for me and nervous it would affect my confidence on vault. They always had my back and always showed they were on my side. The whole experience really drove home how important it was to have people I trust in my corner—my parents, Mihai, and Silvie's constant belief and support got me through everything.

The person's attitude showed me I had made the right

choice by going pro. I didn't want to be coached by people who projected bad results on others just because they hadn't gotten their way.

More than a year later, the person whom I had spoken with on the phone apologized for doubting my potential. In the years that followed, the University of Florida went on to capture three NCAA titles in a row—and I cheered for them wholeheartedly. People make mistakes, I figured. You have to move on, and not dwell on the past.

More offers started coming in after Tokyo. One of the first to reach out was Ralph Lauren. Ralph Lauren! I couldn't believe it. A woman called and said the company was planning a campaign that featured Olympic hopefuls. Might I consider being one of their athletes? It wouldn't take a lot of time, just a couple of photo shoots. They would fly me and one of my parents to Los Angeles for a couple of days, all expenses paid.

My ears pricked up at the sound of that. I called McKayla, who had also been offered a Ralph Lauren contract, and we squealed a little bit over the phone. We had been joking about fashion photo shoots for years, and now here was a company that actually wanted to use us.

"Do you think we'll get to keep the clothes?" she asked.

"I really hope so!" I exclaimed.

McKayla and I had a wonderful time at the Ralph Lauren shoot in LA. They embraced our natural selves and barely applied makeup. Once we were in front of the camera, we got a funny reminder that though people knew what gymnastics was, they didn't actually know too much about the sport.

"Do you have your uneven bars or balance beams with you?" the Ralph Lauren photographer asked pleasantly after McKayla and I arrived at the shoot. When one of his assistants explained that both are very large, heavy pieces of equipment, he looked annoyed. "You mean you can't just pack them in a suitcase?"

McKayla and I burst out laughing.

Going pro was the beginning of a new life outside the gym, but I still had to stay laser-focused on my training. As I began preparing for the year 2012, I couldn't get the University of Florida coach's words out of my mind. As I worked to make my dreams come true, a little bubble of doubt lingered in my brain.

They had been wrong to react the way they had. But what if they were right?

CHAPTER 12

LOWS AND HIGHS

Needham, Massachusetts
Late 2011–Early 2012

That summer, Bubbie's lung cancer returned. By the fall, while I was in Tokyo, she had become very weak, and instead of running around town as she usually did or going to Florida for the winter, she and Papa stayed at home and had her friends and family come to her. She eventually needed oxygen to help her breathe, then a wheelchair to get around. On December 24, she took a turn for the worse.

Dad called to say that Bubbie wasn't doing well, so he and my sisters would be flying home from vacation early, and I should come meet the family at her condo after practice.

That's when I knew: This was my chance to say good-bye.

I went into Bubbie and Papa's room, where Papa was at her bedside. I gave him a big hug and pulled up a chair, keeping them company while a nurse moved around the room attending to Bubbie. I couldn't believe how frail she seemed. I held her thin hand and knew that she felt me right there with her even though she was unconscious.

My parents, siblings, aunts, uncles, and cousins were all there. Throughout the evening, we took turns sitting by Bubbie's bedside and in the living room reminiscing about our favorite moments with her: How she would leave her grandkids in the car while she took her own mother shopping for underwear. How we would giggle as snacks fell out of her raincoat hood onto her face.

My cousins Mikayla and Brooke and I recalled the sleepovers we'd had at Bubbie's house where she would make us tea and cookies and we would sit around the kitchen table, eating and drinking and pretending to be princesses at a tea party. I remembered the vivacious woman in the hot pink tube top at a friend's bat mitzvah, singing and dancing the night away. I thought about how she would tell each of her grandchildren that he or she was her favorite, and even though we all joked about it, she really did make each of us believe that we were her *true* favorite. (She did the same thing with my dad; he, my aunt, and uncle each believe to this day that they are the favorite!)

My family stayed at Bubbie's condo late into the night,

sitting with her and Papa and talking to one another. We eventually decided to go home for a few hours to sleep, planning to come back early the next day—Christmas, so I was off from training. We had just walked in our front door when my uncle called with the news that Bubbie had passed away not long after we left. She was typically selfless even in her final act, waiting for most of the young grandchildren to leave the house before she took her last breath.

I would have liked to have spent several days curled away somewhere, crying quietly and cherishing her memory. Bubbie had so many friends, and she bragged to each and every one of them that her granddaughter would be in the Olympics someday. "You'll see her on television," she'd tell them over my objections. I believed she was still watching me, and I had to make her proud.

On the morning of the funeral, I went to the gym for a brief workout. I was numb. Life seemed so different without Bubbie in it, and at seventeen years old, I felt like I was being forced to push aside this monumental loss. The grief and all the other stress in my life were just too much. I wasn't present in practice, which was dangerous. Silvie said she knew I was upset, but I had to pay attention so I didn't hurt myself. After my workout, I changed into a simple black dress in the locker room. Silvie drove me to meet my family at the funeral service.

In the Jewish religion, when someone dies, you sit shiva, or mourn, at home for a week after the funeral. I respected the ritual as best as I could, though I had to make sure I got my training in. Bubbie would have understood. More than that, I think she would have insisted. "Go get what you want in life!" I could hear her say.

I'll try, Bubbie, I promised.

In the world outside the Brestyan's bubble, the Olympic year was gathering steam, and my world was changing again. For ten years, I'd been Aly Raisman, the gymnast. Suddenly I was Aly Raisman, the Olympic hopeful. While nothing was guaranteed, being identified as a real contender for the US Olympic team did give me an exciting new level of status.

Journalists, photographers, and cameramen were now coming to the gym a few times a week, shooting videos of my practice sessions for news segments. Everyone wanted to know about my training, experiences, goals, even my diet.

Because I was a seventeen-year-old who was not well-informed about nutrition and believed what I saw touted in the media, for several weeks that winter I eliminated carbohydrates like bread and potatoes. I also cut out vegetables, not knowing any better, and thinking that my body only needed protein. I'd eat protein until I was full. Most of my meals involved some combination of grilled chicken and sometimes a little bit of fruit, washed down with a sports drink, water, or coffee.

A few weeks later, I began to crash. Several times I woke up in the middle of the night with terrible cramping pains. I was so thirsty I began keeping a bottle of water near my bed, because my mouth was dry as a desert every morning.

Some days I would call my dad and ask him to come pick me up from the gym, because I was so tired I didn't think it was safe for me to be on the road. Even though I didn't train on Sundays, I had no energy to go out and see anyone on Saturday nights. I'd curl up in bed at 7:30 PM with a movie and be asleep an hour later.

When it got to the point where I couldn't make it through a floor routine because of the cramps, my parents insisted I see my doctor, who administered a blood test. The results were alarming. When I confessed that I hadn't been eating vegetables or carbs, but instead mostly protein, the doctor and my mother looked aghast. "You can't do that," the doctor said.

I started eating more vegetables again after that. Every magazine in America seemed to be talking about the evils of bread, potatoes, and other carbohydrates. I was eager to figure out the food balance that would allow me to feel good, stay fit, and have energy throughout my workouts. Even as a member of the national team, we had no nutritionist. So nobody had actually taught me what foods I needed to put into my body to assure optimal performance in my sport, and I desperately needed guidance.

Only later would I learn that I was cramping from a lack of energy, a lack of electrolytes, and had excessive muscle breakdown from poor nutritional recovery. I also had such a light period that I was in the danger zone, battling two of the three prongs of the Female Athlete Triad (low energy availability, no menstrual cycle, and low bone density). I needed a better balance and to eat smarter.

Basically, I hadn't been eating the right things. But I didn't know that. At the time, I figured I had been doing it for so long—what was a few more months?

With Olympic prep in high gear, the members of the national team all traveled to training camp once a month. We were expected to be in our best shape every month, and to be at our best 24/7 at every camp. Of course, no one can be in top form all of the time. Part of being human is having ups and downs, and learning from them.

February's training camp was just before the American Cup, where Jordyn and I had qualified to compete based on our results at the World Championships. I had also been told I would compete along with Jordyn at the Pacific Rim Championships in Seattle several weeks afterward, and was gearing toward that. I looked forward to traveling with Jordyn. We always roomed together, and Skyped and texted multiple times a week when we were apart.

I felt sick from the long flight and drive, and had a rough practice the first day of training camp. Afterward, I was pulled into Martha's office, where she and Kathy Kelly, the USA Gymnastics vice president at the time, were waiting. As soon as the door was closed, they informed me that they were tempted to pull me from the American Cup and Pac Rims. Head down, I struggled not to burst into tears right in front of them. They were not sympathetic, and I was frustrated that one poor workout erased all of my prior achievements. I heard one message loud and clear: This was an Olympic year, and it was going to be intense; imperfections wouldn't be tolerated.

It was a harsh lesson for a mediocre workout on the first day, and a sharp reminder that even at training camp, you were expected to be at the very top of your game, always just a mistake or bad finish away from being written off.

In the end, they didn't pull me from the American Cup, but I felt like I was still on thin ice. It was my third year at the Cup, but because this was the Olympic year I immediately felt a difference in the air. People who didn't pay attention to gymnastics during non-Olympic years were now interested, since the past few Olympic all-around winners had also won the American Cup in the Olympic year. On competition day, a near sold-out crowd packed Madison Square Garden. People were curious to see whether the streak would hold.

I finished second all-around to Jordyn, but scored my own victory on vault, where I led off by nailing my new Amanar.

Finally. I was elated: It was the first time I'd dared this very risky upgrade in competition since falling on it two years before. I felt on top of the world. There's nothing that compares to the natural high of knowing that years of hard work, of struggle, of nights lying awake, have paid off in the biggest way, on a big stage.

I hoped that my showing would redeem me in the eyes of Martha and Kathy, and they would decide to forgive my poor practice the week before and send me to Pac Rims after all. It didn't happen. I went from New York to Boston, where I was home less than twenty-four hours before heading back to Texas to compete for the spot at a selection camp. In the end, Jordyn, Kyla, and Gabby were chosen to go to Seattle.

It was the first time since I made the national team that I wasn't going to be representing the United States at a major meet. I had packed for camp as if I'd be getting the assignment (as we were always instructed), and now Mihai and I were being sent back to Boston without a thought. To make matters worse, USA Gymnastics had given us the wrong flight time, so we spent a long day in the airport, waiting to be rebooked on a flight home. Dejected and fearful that I was out of favor, I had the longest day of my life.

I spent the next few months sliding between two worlds: the chalky world of Brestyan's gym and the sleek, shiny world of

Olympic hopefuldom, with its photo shoots, interviews, and opportunities to mingle with US hopefuls from other sports, like volleyball player Kerri Walsh and members of the US men's swim team. Having sacrificed so many social plans to go to the gym and train, I was thrilled to spend time with other elite athletes and excited about expanding my circle of friends.

One day I would be sweaty and grubby, my hair piled on top of my head in a messy bun, doing vault after vault and crying in frustration when things didn't go right, terrified that a mistake would cost me my Olympic dreams. The next I would be on a pristine white beach in Florida, wearing the Victoria's Secret Angel wings and being photographed for an upcoming Olympic edition of *Vogue*. The day after that, I'd be back in the gym again, covered head to toe in chalk. Almost every photo shoot, appearance, or endorsement was scheduled around training. Through it all, I think I only missed two or three workouts.

That spring, several world team members were sent to Dallas for a media summit. We sat on tall stools proudly displaying our Team USA gear and did lengthy interviews with journalists. They wanted to know everything about us; I answered questions about my favorite TV shows, my favorite dessert (cheesecake), and even what time I went to bed at night (never after 10:00 PM).

We also did a London-themed photo shoot that featured us leaping and jumping around an actor dressed as a Buckingham Palace guard. The photographer snapped me trying on his tall, furry black hat and peeping over the guard's shoulder. In a few months, I thought, maybe I'd be standing in front of Buckingham Palace for real, a member of the US Olympic team... maybe even a gold medalist.

And then what? A small voice in my mind asked one night that spring as I drove home from practice. As usual, I had been fantasizing about London. All of a sudden it occurred to me that there was life beyond the Olympic Games. *That's right,* the insistent little voice said. *What are you going to do once they're over?*

That was a good question. As I scanned the headlights of the cars ahead of me, I dared to look ahead for the first time. Gymnastics was a huge part of my life—no, that wasn't right, gymnastics *was* my life. Even though it was hard practicing twice a day, taking classes online, and not having a social life, this was what I had chosen to do, and I'd never regretted it.

For as long as I could remember, a single goal had loomed in front of me. It had gotten me out of bed for a decade. Life would be so weird without gymnastics. So very different.

Once the Olympics were over, I'd be able to start fresh, I realized. I could have a life where I wouldn't have to be quite so disciplined about my diet and exercise, where I could take time off and relax and do absolutely nothing if I felt like it.

All I had ever wanted was to go to the Olympics. But when I sat back and thought about it, the Olympic Games lasted for two and a half weeks. Two and a half weeks was not a long time. And then what? What would I live for once the Games were done?

In preparing me for a run at the Olympic team, Mihai surpassed himself. Every little detail had to be perfect—and if it wasn't, he made me do it again.

And again. And five more times after that.

"Mihai, you're killing me," I groaned one night as I lay flat on my back under the balance beam, too tired to even stand up. It was 9:10. Practice technically ended at 9:00 PM. I was drenched in sweat. The evening's assignment had been to execute ten routines. I had two more to go.

Ten sets of leaps and flips and combinations and dismounts one after another on the four-inch-wide beam left me feeling like my legs wouldn't support my body weight. I wasn't sure that I'd be able to walk out of the gym under my own power.

I started to cry. I was too tired. It was too much.

Mihai loomed over me. "Your choice," he said encouragingly. "Do you want to not make it because you could have done a little bit more? You can suffer now and be a champion for the rest of your life. Or you can rest and risk a different outcome. Keep pushing, Aly. You're almost done. Two more."

I chose to suffer. Two more. I stood up, leaving a pool of sweat on the mat below. I saw the outline of my body imprinted in sweat on the chalky blue mat. A sweat angel. *How gross*, I thought. "Look, Mihai," I said, pointing at it. "That's the sign of a hard worker right there."

"Keep going," he said with a smile. "Your hard work will pay off when they call your name at Trials."

After the routines, Mihai insisted that I stretch for ten minutes. By the time I left and got in the car, it would be 9:30, which meant I'd get home a few minutes before 10:00. I would eat and shower and be in bed by 11:00. Somewhere in there I needed to find time for a couple hours of homework, too. *Ugh.*

I turned eighteen the day before the US Classic. Since I didn't like having dessert the night before a meet (to avoid a sugar crash), I blew out a candle next to my salmon and wished for things to go well. My birthday wish came true: I won the meet.

"I celebrated by having a good competition today," I told the reporters afterward, a big smile on my face. It was my third major win as a senior, and the first time I scored more than sixty points, averaging a solid 15.0 per event. To do it at an "Olympic tune-up" meet meant the world to me.

Dressed in a brown V-neck dress with intricate beading across the shoulders and neckline, I pinned a boutonniere on the tuxedo of my friend Jamie in our front yard before we headed off to our high school prom. My parents and Grandma stood off to one side, taking photos, while Brett, Chloe, and Maddie looked on.

Prom was held in the ballroom of a hotel in Boston. To be able to go, I switched up my training schedule, practicing only in the morning and foregoing the evening session. I had no time or energy to shop for a dress, so my mom had picked mine out online and had it shipped to our house. Of course, it was too long (comes with the territory when you're 5'2"), so we had to get it shortened. Despite Mom's urging, I didn't try it on again until prom night—only to discover that the pins were still in and it had never been altered! Luckily, the tailor was just down the street and open. My mom ran the dress over and they fixed it on the spot. Jamie was already at our house, ready for pictures, and Mom couldn't resist an "I told you so" as she handed me the dress to slip on just in time. Grandma Susan laughed, then oohed and aahed over me in my dress.

I was glad to attend the dance. A little normalcy did me a lot of good. Afterward, Jamie and the rest of our group took off for a post-prom party in Cape Cod. Attending an all-night party at that point would have wreaked havoc on my training schedule, so instead Dad picked me up early and took me home so I could get a full night's sleep for the next day's training.

"Did you find a boyfriend?" Mihai teased the next morning.

"Mihai, I left at ten o'clock," I protested.

He understood that meant no. Shrugging, he delivered his verdict: "You should find a boyfriend, anyway," he said.

I rolled my eyes. "Maybe if I wasn't here every Friday night, I'd have one!"

The meet schedule building up to the Olympic Games was a sprint. In a country as competitive as the United States, where fifteen women were competing for only five spots on the Olympic team, nothing could be taken for granted. The US women were so deep that at some point that supercharged spring, I think we all realized that making the Olympic team could be harder than winning team gold at the Games itself.

Instead of preparing for my high school graduation ceremony, the morning of the event, I boarded a plane to St. Louis, Missouri, to compete at the National Championships, the last meet before the Olympic Trials. The major Olympic contenders all competed—all except poor McKayla, who had overrotated a triple twist and banged her head on the floor during warm-up on the second day of competition, sustaining a concussion that knocked her out of the meet. Aware of what was happening and altogether pissed off about it, McKayla was wheeled out of the arena on a stretcher. Her arms crossed and an unimpressed look on her face, McKayla was loaded into a waiting ambulance to get X-rays at the hospital. Left to her own devices, she probably would have competed anyway.

My consistency held through Nationals: I took third in the

all-around for the third year in a row, this time behind Jordyn and Gabby. The whirlwind continued. From St. Louis, we each went home for two weeks to fine-tune our routines. It was getting hot in Boston, and I poured sweat in the gym, which made me feel accomplished and like the hardest worker ever. I gave every practice my all.

Practices flew by quickly. Before I knew it, I was at the airport checking my overstuffed bag for San Jose, California, and the Olympic Trials.

I was doing bar routines in San Jose during podium training when it dawned on me that the preparatory period for the Olympics was over. I had dreamed of this for ten years, and worked nearly every day to make that dream a reality. I had done everything I possibly could to ready my body and mind for the challenge that lay before me. This was it.

As I stood beside the uneven bars, two thoughts hit me at once: One, I was absolutely exhausted. And two, I wanted to make that Olympic team more than anything. At the same time, I knew how unpredictable gymnastics could be. Nothing was ever guaranteed. Old doubts crept back in. What if I wasn't among those selected? What if it hadn't been enough?

The stress messed me up on bars. I struggled and struggled to do my routine, and kept falling. Finally, Martha pulled me aside. *Here we go*, I thought. *She's going to ask me why I'm not prepared and why I keep falling.*

"Relax," she said. "You'll make the Olympic team. Unless

you fall ten times in the competition, I'm taking you. Just relax and do what you normally do." My heart beat a little faster. I held on to her words through the remaining workouts, even though I still felt a little skeptical. I knew nothing was ever guaranteed.

During practices in San Jose, I kept falling on my kneecaps, leaving them bruised and sore. The Olympic Trials had me so nervous that even though Martha had told me not to worry and relax, I wasn't thinking straight, which led to large errors that almost put my body at risk.

The competition was a carbon copy of the National Championships: two days, all events, no holds barred. As usual, I finished third, behind Gabby and Jordyn. At this point, my family joked that I owned third place, and we came to see it as a good omen.

After the competition, the women who participated were shepherded into a small locker room just off the arena, where chairs had been set up in a circle. Our coaches hovered in the background or sat scrunched in cubbies. The minutes ticked by slowly while Martha and the rest of the selection committee held one final conference. I looked around at my teammates, sitting silent and still, uncertain whether their efforts had been enough.

My thoughts turned to my own chances. I finished third in the all-around, though I had had a much sloppier than usual landing on vault, my last event. I worried ending on that note impacted my chances. Although Martha had been reassuring a few days earlier, I knew that every single performance was weighed and taken into consideration by Martha and the selection committee.

After what felt like an hour, I took out my phone and texted my parents. *I'm so nervous*, I wrote. *I hope I make it.*

Several long minutes later, the door opened and Martha swept in. A hushed silence fell as she put on her glasses. We looked at her, knowing that she was about to change five people's lives forever, granting them their most dearly held wish. Everyone seemed to grab somebody to lean on. I clutched Jordyn's hand tight, feeling sick from fear.

With the eyes of so many incredibly hardworking young women looking at her with so much yearning, Martha Karolyi—the most powerful woman in gymnastics—looked around and started to cry. She was about to send five people over the moon, but she knew she would break the hearts of everyone else.

Martha reached into her pocket for a tissue. "Sorry," she apologized. I had never seen this side of Martha before and was shocked by her emotion as she explained that this was always both a special and hard moment for her. She said that it was never an easy decision, or an easy announcement. She reached back into her pocket, this time pulling out a piece of paper.

An eerie silence fell over the room. All of the coaches' and gymnasts' eyes were on Martha. We held our breath. She read the names—Douglas, Maroney, Raisman, Ross, and

Wieber—without fanfare. The silence broke. Nobody attempted to control their emotions. My eyes misted over with tears. Everything after that was a blur.

I was an Olympian: a sobbing, hyperventilating Olympian. We were all crying, except Kyla, who grinned from ear to ear. While it was such a happy moment for the five of us, the majority of the tears in the room were tears of sadness for not making the cut. I tried to control my emotions, out of sensitivity to the other gymnasts and coaches.

"Girls, girls, hurry up! I need the five girls; I need the five girls!" An NBC producer was calling us.

We stood up, hugged one another, then turned to our coaches. I gave Mihai and Silvie a quick hug. This was their accomplishment as much as mine.

"Stop crying," Mihai said, sniffling. "You're going to be on the front page of every newspaper tomorrow morning. Smile!"

"Why are you crying so hard?" Silvie asked, puzzled. "Don't you understand you've made the team?"

But there was no time to explain. I laughed and ran out the door, grabbing a waiting bouquet of roses as we were rushed out for the public announcement. NBC cameramen ran alongside us as we half jogged the short distance between the back room and the darkened arena, where the floor was now lit by spotlights.

I reentered the arena with one hand over my mouth, the other waving to the crowd as tears of pure joy streamed from my eyes.

Already on the floor, members of the men's team (announced the day before) joined the massive figure of the emcee, who held a microphone in his hand.

"Good evening, please welcome the five members of the women's 2012 US Olympic team!" he boomed. "Gabby Douglas, McKayla Maroney, Aly Raisman, Kyla Ross, and Jordyn Wieber!" A resounding roar of approval greeted each girl's name as she appeared on the Jumbotron high above. The whole arena broke into chants of "U-S-A! U-S-A!"

In this supercharged atmosphere, we ran up the steps of the podium and hurled ourselves into the arms of the first people we saw. A moment later, music came on and it began to snow red, white, and blue confetti. I opened my mouth, playfully trying to catch some on my tongue. The moment a childhood dream comes true, I guess you become a little bit of that same child again. I was living my childhood dreams, living the same moment the Magnificent Seven experienced. After savoring the moment with my teammates, I spotted my parents and ran from the podium and into the stands. They were shouting and crying as hard as I was. I hugged my parents over the barrier. We were beyond words.

I went back to Boston for three days, just enough time to do laundry and repack my suitcase in between workouts. Reverently, I placed the new Team USA warm-ups that we would wear in London in with a mound of practice leotards, shorts, tops, and Team USA gear. We would be gone for about a month, so of course my bags were stuffed to bursting. Even so, I made sure to leave a little room for souvenirs. Our team had its eyes on one in particular: a golden one.

CHAPTER 13

THE FIERCE FIVE

London, United Kingdom
July 2012

"The fantastic five," Jordyn suggested.

"Isn't that something already?" McKayla asked.

"The fearsome five," I tried.

"Ehhhh..."

"The friendly five!" Gabby exclaimed.

We all laughed, knowing she wasn't serious. "The frrrreaky five!" McKayla said, executing a little shoulder shimmy.

"Mack, that is ridiculous," Kyla said, covering her eyes with her hands.

We were sitting in our townhouse in the Olympic Village. With the opening ceremonies of the 2012 Olympic Games approaching, we had settled down to the important business of giving ourselves a team name. The media had initially dubbed us the "Fab Five," but that nickname already belonged to a basketball team. We wanted something different, something that represented what we were. We were combing our brains—and several online thesauruses—for the right moniker.

We had arrived in London the morning before, five determined women with a mountain of Team USA suitcases and bags. Ever since we'd touched down in London, butterflies had been flapping away in my stomach. Partially pre-competition nerves, but also something more. "I have a good feeling about this," I told McKayla, smiling.

"Me too," she said, leaning over for a quick hug.

At the Houston airport, we'd made a surprising discovery. As we wheeled our luggage past a bookshop on the way to the terminal, a flash of red caught our attention. "Oh, look, those girls on the cover of that magazine are wearing red leos like ours," I said, pointing. One of our competition leotards was a bright, fire-engine red, studded with crystals that shimmered brilliantly when they caught the light. My brain was just catching up to my mouth when Kyla, who was walking in front of me, stopped dead.

"You guys," she said. "That magazine. It's *Sports Illustrated*. It's *us*."

We dropped our bags and rushed over to the newsstand. Kyla and I gaped at each other, jumping up and down. There we were, posed around a balance beam in our red leotards on the cover of *Sports Illustrated*'s Olympic preview edition. The photographer had shot the cover the week before at the ranch. "Okay, can we get three girls standing on the bar, please?" he'd asked, pointing to the beam, and we had fallen over ourselves giggling. "Five Stars: America's Game Changers," proclaimed the headline. Inside were profiles not just of us, but of Michael Phelps, Usain Bolt, and the US men's basketball team. And from all those stars, they had chosen to put us on the cover.

I was so excited to be going to the Olympics that I couldn't think straight. "What nationality are we?" I asked Jordyn as we filled in customs forms on the plane. I was so tired and overwhelmed that I thought "nationality" meant where your ancestors had come from. "I want to put Russian, Romanian, and German, but there's not enough room," I explained, still confused. That one proved to be almost as good as McKayla mixing up the national anthem and the Pledge of Allegiance. Jordyn laughed until she was gasping for air.

There had been a lot of laughter on this trip so far. To keep from getting stiff over the twelve-hour journey from Houston, we did sit-ups and stretches in the aisles. The flight attendants fussed over us, took photos, and politely asked us to sign napkins before we got off.

We loved London from the moment we set foot on British

soil. The city was "brill," the word McKayla used (with a British accent, of course) to describe everything we saw. When someone tweeted photos of the inside of the arena and we saw that the podiums were hot pink, our lucky color, we were delighted. "It's like they knew we were coming," Kyla said.

When we weren't in the spacious training halls, we were confined to our three-floor townhouse in the Olympic Village. Martha stayed on the first floor, while Kyla's coach, Jenny, and USA Gymnastics vice president Kathy Kelly slept on the second. Part of the second floor had also been converted into a trainer's room since we weren't allowed to use the USA athletes' Olympic training room (excited to meet many of the other athletes, we asked to receive therapy there, but our request was turned down).

The third floor was all us. Sleeping arrangements were assigned, I suspected, based on the nap schedules of each girl. Jordyn and I, who took afternoon naps at similar times, had a bedroom overlooking the Olympic cafeteria. McKayla and Kyla, who never slept between workouts, were given another room. Gabby had requested the last room for herself.

Pushed up against the wall in the hallway connecting our rooms was an ever-growing pile of stuff we had started collecting right after arriving in the Village. There were backpacks, T-shirts, and shoes in a rainbow of colors, all emblazoned with different sponsors' logos. Surveying this mountain of Olympic swag on my way to brush my teeth one morning, I realized I would need yet another suitcase to haul all of it back to Boston. I wondered if extra suitcases were being given away somewhere as well!

We spent most of our limited downtime sitting in the common area on the second floor. The doors opened onto the Village street, making it an ideal spot for people watching—and talking to the men's team, who were briefly housed in a townhouse next door. (When a pipe burst and flooded their apartment, they were moved to a different location. We joked that Martha had been behind the whole thing in order to keep us focused.)

Inside the Olympic Village, fruit and drink stands dotted the walkways, and every athlete was given a special keycard to swipe in vending machines for as many free bottles of sports drinks as we wanted. Whenever we had a team meeting with Martha, we would sit meekly and nod at whatever she said. If we talked, she might see that our tongues had turned bright blue from the forbidden sugary drinks we'd been sneaking. Each time Martha left, we would cover our mouths to stifle the nervous laughter.

All day long, the training and demands of being prominent members of the US Olympic delegation were intense. We were all feeling the stress, evidenced by the amount of hair we lost before and during the Games—the shower drain in the apartment was clogged with it. So when we were alone, a slumber party atmosphere prevailed: We hung out in our sweats, on our laptops, scrolling the Olympic profiles of the guys we met in the dining hall. We met fencers, volleyball players, and swimmers, all of them "adorable," as McKayla would say. We were confined to the townhouse most of the time, but we used our trips to the cafeteria to exchange hellos with everyone we could. When we were asked what time we wanted to go eat dinner, we chose 7:00 PM, because that's the time when everyone else seemed to be eating.

One day we were in the cafeteria when we realized a group of swimmers, including Michael Phelps and Ryan Lochte, were seated several tables in front of us. Both were high on our list of athletes to meet.

"Hi!" we called brightly, flashing our biggest smiles. "Excuse us, but can we take a photo with you?"

"Sure!" Ryan and Michael said kindly, grinning as they peered down at five girls about half their size. McKayla sidled up to Nathan Adrian, another swimmer whom we had met at a pre-Olympic media conference. "'Sup, Nathan," she said, all casual.

All the way back to our rooms, we discussed how cool it was to meet the swimmers, giggling all the way. "You guys can have them; I'm going to date Justin Bieber," Jordyn joked.

Gabby chimed in, "You guys are so silly; we'll find boyfriends after the Games!"

We trained for about ten days in the Olympic training gym before setting foot in the competition gym. In workouts, I stuck to the formula that had become second nature by this point: two layout Yurchenkos, followed by two with a double twist, and three Amanars on vault. I would do four routines on bars, six to eight beam routines, and one floor routine every day. This was fewer routines than I was used to doing in the gym at home, because we didn't have rest days when traveling internationally. Plus, our skills were so refined at this point that the practices were for fine-tuning and keeping up muscle memory.

Mihai was pleased with my bar routine, which we had worked hard to polish up in the months before the Games. "Very clean, Aly," Martha said approvingly one day, patting me on the head. Since she didn't give compliments unless she really meant it, I took it as a good omen that I was ready to compete.

Bela came in one day and watched our workout. Afterward, he took Mihai aside and said my bars looked much better and he privately believed I'd make the all-around final. When Mihai told me, I couldn't stop smiling!

We held a special team meeting in the townhouse, where we each took a sheet of paper and wrote down the name of who we thought should be team captain, then folded them and handed them to Martha, who looked at them quickly. "Aly," she said with a smile, "you have been named team captain. Congratulations." I was honored. Being the team captain meant that I was expected to lead and set a good example, that my teammates could look to me for guidance and support.

Our focus, we emphasized, would be on earning team gold. Anything after that would be icing on the cake, though the goal was to earn as many medals as possible for the United States. Having that common goal helped shift the pressure off of ourselves. It was the team's job, and we were working for the team.

I was slated to lead off the American gymnasts' Olympic effort as the very first person to perform on vault, our first apparatus, with my Amanar. I would also close out the team on floor, our last event. I began feeling impatient for the workouts to be over and the competition to begin. This was our time. We were prepared. We were—

"Fierce!" McKayla exclaimed. She shut her laptop with a snap and looked up, her eyes shining. The rest of us stared at her. "That's it! Fierce—the Fierce Five," she said. "That's what we are."

And that's what we became.

CHAPTER 14

GOLDEN SUMMER

London, United Kingdom
July–August 2012

Gymnastics is one of those rare sports where you compete individually but also as a team. A gymnast's scores in qualification actually serve two purposes: They help determine the team score, and they also decide who qualifies for the all-around and individual event finals. The top twenty-four gymnasts advance to the individual all-around finals, while the top eight per event go on to the event finals—with one big caveat.

To prevent any one nation from dominating the podium, only the top two gymnasts per country advance to any given final. Even if every gymnast on a team scores among the top eight (or top twenty-four, in the case of the all-around) only the best two can compete in the final. For the gymnast who ranks third on a really good team, it's always a heartbreaker.

At the 2011 World Championships, Gabby had the fifth highest score in the all-around qualifications, while Sabrina had been ninth and McKayla twelfth. But since Jordyn was second and I was fourth, only Jordyn and I had advanced to the all-around final. Despite ranking well within the top twenty-four in the world, Gabby, McKayla, and Sabrina had watched the final from the stands.

In London, three of us were vying for the all-around spots. McKayla injured her foot on beam during one of the early training sessions, which limited her to vault, her best event. Kyla would be doing bars, beam, and floor. Jordyn, Gabby, and I were all slated to do the all-around in qualification. It was likely all three of us would place in the top twenty-four. We understood that only two would advance. It was an awkward reality, and we didn't really feel comfortable talking about it.

I knew the media predicted me as the odd gymnast out. Some even took it as a given. As my mom set the DVR to record the gymnastics events before leaving for London, she noticed that the summary description of the all-around final read "Watch Jordyn Wieber and Gabby Douglas battle for all-around gold."

The assumption was logical given my past competition results. Third place seemed to be my spot. While my mom didn't tell me about the TV description for years, I felt everyone writing me off. *We'll see*, I thought. Beating either Jordyn or Gabby to earn one of the two all-around spots would be very tough, but deep down I believed I had a shot. My teammates were my friends, but each of us wanted individual success in addition to USA gold. My first priority was gold for the team. After that, I wanted to show the doubters that they were wrong to count me out.

As the shuttle bus rolled toward the arena on the big day, McKayla and I unwound by taking selfies on the bus and laughing at the ridiculous faces we were making. We were distracting ourselves from the nerve-wracking reality settling in: We were going to compete in the Olympics! In spite of the enormous pressure of representing the United States and the years of work, we were excited. Before we left, I had called my parents, as I always did before meets, to say I love you.

"We love you, too," Mom and Dad said. My mom added, "Show the equipment who's boss." I laughed, and loved her message: I was in control of the day.

Poised high above the North Greenwich Arena floor was a giant four-sided Jumbotron scoreboard that flashed up-to-the-minute standings on all events. If you wanted to know what was going on, all you needed to do was look up.

I avoided looking at it during that tension-filled qualifying round. I had learned the hard way that getting ahead of myself could be a huge distraction. When you know, you start thinking about outcomes rather than just doing a good routine, which often leads to mistakes. At the Olympics, nobody wanted to make any mistakes.

The tension in the arena was palpable. My teammates and I promised ourselves that whatever happened, we would go out, give it our all, and support one another. Our performances would decide who ended up where.

I landed my Amanar with just a tiny hop forward. *Yes!* I thought as my feet touched the mat. That was the way I'd hoped to begin.

In the middle of my bar routine, the crowd erupted. But their cheers weren't for me—a British gymnast was performing on floor at the same time, and the hometown crowd went crazy every time she hit a skill. I was so used to doing the routine in a quiet gym with my coaches, and the intense noise and distractions of an Olympic audience aren't something you can prepare for. I tried my best to block it out, but the noise was so loud, it was impossible to ignore. Thankfully, years of practice and having done the routine endlessly allowed muscle memory to kick in. I delivered.

My parents' reactions to watching me as I did my bar routine in qualification were broadcast during the primetime coverage. They looked like crazy people, swaying back and forth in time with my swings as though their movements could help me, yelling encouragement, and shooting to their feet in relief when

I landed my double front dismount. NBC loved it and aired it during the broadcast, turning my parents into internet celebrities overnight.

Because I was first on bars and last on beam, I had to find the tricky balance between keeping myself focused and allowing myself to relax and stay calm during the wait. I spent my waiting time pacing back and forth and trying not to psych myself out. Finally, it was my turn. Before each skill on beam, I reminded myself to take a deep breath, to not get ahead of myself because the competition had been going well. It worked.

Next up was my best event, and I was the last American to go. I was favored to medal on floor, so there was extra pressure to qualify. I paced to calm my nerves and stay in the zone. I couldn't watch my teammates, but I cheered them on, hoping that everyone was satisfied with their Olympics so far.

I wanted floor to be my moment. In practices, I'd focus on every little detail, pointing my toes, extending my arms, making sure my leaps and dance were crisp and precise, my landings as consistent as possible. Now, I found I needed to almost turn my brain off, and just let my body do what it had done so many times before. From the first second my music came on to the last pose I struck, I trusted my training. I blocked out the fear, but I allowed myself to take in the crowd, clapping and cheering for me.

Though I appeared calm and focused from the outside, before every routine I felt a draining combination of heart-pounding adrenaline and heart-stopping fear. After every landing, a tsunami-sized wave of relief washed over me when I realized I hadn't messed up. I hadn't let my teammates, my coaches, my country, or myself down.

As I came down the steps to rejoin my teammates and Mihai, I figured I had done enough to get into the floor final. For the first time that day, I looked around the pink arena and let myself take in some of the splendor of the Olympic Games. I was still taking in my surroundings, feeling relieved that the day's competition was over, when Mihai turned to me.

"You did it!" he cried, throwing his arms out and enveloping me in a huge bear hug. I grinned. *A final!* I thought. My heart leapt into my throat at the possibility.

"How do you know?" I asked.

"Look," Mihai said softly, pointing up at the Jumbotron I had been avoiding all day. "You're in the all-around final!" I allowed myself a peek, but at first I didn't see what had made him so excited. "Where does it say that?" I asked, searching.

Anyone following the scores was aware that the results of my floor routine would determine whether Jordyn or I advanced to the all-around final. Gabby's four-event total had put her ahead of Jordyn, so when I stepped onto the floor, my score would determine who advanced and who didn't. Regardless of my score, Gabby had secured her spot.

So when Mihai came up to me after floor, I thought he was just celebrating what had been a good routine and a good competition.

But then I saw it. Under the words "All-around qualification" was a list of names. And beside the number one was my own. What felt like an electric current surged through my body.

I was in first place in the all-around at the Olympic Games.

Even in a qualifying round, seeing your name at the very top of an Olympic scoreboard is a deeply emotional, deeply thrilling experience. Only in my wildest dreams had I imagined being the top American going into the all-around final. I was in tears as I gazed up at that scoreboard. My heart dropped a little when all at once I remembered the qualification rules.

If I was in, that meant one of my teammates was out.

That's when I saw Jordyn. Cameramen were clustered around her, and she was devastated, her hands covering her face. Standing between her and the scoreboard, Kyla's coach, Jenny, wrapped Jordyn up in her arms. Jordyn buried her face in Jenny's shoulder. Her shoulders heaved with soft sobs. And the cameramen were hovering right in front of her, capturing every second. In that moment it became clear: Jordyn Wieber, the reigning world all-around champion, would not get a shot at the Olympic all-around title.

At that moment, Jordyn was third in the all-around qualification behind myself and Gabby. Yet just because she was third on the US team, she would not be one of the twenty-four women competing in the final. She would sit in the stands with Martha and the rest of the team, knowing that if she were allowed to compete, she would have had a good shot at winning the gold medal. Everyone had expected me to be in that position, and though I was excited to move forward, my heart broke for Jordyn. *Two per country is the dumbest rule ever*, I thought angrily. It's totally unfair.

The qualification rounds were divided into several sub-divisions, with four teams competing per subdivision, and the Russians competed after we did. In the final qualification standings, Viktoria Komova finished first in the all-around. I was second, Gabby third, Jordyn fourth. Aliya, recovered from her knee injury, finished fifth.

What do you do when you set a goal and work toward it for so many years, just to come up a little bit short? How do you deal with something like that?

Our room was quiet as I gently opened the door later that day. Jordyn was sitting on her bed, staring off into nothing. "Hey," I said.

"Hey," she answered. We smiled at each other, but I understood my friend needed space. Jordyn stood up and grabbed her toiletries case. I watched as she disappeared into the bathroom, remembering Martha's words: *You have to turn the page.* Jordyn must have heard this, too, at some point, because after a full night of sleep, she rallied. In the middle of the most important and difficult competition of her life, Jordyn Wieber didn't let disappointment get the best of her. She seemed to give herself a few hours to mourn what had happened, then moved past it. She's a class act.

After our ritual Pledge of Allegiance—if it had worked in 2011, we didn't want to tempt fate by not doing it in 2012—Jordyn led the United States off on vault in the team final. And she nailed it.

Jordyn's vault was just the beginning. Gabby followed with a terrific Amanar herself. That set up McKayla, who stepped up and did the best Amanar anyone had ever seen, a vault so perfect that the American judge Cheryl Hamilton's mouth dropped open in sheer disbelief as McKayla stuck her landing. The crowd gasped and whooped and shrieked as though they could feel in the air that it was our turn. So could we. McKayla left the podium practically jumping up and down. The five of us were so confident and excited. Even with three events to come, in that moment we knew the night was ours.

The vault rotation electrified us. I kept my warm-ups on, jogging in place to keep warm, and stretching to stay loose for beam, my first event in the team final, as Jordyn, Kyla, and Gabby all delivered excellent bar routines. Since it would be almost an hour before I would compete, I had to figure out a balance between watching my teammates on bars and focusing on the beam routine to come. I knew that by focusing on myself I would help the team the most. Watching the other girls made me even more nervous, so I would turn around and face

McKayla, who was done competing and screamed and cheered our teammates' every move. McKayla's expressive cheers told me all I needed to know: Everyone was hitting.

We were standing and waiting to march over to beam when I felt a tap on my shoulder, and Gabby stood there. "I'm really nervous," she said. "I don't know if I can do it."

I placed a hand on each of her shoulders and looked into her eyes. "Your beam is great. You can do it," I reassured her. "I'm nervous, too. We just have to be our normal," I said.

"Normal" was a word we shouted during each other's routines, a reminder to do things just like we did in practice. Almost instantly, Gabby's face cleared and she breathed a sigh of relief. She wound up turning in a terrific beam routine. Sometimes you just need to be told everything is going to be okay. We all hit solid routines. After I finished my beam, Gabby ran over and gave me a big hug.

Kyla had been first up, and now she ran over to join our hug. She was proud of our routines, but she was even prouder that— after not showing emotion even when her name was called at Olympic Trials—she had finally learned how to cry. "Look," she said, pointing to her face, "happy tears!" Gabby and I laughed and congratulated her.

It was during the one touch on floor—a brief, ninety-second warm-up that each team shares before competing on each event—that I hit a speed bump. I needed to practice my first pass because of the difficulty, but at the same time, I needed to make sure I was sufficiently warmed up before going for such an intricate pass. The problem was that this all had to be done in a minute and a half, so I was stressed and tired from trying to fit too much into such a short warm-up period. I was practicing my first pass, but when I punched into the last skill, a front layout, my legs gave out, and I went forehead first into the ground. My head was already pounding as I picked myself up.

I went down the stairs and over to Mihai and started tearing up. He took me by the shoulders and bent down so his face was level with mine. He looked me straight in the eyes. "I believe in you, Aly," he said. "You can do this. Yes, you can."

I paced back and forth for much of Gabby's routine. I couldn't get the fall out of my head, but there was no more time to go back and do the pass once more. When Gabby finished, she came to stand beside me. "What's wrong?" she asked, her face puckering in concern. She had been preparing for her own routine and hadn't seen me fall, but took one look at my face and understood what I needed to hear. "Don't worry, Aly, you got this," she said. I smiled. Normal.

There was no time to argue. Jordyn had finished, delivering another hit, and now it was my turn. I climbed the short flight of stairs to the podium, gave Jordyn a hug (as we had done the year before), and waited for the green light, trying desperately to stay focused. *This is it. We can be Olympic champions.* My teammates were standing just off the podium, screaming and cheering before I even assumed my starting pose. Hearing their voices gave me strength.

Do your normal, I repeated to myself as I listened for the familiar sounds of a violin warming to "Hava Nagila." When the music came on, I switched onto autopilot.

To be honest, I don't remember much of the routine that sealed the United States' first team gold medal in gymnastics in sixteen years, and first win on foreign soil. I took the punch front layout out of my first pass to reduce my risk of falling like I had moments before. It worked. *Keep going,* my mind ordered my body. My body obeyed. I had done it so many times during so many hard training sessions that it was all second nature.

Our coaches once told us that in the Soviet Union, gymnasts had to get out of bed at 3:00 AM and go do a cold routine in the gym, just to prove that they were ready to perform at any time. They said that to motivate us, letting us know how "easy" we had it, but we were never quite sure if they were joking or not. By that point, if a 3:00 AM routine had been necessary, we could have done it.

But for a split second before my third tumbling pass, I felt like a deer in the headlights. I almost panicked, as the pressure I was under threatened to crush me. I snapped myself out of it, and the pass went great. Now, onto my fourth and final tumbling pass—a double pike that rebounded into a split jump.

One tumbling pass stood between the team and Olympic

gold. Standing in that corner before my last pass, I felt no fear. I took a few steps and hurled myself into the roundoff. Then the back handspring. I shot for maximum height on my double pike. It was over in five seconds. I struck my ending pose. At that point I couldn't hold back the tears. The joy and excitement of the moment were overwhelming. With trembling lips and a quivering chin, I turned to salute the judges.

Mihai and Jenny were right there at the bottom of the steps. Mihai was jumping up and down. I was astonished—I had never seen him like that before. My teammates, Mihai, and Jenny hugged me so tightly I couldn't catch my breath. I squeezed back as my tears flowed and I struggled to breathe normally.

The five of us stood close together in the middle of the arena. We waved at the cheering crowd. My score still wasn't posted, so we clutched one another's hands, our eager faces turned upward toward the scoreboard. The Jumbotron was the only thing we saw as we waited for the scorekeepers to make it official. Around us, the coaches smiled jubilantly. Above us, the crowd was on their feet and going nuts. A chant of "U-S-A, U-S-A" had gone up around the arena. We stood together and watched it unfold. Then there was a whoop as the scoreboard flashed the final results: USA gold, Russia silver, Romania bronze.

The Fierce Five of Team USA, Olympic team champions.

The song "Firework" by Katy Perry was blasting. My teammates and I tightened our circle, as our eyes searched for our parents in the stands. We were screaming and hugging one another and jumping up and down with joy.

A few minutes later, there would be a medal ceremony. As we advanced to the podium, we stopped to shake hands and congratulate each silver and bronze medalist. Then, one by one, we bent our heads as the long dreamed of Olympic gold medal was placed around each of our necks.

We held the medals and turned them over and over in our hands, flipping them over to see both sides. On one side was the 2012 Olympic logo, with the year in jagged-edged numbers. On the other side was an engraving of the goddess of victory, stepping forward below the Olympic rings. We looked at one another and smiled, knowing we had handled all the pressure and fulfilled our potential. All the hard days were for this moment. We stood reverently as the sounds of "The Star-Spangled Banner" filled the North Greenwich Arena.

I ran to find Mihai, and put my medal around his neck. Naturally, he was crying as hard as I was! We hugged, and nothing needed to be said—there were no words that could sufficiently thank him for believing in me, and for all of his hard work. My brain was running a mile a minute, thinking of all the people I wanted to share this moment with, wishing my parents, Brett, Chloe, and Maddie were standing beside me. I wanted to pinch myself, because it felt that much like a dream. I was smiling from ear to ear, trying to soak it all in.

People sometimes ask me what our team did after winning Olympic gold. Did we go to the USA Olympic House to mingle and celebrate with fans? Did we venture out to the London hot spots to let our hair down and live it up?

None of the above. We went to a press conference in a big room high above the arena, then to the NBC house for more media interviews. When we finally made it back to the townhouse, we went to our rooms. Exhausted, each of us fell into a dead sleep.

When I woke up, it was morning. I lay there smiling for a while, then reached for my phone. My mom had sent a short and awesome group text to the team: "Good morning, Olympic champions!" I smiled even harder. So it all *had* been real.

Then, mechanically, I swung my legs over the bed and began getting ready for workout. Olympic gold medalist or not, the competition wasn't over.

CHAPTER 15

THE NUMBER FOUR

London, United Kingdom
August 2012

Mihai was in a great mood on the morning of the all-around final two days after the team competition. He walked the length of the dining hall with a spring in his step, and when he got to our table, he greeted me with a hug.

"What celebrities are tweeting at you today?" he asked with a grin. I listed them: Taylor Swift, Lady Gaga, Joe Jonas, and even Justin Bieber, a.k.a. the Love of Jordyn's Life. "That's good," Mihai said approvingly. "Today is a good day," he added before getting in line for an omelet.

I looked down at my hands. The day of the all-around final had finally arrived, but I just didn't feel the same confidence that I had before the team final. Maybe I was just tired from only having one day between the team and all-around finals.

"Hey," Mihai said. I looked at him standing there with his breakfast, and saw he had guessed what was running through my mind: that I had somehow stolen Jordyn's spot. "You earned this chance fair and square," he said. "Believe in yourself, Aly. This is for you."

When we got back from breakfast, we had some time to kill before the competition later that night. Jordyn gave me and Gabby hugs, and said she couldn't wait to watch us compete. She is a great friend, with a great heart.

We walked into the arena later that afternoon like gladiators marching out into combat. The competition was fierce, especially among the top group, who rotated together. Viktoria, Aliya, Gabby, and I all wanted very badly to win. Each one of us had dedicated years of her life preparing for this competition, dreaming of it, using it as motivation to get through the toughest days. Nobody held anything back.

Gabby and I started off on vault. We both had strong performances there, and I felt relieved to have finished strong on our first event. Gabby was radiating calm and confidence, and I wanted some of that to rub off on me. I started singing to ease the tension, and Gabby joined in. When it hit us that we were at the Olympics, surrounded by cameras, we laughed and stopped singing. We put our grips on and got ready for bars.

For two years, the uneven bars had been my undoing in the World Championships all-around final. When I finished my bar routine without a mistake, I was so proud and allowed myself a moment of thinking that tonight might be my night.

Then, a dangerous thought crept into my mind. Since I went up first on uneven bars and was set to be last on beam, I would have about an hour with nothing but my thoughts. *What if I mess up? What if I forget how to do a beam routine? What if I can't stay on that four-inch space?* I paced back and forth, trying not to watch or listen to the other competitors, knowing that would just make my thoughts spiral more. *You'll be fine, you'll be fine*, I repeated to myself.

My pacing brought me in front of the beam at the worst possible moment, just as Aliya fell. She had come off on a standing Arabian, a very difficult skill where a gymnast jumps backward, does a quick half twist, and then a front flip. Knowing she had fallen, I put pressure on myself to be even more precise. By the time I mounted the beam, I was so focused on not making a mistake that I psyched myself out. Seeing the fall, knowing it would be a big deduction for her and that it could happen to any one of us, terrified me.

I felt sick from nerves. *Deep breaths.* My first two tumbling sequences were dead on. Then, midway through my routine, I bent forward on a front flip and narrowly avoided a fall. I grabbed the balance beam to stay on, an eight-tenths of a point deduction (very close to the deduction for a full fall, which is one point). The rest of the routine was shaky. I only remember feeling really sad and embarrassed. I don't remember the rest of anything that happened during the competition. I knew I had given away my chance, and it devastated me. As we moved to floor exercise, I was crushed.

I assumed that, yet again, I had failed in the all-around final. I didn't realize, though, that I still had a chance for bronze. After three events, Aliya held a slight lead for third place, with me chasing her in fourth. The beam mistake really got to me, and I forgot my parents' sage advice that nothing was over until it was over. I didn't have the same sparkle and confidence I usually did going into floor. Because I was so afraid of making another mistake, I decided to take out the last skill in my first tumbling pass, like I had in the team final. After the routine, I stepped off the podium with my head down, afraid to look up at the scoreboard, but praying I had done enough for a medal.

When I finally gathered the courage to look up, I saw that Gabby Douglas was the 2012 Olympic all-around champion. Viktoria Komova got silver. And Aliya and I were tied for third.

Confusion broke out, because there are no ties in gymnastics at the Olympic Games. I learned later that when two athletes tie in the all-around, the lowest score of each is dropped and the total of the best three are tallied. The total of Aliya's best three outscored mine. But in the moment, all I saw was my name dropping to fourth.

The cameras swarmed around Gabby and me. Pale and hollow-eyed, I gave her a hug and moved away. I recognized that it was Gabby's day, and was happy for her.

At the same time, slipping to fourth was one of the hardest moments of my life. To be so close to getting a medal, and to then wind up empty-handed, was physically painful. I tried as hard as I could not to show it. The goal had been to get the most medals for the United States. I felt I had let my country down.

After it was all over, I was scared to face Martha. I was so afraid of her reaction. To my surprise, I found her almost in tears. She cupped my face in her hands, tilted her head down toward me, and hugged me close. "Oh, Aly," she said, "when will you ever learn to compete for yourself? You always do so well in the team final, and then you put too much pressure on yourself individually."

Mihai tried to cheer me up. "It's okay—you'll get a medal next time," he said. I smiled weakly. It had been hard enough making one Olympic team. Though neither of us said it aloud, we both knew there was unlikely to be a next time.

CHAPTER 16

A GOLD OF MY OWN

London, United Kingdom
August 2012

Our days of introducing ourselves to people in the cafeteria were over: After we won the team gold, everyone seemed to know who we were. Athletes from around the world started coming up to us, offering congratulations and asking to take photos. I became obsessed with trading pins; every athlete got a number of distinct pins for their country and sport, and it became a game to trade them with new people. It was such a great way to meet people, and to learn about other cultures.

Despite the disappointing all-around finish, I reminded myself that I had two more chances to win an individual Olympic medal. Beam and floor had been my best events since I began competing elite, but in the workouts before the competition, I was starting to get tired. Our hours were divided between sweating in the training gym and napping in the townhouse.

Survival of the fittest, Mihai had once said. He was right: By the time event finals came around, the physical and emotional toll of the Games has begun to take hold. With so many competitions in a row, it is very hard to recover. Luckily, I had multiple days between the all-around final and my next event.

Mihai and Martha were working to help me lift my spirits and regain my typical confidence before competition. All three of us had the same lucky number, seven, so they made sure to remind me that it was a great sign that the floor and beam finals were both slated for August 7. I smiled, thinking that they had to be right.

Meanwhile, Kathy Kelly told my parents that if they found coins around London, it would be good luck for me medaling. She said to be sure that they found a gold one for floor. My parents began their task of looking for coins! Sure enough, they found a gold and a bronze on the streets of London. They didn't tell me this story until after the competition, and we still have those good luck coins today.

On August 7, I woke up at six in the morning without an alarm. I took a deep breath and smiled. Today was going to be my day.

Starting order for event finals is chosen by random draw,

and I had drawn the eighth and last spot to compete on beam. The difficulty was mostly mental: I had to stay warm and wait my turn while everyone else performed their routine.

Since the long wait and seeing my competitors perform had put so much pressure on me during the all-around, Mihai and Martha decided that I should spend the waiting time in the warm-up gym, practicing my routine. The event finals require a different type of mental toughness—you have to trust yourself more than ever, because there's no thirty-second warm-up on the competition equipment. So I focused on calming myself. By the time I stood on the podium watching Mihai set my spring-board, I was feeling collected, happily unaware that three of the seven before me had fallen and that Catalina Ponor, who sat in third place, had two big wobbles during her routine. It was just me and the beam.

Once I was on, two sounds penetrated my consciousness. The first was the clicking of the cameras from the pool of photographers stationed fifteen feet from the beam. With each skill or pose, I'd hear a chorus of *clickclickclickclickclick*. The other was McKayla's voice, which comforted me. Her loud cheers rose above the sound of the rest of the spectators, and they made me feel like I was back in practice, and that everything would be okay. Her support helped me push past my fears of repeating the mistake from the all-around final a few nights earlier.

I landed my dismount to see Mihai screaming with happiness. His reaction made me think I had done even better than I thought. The judges, however, gave me a 14.933, which put me—you guessed it—in fourth. Mihai was livid, and disappointed that my score hadn't earned me the bronze medal.

Is it my destiny to be eternally fourth? I wondered to myself.

That was when I heard the unmistakable voices of Kathy, Bela, and Martha in the stands right above us. They were all screaming...for Mihai. I tapped his shoulder and pointed at the Karolyis. Martha and Bela were shouting, "It's the wrong start value! Get your papers!"

"For what?" Mihai asked.

"You have to put in an inquiry. She deserved a higher score," the three of them yelled from the stands.

"For what?" Mihai asked again. "They'll never accept it."

"Just do it!" Kathy shouted. Mihai dashed off across the arena toward the head table.

It is the judges' job to determine the difficulty score of an exercise. Of course, the judges are human, so sometimes they miss a connection, which will impact the difficulty score. If a judge doesn't give a gymnast proper credit, and the coach feels that an error has been made, the coach can appeal the score.

That's what happened. When the score came up, Bela and Martha looked at each other and thought, *That's too low.* They realized I hadn't been credited for all my connections, and called to Mihai to challenge it.

Martha always had coaches fill out inquiry forms before the

competition, just in case they needed to be submitted. That was good, since gymnasts and coaches have a short window of time to file an inquiry for a score. But in the commotion, Mihai had left his inquiry form in the back gym. Now he raced off to fill out a new form because he didn't have time to go and get it.

I was the last to compete and gymnasts were already being gathered for the medal ceremony. Inquiries were rarely accepted. I collected myself and went to congratulate others on the final.

A message flashed on the scoreboard announcing an inquiry had been made on my behalf. Everyone stood around and waited while the superior jury reviewed a video of my performance. After several tense minutes, a new message flashed on the scoreboard: INQUIRY ACCEPTED: 413 ALEXANDRA RAISMAN, USA. D SCORE CHANGE 6.3. My score had been raised! The superior jury agreed that I should have received credit for the combination, and they changed the score. Instead of 14.933, I now had a 15.066, the same score as Catalina Ponor from Romania.

That put us into a tie for bronze. *Wonderful,* I thought, *tied again.* On beam, unlike in the all-around, the judges look to the execution score to break the tie—and mine was higher. I paced nervously, waiting for the officials to award one of us the bronze medal. "Don't worry," Mihai said. "You have the higher execution—it will be you." But I needed to see it on the scoreboard.

After what seemed like an eternity (the longest five minutes of my life), the score change flashed on the Jumbotron and it was official: I had won the bronze medal! I jumped into Mihai's arms, giving him a big bear hug. I closed my eyes, cherishing this special moment. On beam, where it is so easy to make mistakes, medaling was a sign of mental toughness.

During the medal ceremony, I looked around and took in the moment of my first individual medal. I flipped the medal over in my hands, thinking back to my "sweat angel" at the gym with pride, and how it was all worth it to get to this moment. At the same time, I reminded myself that there was still more to do, and I started mentally preparing for the floor final.

The floor final would begin in about an hour. Mihai and I rushed back to the training gym to warm up my tumbling passes while the men's high bar final was taking place in the main arena. High bar, with its spectacular sequences of release moves, was the most thrilling men's event to watch, and I knew the crowd would be amped up when we returned.

Back in the training gym, I told Mihai I wanted to water down my first pass like I had in team finals. "Let me play it safe," I begged Mihai. "I'm just too nervous."

Mihai looked me straight in the eyes. "Today is not the day to be a chicken," he joked, before turning serious. "For a minute and a half, don't think. Do what you do in practice. Do what you've trained to do. Go out there and get your medal." I nodded and warmed up that pass.

I walked up the few steps to the podium, and bent down to

grab chalk for my legs. *I can do this*, I thought. *My moment is here.* I looked to Mihai. He smiled and gave me a nod. With a deep breath, I stepped onto the floor.

My first pass started exactly as I had practiced: a short first step into the roundoff and the other five elements. When I stuck the landing on my first pass, I knew this was going to be a routine I'd always remember. *I'm going to be an Olympic champion*, I thought. Fifteen seconds into the routine, I could already feel it.

The rest of the routine was better than I had ever dreamed of. For the first time ever, my floor routine felt effortless. It felt *right*. In that minute and a half, I didn't feel nervous, I didn't doubt myself—I just felt powerful. I stuck every pass.

There were no tears this time. In fact, after I landed my final pass and assumed my ending pose, I murmured "wow" to myself as I turned to salute the judges. When the score flashed, it was 15.6, even better than the 15.325 I had scored in qualifying, which had been the highest of the meet. I let out a quiet "yes!" when I saw the score, and ran to celebrate with Mihai.

I was putting my warm-ups on when I felt a tap on my shoulder and turned around. It was Aliya. "That was the best floor routine I've ever seen," she said, giving me a thumbs-up.

"Thank you so much," I said. "You've done great, too."

It's surreal to hear your name called as the Olympic champion, then to step up to the top of the podium and stand there while your national anthem is played. No American woman or man had ever won individual gold on floor before. As I stood on the podium, I kissed the medal and bit it, just as I'd seen so many of my Olympic heroes do. I thought of Liliya and how I had watched her when I was eight and dreamed of this moment. I also thought about my family and my coaches, and everything they'd done to help me achieve this dream.

Catalina, the veteran of the Romanian team at twenty-four years old, took the silver. She was one of the gymnasts I had watched over and over again and had admired so much growing up. (My first optional floor routine was a version of the music she had used in 2004 when she was Olympic champion on floor. She won gold on beam, as well.) To win a medal alongside one of my idols was amazing. *How cool.*

During the press conference after the floor final, an Israeli reporter asked if I wanted to dedicate my gold medal to the memory of the Israeli athletes who had been murdered in the terrorist attack at the 1972 Olympic Games in Munich forty years before. The International Olympic Committee had opted not to honor them with a moment of silence. Of course, I said yes immediately. At the time, I didn't realize the impact my words would have on the Jewish community around the world, but people still come up to me today to talk about it.

I was standing in the hall after the last press conference when Martha strode up to me. She admired the gold and bronze medals on their purple ribbons and gave me a hug, cupping my face in her hands. "You finally did it for yourself," she said, smiling broadly.

I slept for twelve hours straight, better than I had in years. *This must be what it's like not to have anxiety before bed*, I marveled when I woke up. The thought that I was finally done— and would come home with two golds and a bronze—made my heart flutter every time I thought about it. That morning, I had a round of press interviews. I also texted a bit with singer Joe Jonas, who offered his congratulations and told me to look him up the next time I was in LA. I blushed deep red at the thought.

A few days later, I moved from the Village to a hotel room with my mother. Mom and I spent several afternoons just hanging out, enjoying delicious English teas and cakes, and quality time after the long weeks of separation. My teammates and I invaded a London mall and enjoyed a shopping spree. It felt so, so good to kick back. Everywhere we went, people knew who we were and asked us to sign something or take photos with them. What's hilarious is that my mom was recognized almost as much as I was, thanks to that viral video.

Toward the end of the Games, I went with the Octagon team to see the gold medal soccer match between Brazil and Mexico.

Sitting in the stands, I got a glimpse of the spectator experience, which included a video montage of Olympic athletes in London just before the match began. I had never seen it, because it was always played in the arena before the athletes marched in to begin the competition.

The video was set to "Survival" by Muse, the official song of the Games. There was Usain Bolt tearing down the track, and Michael Phelps splashing powerfully through the pool. With a jolt, I recognized myself on the screen, flying through the air, suspended in super slow motion. Standing there watching it with the tens of thousands of other people in the stadium, it truly sunk in that I had competed at the Olympic Games.

A day later, the Olympics came to an end. We walked into the Olympic stadium with all the other athletes from nations around the world who had competed at the London Games, taking photos, trying on each other's medals, and enjoying the moment. Most of the closing ceremony was a concert: Several famous musicians performed, including Jessie J, Ed Sheeran, Muse, and the Spice Girls as part of a reunion (though we arrived too late to hear One Direction, and Kyla was devastated). We danced and sang to the music.

The whole thing was incredible, I marveled as we mugged for cameras and took in the packed stadium and the awesome ambiance that can only be generated by an Olympic Games. I looked over at my teammates and smiled. Olympic champions.

CHAPTER 17

THE FAMOUS FIVE

All Over the United States
Fall 2012–Winter 2013

"Hello, is this Aly?" asked a familiar male voice on the other end of the line. "This is Justin Bieber."

I nearly dropped the phone. "You guys!" I squealed excitedly, grabbing my teammates, who were all staring like I'd gone crazy. I motioned frantically at the phone. "It's JUSTIN BIEBER!"

Normally I would have tried to play it cool, but... *Justin Bieber.* The biggest pop star on the planet. Jordyn, Gabby, McKayla, and Kyla all stopped vogueing for the photographers and dashed over. We crowded around the phone, hanging on to his every word.

"I just wanted to tell you all that I'm sorry I couldn't be there tonight," Justin was saying. "I was really looking forward to meeting you all, and I hope I'll get another chance soon."

We stammered some incoherent sentence fragments in reply, and Justin said good-bye. When he hung up, I stared at the phone, my heart pounding. I thought I might faint. A playful shove from McKayla snapped me out of it. "You didn't play it cool at all!" she said. "Now he's never going to date us!"

"Date *us*? He's mine!" Jordyn said. We cracked up.

We were at the MTV Video Music Awards in Brooklyn. I was wearing a navy and silver long-sleeved mini dress accessorized with hot pink heels, matching bright lipstick, and a silver clutch. We'd all spent hours at a hotel nearby with our families, getting our hair and makeup done, laughing, and talking about who we might meet at the VMAs. Now we were surrounded by people we'd seen in magazines or watched on TV, and doing our best not to point and squeal (Justin Bieber aside).

The amazing thing was that these famous people recognized us, too. When we arrived and stepped out of our limo and onto the red carpet, we found ourselves next to Miley Cyrus. We gaped as she waved and walked over to say hello. "I absolutely loved you guys at the Olympics. You were terrific!" she said, flashing a huge smile. "Thanks," we managed. Later, Rihanna was friendly to us backstage. We stared at one another openmouthed. *Rihanna knows who we are. What is even happening?* We also met Taylor Swift and Katy Perry (who kissed Jordyn's bicep!), among many others.

The Olympics set off a whirlwind. For the next few months, we lived like rock stars.

Right from London, we had headed to New York for a round of press calls and TV appearances. We had gone on *The Colbert Report, The Today Show,* and *The Late Show with David Letterman.* We did publicity shots at the top of the Empire State Building, which were later displayed around the building's famous observation deck. We rang the closing bell on the New York Stock Exchange. We were presenters at the VMAs. In the months to come, we would ride on a special float in a Thanksgiving Day parade and do a guest appearance on *Dancing with the Stars* in LA.

We were invited to the White House by President Barack Obama and First Lady Michelle Obama, who were so gracious to us. We took some pictures with them, and then the president of the United States asked if he could take one with McKayla, with both of them making her famous "not impressed" face.

"I make that face at least twice a day when my advisors tell me things," he joked, and we all laughed.

It was amazing to go from training and never staying out past 10:00 PM to a life where we were doing photo shoots, appearances, and living it up—a heightened version of the normal teenage things I'd dreamed of for so long.

Amazing, but dizzying, too. It wasn't long before we all began feeling some whiplash.

USA Gymnastics organizes a "tour of champions" after each Olympic Games, and we had all signed on to participate. The forty-city tour, beginning in California, would span one coast to the other. Tour life was different and cool. We were reunited with the men's team, as well as with some of our national teammates and past Olympians, for about a week of rehearsals and then the tour. In addition to the current Olympic team, other national team members—including Sabrina and Olympic team alternates Elizabeth Price, Sarah Finnegan, and Anna Li—joined us for some or all of the shows. Everyone knew each other really well, and after the Olympic rush, we were all relishing the opportunity to travel together, perform, and have some fun.

After each show, we would sign autographs and greet fans, then pile on to tour buses that would drive half the night to the next city. Performing to cheering crowds was fun, but the best moments actually came between the shows, in transit from one city to the next. The five of us had a tour bus all to ourselves. The buses were equipped with beds, and every night was like a huge slumber party: We stayed up late playing music and having dance parties or watching movies in our pajamas as the bus rolled from one city to the next.

Around 4:00 AM we would arrive at our next destination, check in to a hotel, do cartwheels up and down the hallway, and grab a few hours of sleep. We usually got up after four or five hours to make sure we took advantage of each hotel's free breakfast buffet, piling our plates with French toast, eggs, or bagels, whatever we felt like eating. Then we would head to the arena for rehearsal before the evening show. There was a lot of pressure to do difficult skills to please the crowds. But it wasn't wise to attempt those skills given the intense schedule and absence of the coaches who knew us (and our limits) best.

On days when there was no show, I would usually travel—sometimes by car, sometimes by plane—to do an appearance or speaking engagement, and would rejoin the tour in the next city. The shows were Thursday through Sunday nights, so I spent Monday through Wednesday traveling. Some days would be dedicated to photo shoots for endorsement campaigns, including an especially fun one with my mom for a jeweler's Mother's Day ad. I worked with the nonprofit organization Century Council to speak with middle schoolers about choosing a healthy lifestyle and saying no to underage drinking. I started working with a leotard company, GK, to create my own line of leotards, which is something I still love doing today. I spent most of these travel days holding gymnastics clinics, meeting with kids at school events, and speaking to crowds of all ages.

I would often speak at Jewish Community Centers, and the responses there made me realize the impact I had as a Jewish athlete. For example, an Israeli Defense Force soldier publicly posted a letter thanking me for standing up for the Munich Olympians, and saying that he saw an officer saluting my image on television. Shortly after the Olympics, my rabbi received a letter from a woman whose mother was a holocaust survivor. When her mother saw me perform to "Hava Nagila," she told her daughter, "I never thought in my lifetime I'd see a Jew at the Olympics dancing to 'Hava Nagila' in front of Russians, Germans, and people of all nations, and it was no big deal, everyone is okay with it. More than that, everyone says she is doing great." It became clear to me that when I competed, I was representing not only my country, but also the Jewish community. It gave me an even greater appreciation of the Olympics, a place where the whole world and people of all nationalities came together to support one another.

Everywhere we went, we met people who told us how much they had loved watching the Olympics, how much they loved gymnastics, and how proud they were of us. The Olympics had always been a big deal to me. But I hadn't realized how many other people felt the same way. A few people cried when they met us. It was always a shock to be recognized. Interacting with fans more and more really drove home my parents' lessons about how much the kind of person you are impacts other people. I started to become aware of the person I wanted to be and hoped that my fans would look up to me and think highly of me.

Doing gymnastics in a show is very different from doing it in competitions. For safety, many of our routines were watered down (at least compared to our Olympic routines), but we were still pressured to do difficult skills and tough routines and expected to execute them flawlessly day after day in unfamiliar surroundings. We performed under spotlights or in semi-darkness, and had to get used to bright flashing light effects for some numbers, which made it hard to see when we were doing gymnastics.

I arrived for the tour without grips, because I wasn't expecting to have to do bars—and didn't want to do them. I thought I'd be able to focus on my stronger events, and bars wasn't one of them, so I wondered why I'd have to perform it every night. Plus, without Mihai around, I didn't feel safe. Despite my concerns, the tour directors said we all had to do bars, no exceptions.

During our second show, in Ontario, California, I learned how important it was to be firmer in sticking up for myself. We were in the middle of a number set to Beyoncé's "Run the World (Girls)." The routine starts with a group of us doing a dance performance on floor before shifting over to take turns doing pieces of our routines on the uneven bars, bathed in violet light. Jordyn, Kyla, and Gabby were on one set of bars, while McKayla and I were on the other.

McKayla did her routine and dismounted with a single back layout salto. When her feet hit the mat, she fell backward, grabbing her knee. For a moment I thought she must have rolled an ankle. But when she didn't get up, I took a few steps toward her and saw that her face was contorted in pain. She was still clutching her knee. One look at her leg showed me that her shin bone was sticking up, way out of place.

Oh no. I wanted to yell for help, but I didn't know who to turn to. Fortunately, the tour medical staff had seen McKayla fall, and when they saw that she didn't get up, two of them appeared, picked her up, and carried her off the mat and out from under the lights. She wasn't even crying. I was amazed at her bravery, but I also wondered what the crowd must be thinking.

The music jolted me back to the performance. Thinking it was my duty to provide a distraction, I hurriedly mounted the bars for my turn. Seeing McKayla get injured had freaked me out, and I was so upset I couldn't think straight. Mechanically, I cast into a handstand, but went too far over and swung back to my starting position, mentally shaking my head. I put my feet on the bar and swung into a skill known as a Shaposhnikova, in which the gymnast swings backward on the low bar and shoots her feet upward, letting go of the bar at the same time. Her backward and upward momentum carries her toward the high bar, which—if all goes well—she catches.

I mistimed the skill, shooting my heels too soon. That didn't give me the height I needed to firmly grasp the high bar. My hands brushed it and gripped for a second, but I couldn't hold on. Suddenly, I was unanchored and hurtling backward through space.

Normally I would have belly flopped onto the mat below and suffered nothing worse than embarrassment. But this time, the lower half of my body landed where there was no mat. My bare knees smacked down hard on the concrete floor of the arena. *Bam.* Excruciating pain—pain like I'd never experienced—hit my legs.

If I could have, I would have crawled out of the arena. But the floor digging into my kneecaps hurt so much that I summoned all of my willpower and pulled myself to my feet. Shakily, I walked over to the chalk bowl and stood for a few seconds, waiting for someone to come and see if I was all right. I would tell them how much pain I was in and get some help.

But no one came. There weren't a lot of people on the medical staff, so all of them were with McKayla. Gingerly, I limped off to find a trainer. I encountered one of the tour's creative directors, who took one look at me and told me to go back out and finish the routine with the others.

I shook my head. "Did you see me fall?" I asked, shocked that no one was helping. I couldn't believe that after asking not to do bars, asking for more mats, and then being injured because neither request was met, now I was being told to just go back out there.

Ice. I needed ice. The hallway just off the arena floor was deserted. *Where was everyone?* I wondered. I limped around for several minutes before I found the training room. McKayla was lying on a table, her left leg already in a splint. Her eyes widened when she saw the pain on my face as I came gingerly through the doorway.

"What happened to you?" she asked.

"I fell onto the cement," I said simply, collapsing on the other table. I felt like I might pass out from the pain.

We held hands as we waited for the ambulance that would take her to the hospital. The trainer dashed around, shoveling ice into two big plastic bags for my bruised kneecaps. As the heavy bags of cold ice touched my skin, I closed my eyes in pain.

Sufficient mats weren't arranged on the floor before our performance. I was very angry about the oversight, which had caused my injury. After that, mats were added.

"You know," Mom said during a phone call, "you trusted that those mats had been set up correctly. Why wouldn't the performance setup match a competition's? Going forward, if something doesn't seem right to you, it's important that you speak up."

Mihai called, too. He was worried. He had kept me healthy and injury-free for years, and couldn't believe I had been injured so quickly the moment I wasn't under his care. He made me promise to stay away from difficult skills on bars.

For the next several months, I applied topical cream twice daily to bring the swelling and internal bruising down. I was lucky that I was able to rejoin the tour almost right away. Even McKayla eventually rejoined the tour, though her injury limited what she was able to do. We were all just glad she was back.

A few months later, I lay in a deck chair by the pool at a resort in Puerto Vallarta, Mexico, watching the sunset streak the sky orange and purple and pink. The tour had wrapped, leaving me and my family free to finally take a long-anticipated vacation the following February, our first time taking a trip all together in many years.

I spent most of my days lounging by the pool, thinking how wonderful it was to finally be somewhere where the most physically demanding thing I had to do was apply sunscreen! It meant so much just to spend time with my parents, Brett, Chloe, and Maddie, and to do absolutely nothing.

With a few months away from the gym, I was free to really contemplate the future for the first time. In the short term, I had an exciting new project to look forward to: being a contestant on *Dancing with the Stars*. Following the Fierce Five's appearance on the show during the All-Stars season, producers had expressed an interest in having another gymnast do the show. I had a blast during our guest appearance, and I made it very clear to the producers that I hoped they would pick me to be a contestant. My whole family was excited when they chose me—my dad even burst into tears because he knew how much it meant to me and how much my Bubbie would have loved to be part of the excitement.

So far in the months after the Games, the press had been content to let us relive the awesome achievement of winning Olympic gold medals and going on tour. But now they were focused on one question: Will you go back to the gym and train for Rio?

I would explain that I was enjoying my time off and keeping a possible return in the back of my mind. I would absolutely love to compete in Rio—who wouldn't? But I felt like I needed more time.

That March, the American Cup was held in Worcester, an hour's drive from my house. Gabby and I had been invited to make special appearances there. We watched the competition seated at the head table. When familiar music came on, we broke into the popular Harlem Shake dance, which they broadcast on the Jumbotron. We couldn't stop laughing! As we sat back down and stared at the blue floor mat, I turned to her and asked, "Do you miss this?"

Slowly, she shook her head. "I just need a break," she said. Then she looked at me. "Why? Do *you* want to be out there?"

"Not yet," I said honestly. We sat quietly after that, each lost in our own thoughts. I had trained and competed and dealt with the pressure for years. I tried not to think about the all-around final and the medal that had eluded me. *I wish I could do it over,* I thought sometimes. Maybe next time, I wouldn't be so afraid.

Other times I thought, there's nothing left to accomplish.... Was there?

CHAPTER 18

DANCING INTO A NEW ME

Los Angeles, California
March 2013

"You know what we're going to do?" Mark Ballas, my professional dance partner, told me during one of our first training sessions for *Dancing with the Stars*. "We're going to model. I know you can model. Vogue for me!" He jutted his hips out and strutted around the dance studio, doing a perfect imitation of a runway model. "Your turn—shake those hips and give me a shimmy!"

I took two steps and crumpled to the floor in a puddle of giggles. Mark was absolutely determined to get me out of my shell, but I was so used to being serious and focused in the gym that what he was asking was totally foreign to me. He wanted me to flip a switch and bring my well-hid emotions out for the world to see.

Mihai had been my coach since I was ten years old, and I was used to his way of doing things, but now Mark was my coach—in a whole different arena. I was also used to listening to Mihai and following his instructions exactly, because my safety depended on it, and now Mark wanted me to let loose and improvise. "Aly, you're not at the Olympics anymore! You can relax. There's no right or wrong answer in dance. In dance you need to feel the music."

Another one of the many big differences between Mark and Mihai was that Mihai would watch from the sidelines, but Mark was my dance partner, and we needed to learn to move as one. Mark would choreograph the routines to my strengths. Mark and Mihai were similar in one way: They both expected me to give 100 percent every day.

The twelve contestants on season sixteen of *DWTS* came from different worlds. They included Disney Channel star Zendaya Coleman, singer Kellie Pickler, recent *Bachelor* star Sean Lowe, comedian Andy Dick, and NFL wide receiver Jacoby Jones. We had all lived unusual, diverse lives, but got along surprisingly well. From the first day, it was clear that some of us came into the show with some preconceived notions about Andy Dick, for instance, who got a bad rap in the press. But Andy turned out to be one of the sweetest, kindest people on the show.

He was a walking reminder of the importance of reserving judgment and getting to know people for who they are. People can
be so quick to judge, but everyone goes through ups and downs
in their lives, and it's important that we all lift one another up.
If Andy was the comic relief on set, Kellie was the one I bonded
with over her great energy and consistent warmth, and Jacoby
was like the big brother I never had. We often joked about how
far outside of our comfort zones we were.

During my twelve weeks living in Los Angeles and performing on the show, counting music and showing the emotion of
the dances quickly became my biggest challenges. Another one
was dancing in heels, since gymnasts are always barefoot, and
sharing the stage with another person. Dancing with a partner
is much harder than it looks. For the first time, I had to focus on
someone else while also concentrating on my own movements.
More than once during our first rehearsals, I kicked Mark or hit
him by mistake. He must have felt like my mom when I was five
and was knocking into everything as I did cartwheels.

The other thing that took some getting used to was being
part of a hit TV show. Everything was a secret at first, including
the identity of the other cast members and then of our dance
partners. I was begging the producers to tell me who my partner
was (everyone who knows me will tell you how persistent I can
be!). Of course, they kept saying I'd have to wait and see. The big
reveal was all meant to be captured on film. But things didn't

exactly go as planned—when I went to wardrobe prior to the big reveal and went to pick out my shoes for week one, someone said, "Go with those, the height is better for Mark."

"Mark is my partner!?!?!" I exclaimed. They looked at one another, hands over their mouths. We all started laughing. Hungry for more details, I scanned the room as I was being ushered out and a label on a garment bag caught my eye. "Jacoby Jones will be here, too?!?" I exclaimed, excited because I remembered watching his touchdown dance at the Super Bowl and thought that he would be fun competition if we did the show together. "Get out of here," the producers cried, only half joking.

From that day on, we wore tiny microphones on set at all times, and every second of rehearsal was filmed. Mark and I had lots of fun teasing each other. I would try to imitate his British accent, which I loved. He teased me about boys. Whenever we had to dance nose-to-nose, I wasted a lot of time giggling. I was *not* used to having a boy's face so close to mine.

When it was showtime, however, Mark turned dead serious. "We get one chance—that's it, one time," he reminded me as we walked onstage to do our first dance, a cha-cha, and just for a second it was like I was taking the floor at the National Championships.

I was pleased that my very first dance went well, and the judges—dance masters Len Goodman, Carrie Ann Inaba, and Bruno Tonioli—scored us a respectable 21 out of 30. "I really like the sass and the frass that you got going on," Carrie Ann told us. "But I do think I want you to not be so safe. I think you need to push just a little more."

The life cycle of a *Dancing with the Stars* dance is one week, Wednesday to Tuesday. On Wednesday you learn what dance you'll be performing on the show the next Monday, and Thursday, Friday, and Saturday are completely taken up by rehearsals, with each couple in the studio around eight hours a day. First comes a crash course in the basic steps of the dance. A few hours later, you get to work on the routine you'll perform on air the same week. On Sundays, we had camera blocking, where we could practice the full routine in the ballroom without our costumes, to figure out the best camera angles, lighting, and props for the show. Dress rehearsals were early Monday afternoon, when everyone would be on set to make last-minute adjustments before the show. The wardrobe team was especially impressive—I always said it was like magic that they were able to come up with such amazing costumes in such a short amount of time, and make adjustments on the spot.

Dress rehearsal was my favorite part of the show—we could be more playful, teasing each other through the practice interviews that we knew would never air. Plus, there were stand-in judges, so we didn't need to worry about scores and we could make funny faces and jokes to the stand-ins. We might not have been the most mature group of contestants, but we knew how to have fun!

At the beginning it always seemed like the dances would need a month or longer to master. Mark understood the time crunch: He was a master at time management. The pros could listen to a song a few times and an incredible, original idea would pop into their heads. They could choreograph numbers in half an hour. Their quickness amazed me. Mark choreographed numbers around my strengths, but would change the choreography on a dime if it was taking me too long to pick something up.

Sometimes it would take me a while to learn a particular sequence, or counting the music would trip me up. I was so used to blocking out the world when I competed, but you can't be on autopilot in the ballroom. Luckily, what had made me successful in gymnastics applied to dancing as well: I never gave up. I would work until I had mastered whatever I was being asked to do. It wasn't long before my feet were covered in blisters, which were so uncomfortable that I eventually started wearing socks with the heels. At night, I'd go home to the apartment across from the Grove shopping complex, a terrific sunny row of boutiques and cafes.

My parents worked it out so that one of them was always there with me, while the other stayed in Boston. A few times, my whole family flew out for the Monday taping of the show. Often after the show wrapped, my family and I would go out for dinner, taking advantage of a delicious LA hot spot. Sometimes the show would be playing on a nearby TV as we ate, and we'd sit and gawk at how much bigger the ballroom looked on camera, and laugh at the things that had happened behind the scenes that didn't make it onto the program.

My extended family, including my cousins Mikayla and Brooke and their parents, also came for a short while. My little sisters, particularly Maddie, had a great time exploring chic, offbeat LA hangouts, which were so different from what they were used to in Needham. The food scene in LA was especially appealing, since there are so many restaurants that serve fresh, healthy options. Almost all of them were good, though we reconsidered our favorite sushi restaurant after noticing the health inspector's subpar rating posted on the door one night as we were leaving. We never ate there again!

Being in the ballroom week after week, my family got to know some of the other contestants' friends and family. Jacoby's mom and cousin were in the audience every single week, as was Sean Lowe's fiancée, Catherine.

The third week of the season was a prom night theme, where Mark had me reminiscing about my own prom. I told him about my date. "Did y'all make out?" he asked playfully.

"None of your business!" I yelped.

"They made out," Mark grinned.

"We didn't!" I insisted, covering my eyes in embarrassment. "I left early because I had to practice the next morning." As he started googling my prom date's name, I grabbed the phone, blushing.

For prom night, Mark and I showed a dramatic Viennese waltz, based on the idea of two people without prom dates who find each other and fall in love. "What I want to see you work on is staying in the character," Carrie Ann said.

For the "my most memorable year" week, I chose 2012, and Mark had the idea to do a raw, emotional contemporary piece that allowed me to relive what it was like to prepare for and compete in the Olympic Games. Mark set the tone by comparing it to preparing for London.

"Training for the Olympics, was it fun and cupcakes?" he asked.

"It was the hardest thing I'll ever do in my life," I replied honestly.

"Mentally, that's how you need to feel during this dance," he said. "This is about the years of hard work that you put into it—all that pain and repetition that created that moment for you."

For the video introduction to the dance, I did a long interview talking about my experiences in gymnastics and at the Olympics. I was surprised that more than six months later, I still felt vulnerable talking about the all-around competition. That, in turn, made me feel guilty. I had three medals, including two golds. What more could I possibly want?

The song was David Guetta's "Titanium," one of the songs that I'd listened to before training every day in London. The choreography told the story of a girl who faces numerous challenges and setbacks as she strives to achieve her dreams. It was therapeutic to let all the things I felt about my experiences come out in a dance—all those moments of being hurt, exhausted, stressed, scared, and frustrated. At one point in the dance, Mark appeared to put weight on my ankles as I struggled to move forward. At the very end, I finally broke free of the bonds holding me back. As the music faded away, I was walking slowly offstage, toward a brighter future.

I especially loved the ending to that dance, because it was about breaking through, conquering fear, and empowering oneself. The contemporary dance helped give me a newfound appreciation for how strong I really was. Sometimes we forget to appreciate that, I realized, because so often we dwell on what's negative about an experience rather than how it made us stronger.

I poured all the doubt and uncertainty I was feeling into the contemporary dance. We received our highest score yet. Mark and I jumped up and down in excitement. Later, off camera, he told me how proud he was of my progress. The compliment meant a lot.

The contemporary dance was a turning point. I had taken a risk and let people see vulnerability, which you just don't show in gymnastics. And the judges and the audience had celebrated it.

The next weekend was the beginning of my siblings' April vacation from school. Brett went on a trip to Italy with several classmates, while my parents, Chloe, and Maddie flew to LA to spend the week with me. Early Monday morning, we heard the terrible news about what had happened back home in Boston. During the Boston Marathon, an annual event held in Boston, Massachusetts, on Patriot's Day, on April 15, 2013, two bombs went off near the finish line, killing three spectators and wounding more than 260. It is hard to describe how horrible and awful it was and how sad everyone felt. It disgusts me that we live in a world where people are so cruel and use their hate to justify such unspeakable acts.

Being across the country from my beloved hometown and watching the coverage of the bombing on the news left me feeling sick. It felt wrong to be so far from Boston when my city was hurting. Throughout practice, I was glued to my phone, following the news as it came in, and texting with family and friends to make sure they were okay. It was a heartbreaking day.

With each week that passed, the competition became more intense. Although *Dancing with the Stars* was not nearly as competitive as the process of making an Olympic team, I badly wanted to do well. In gymnastics, only the judges determine your score. On *DWTS*, the public also weighs in by voting and posting comments on social media. And it wasn't long before my body became a topic of conversation.

On Twitter, Instagram, and YouTube, people commented on

whether they liked my hair, my makeup, my costumes, and my body. Some of the comments, particularly ones that discussed my weight, were hard to read. My figure had filled out since the Olympics, and it was difficult adjusting to what often felt like a whole new body. Knowing the cameras captured everything, it was hard not to obsess over how I looked. For every unkind thing someone said, there were thousands of positive remarks. But every now and again, one of the mean ones would get under my skin. I'd find myself thinking about it hours, even days, later.

"It's like people assume that the more followers you have, the fewer feelings you have," I confessed to my friend Samantha Peszek. Samantha, a member of the 2008 Olympic team, was now going to UCLA. "I know I shouldn't care what's being said on social media, but I do," I continued, close to tears. "I actually feel anxious when I open Twitter or Instagram these days because I'm so worried that someone will have said something mean about me."

Samantha understood. "Everyone always says, 'Oh, I'm not going to be that person who gains weight,'" she said. "But guess what? Everybody does. You have to get used to it, and you have to accept it. Think about how many days we spend on this earth. If we didn't all gain or lose a few pounds here and there, it wouldn't make sense! So what you're going through is completely natural, trust me." What she was really saying was, *You're not alone.*

The weeks went by in a blur of dance steps. One by one, contestants were eliminated. It was crushingly hard to say good-bye to them. Even though we'd known each other a very short time, the experience was so intense that we'd become like a family. It was a little like gymnastics that way: Yes, everyone wanted to win, but everyone also recognized the hard work the others were pouring into their routines, and respected it.

Before I knew it, we were preparing for the final. Jacoby, Kellie, Zendaya, and I made up the final four. Our finale routine was so physically taxing, and Mark exerted himself so much in practice, that he ran to a trash can and threw up the second the dance was over! A moment later, he was back and joking around. "You're not the only tough one here," he said. A few minutes later, we had to do the dance again for the camera blocking, and then the next day it was showtime.

And I finished—you guessed it—fourth. Mark and I were the first pair eliminated during the final. *How ironic*, I thought. *This number is meant to haunt me.*

I was so happy that Jacoby, Zendaya, and Kellie—all of whom were awesome dancers and very worthy of the Mirrorball trophy—got to continue in the final. At the same time, it broke my heart to see the disappointment written all over Mark's face when the host announced that we would be the first pair eliminated in the final.

Dancing with the Stars was an eye-opening experience for me in more ways than one. There was so much media attention surrounding costumes, hair, and makeup, and the way that we looked. Having that level of exposure naturally made me self-conscious and uncomfortable at times. Still, the whole experience showed me that having fun and meeting new friends is more important than worrying about looks and perception. I'm grateful to have had the opportunity to do the show, which helped me come out of my shell on camera and connect with a whole new group of people.

CHAPTER 19

TOGETHER AGAIN

Hartford, Connecticut
August 2013

"Aly!"

"Mack!"

We raced across the hotel lobby and caught each other up in a big hug. I was so glad to see her. The Fierce Five were reuniting at the 2013 US Championships in Hartford, Connecticut. McKayla and Kyla were competing at the Championships, while Gabby, Jordyn, and I were just there for the Fierce Five's induction into the USA Gymnastics Hall of Fame. I was especially looking forward to seeing old friends and coaches, as well as the new generation of top US gymnasts.

It wasn't just the five of us who were happy to be back together—our families were thrilled to all be in the same place once again. Our siblings, especially, had a great time at the hotel. Late one night, I ran into Chloe, Maddie, McKayla's sister Tarynn, and Kyla's brother Kayne in the lobby, their arms full of candy. "What are you guys doing up? Where did you get all that candy?" I asked.

The youngest of the group, Tarynn, proudly proclaimed, "If you just give the hotel your room number, everything is free!" not realizing that the rooms were being charged for every "free" purchase!

Before the Hall of Fame ceremony, we all sat around chatting and catching up. McKayla, whose injury had healed, had returned to training and was eyeing a spot on the team for the World Championships in Antwerp, Belgium, that fall. So was Kyla, the only one of us not to have turned pro, instead returning to school and the gym shortly after the Olympic Games. She had grown five inches since the Games, blooming into a tall, elegant gymnast. She, too, was expected to have a big impact on the World Championships stage.

Jordyn had decided to take a break from full-time training and enroll at UCLA. Having turned pro before London, she was not able to compete for the UCLA gymnastics team. Instead, she had become the most overqualified team manager the school had ever had in any sport. Gabby had recently moved to California with her family. I had enrolled for fall semester classes at Babson College, not far from my home, while continuing to take advantage of professional opportunities like speaking engagements and endorsement deals. I had also been going to Brestyan's a little bit here and there. Just for some light training.

As the captain, I spoke at the Hall of Fame ceremony on behalf of our team. I talked about how proud we were of what we had accomplished at the Games, for ourselves, for our families, for our coaches, and for our country. It was hard to believe how far we'd come—I told the gathered crowd about the time I ran around a meet just like this one, collecting autographs, including Jordyn's. And then she turned out to be my Olympic teammate, roommate, and one of my best friends.

Afterward, Mihai and I reminisced about our first international assignment together, in Brazil back in 2009. "Wouldn't it be special to go back to Brazil for the 2016 Olympics?" he said. "You could return to where it all began."

The words stuck in my head. In my room that night, I allowed myself to really think about making a comeback. *Maybe going back to training wouldn't be such a bad thing*, I mused. I remembered all the girls and all the fun we'd had, even cut off from the world at the ranch. Sure, preparing for the Olympics was grueling work. But we'd also had too many good times to count.

I wasn't ready to turn away from that.

The next day, I met Simone Biles for the first time. We took to each other immediately. "You inspire me," she told me, flashing a bright smile when we were introduced. "When I watched you at the Olympics, I thought, 'Hmmm, she has boobs. So do I! And she's not that great on bars. Neither am I! If she can make it, maybe I can, too.'"

Her honesty impressed me almost as much as her energy. "I think you're going to do all right," I told her, laughing. We had texted before I met her in person, and years later she showed me a video someone had taken of her reaction when I texted her the first time. She screamed, fell on the ground, and was her typically hyper self. Her reaction was almost as big as when Zac Efron tweeted at her years later!

I sought out Mihai. I felt a sudden desire to be back on the floor, warming up with the girls, feeling the butterflies of anticipation. I missed being in the gym working toward a goal, even being exhausted at the end of a workout! Some part of me had become accustomed to the hard work and drive that surrounds an Olympic dream. And there was another little voice in my head now, one that kept saying, *You're not done yet. There's still more to accomplish.*

I took a deep breath. "Mihai," I said, "I think maybe I'd like to try to come back."

He didn't look surprised. "Yeah, you can come back," he said, in the same nonchalant tone he'd use when I'd ask to be spotted on a tumbling pass. "But you realize," he said, turning to look at me, "if you're serious about coming back, you will have to be even better than you were last year. And that's going to take a lot of work. Can you do that?"

I swallowed. "I think I can," I said.

Mihai went to the ranch a few weeks later to survey the world team, which included Kyla, Simone, and McKayla. "Aly tells me she wants to come back," he told Martha casually.

"That's interesting," Martha said. "Let's see if she has the desire to prove herself again. Nothing is impossible."

CHAPTER 20

THE RETURN

Needham, Massachusetts
2014–2015

Winter sunlight was filtering through the blinds in my room as I yawned and stretched my arms toward the ceiling, feeling recovered and energized. Giddy anticipation coursed through my veins.

Today, I thought, *I get to go do gymnastics!* Excited already, I pushed the covers back and hopped to my feet.

After so many years of eat-sleep-breathe gymnastics, I was surprised to find that the prospect of going to practice filled me with joy. In the gym I felt like a kid let loose in a candy store— exactly the way I had ten years before.

It was like someone had pushed a "reset" button some- where. All my old dreams had become new again. Even during my classes at Babson, I found myself longing for 4:00 PM so I could hop in the car and make the half-hour drive up the highway to Brestyan's for the five o'clock practice.

But when I went to get out of bed, it hit me just how sore you can get from doing gymnastics. *Oof.* I started seeing a chiropractor, Dr. Miller, who helped build a whole team to address my aches and pains and help me perform at an optimal level. I felt so much looser and more comfortable after my first adjustment with Dr. Miller—my body felt brand new.

Since I'd been out of the gym for nearly a year, I knew better than to start working double backs and full bar routines at once. That would be dangerous and, for me, impossible. For three months, I hardly did any gymnastics at all. I would run around the floor for an hour with my headphones in to build up endurance. Then I'd attack the old conditioning routine: jumping exercises to get the spring back on floor. Chin-ups and leg lifts on bars. And many, many rope climbs. I did one-minute handstand holds against the wall, trying to have every part of my body flat against the wall to make sure I was going to have better bar form this time around. I did toe raises, squat jumps, lots of kicks for flexibility, and so much more.

When I thought I was finished with conditioning, I'd ask Mihai what to do. My coach, a world-renowned expert on conditioning, would unfailingly have another exercise on hand for me. Sometimes I'd go up to him thinking he couldn't possibly have one more in mind, but he always did. When he finally thought I was done, he would send me off with Silvie for ballet and flexibility exercises. My coaches did everything but stretch me. I've known coaches to stretch their athletes to the point of tears, sometimes causing serious injury. When it came to flexibility, Mihai and Silvie trusted that I knew my limits. To distract myself from the discomfort of stretching, I asked Silvie to help me learn Romanian. But no matter how much I practiced, every time I said good-bye to Mihai in Romanian, he teased me that my accent was horrible. But at least I made him laugh.

When I returned, I didn't do double sessions. I also took weekends off that summer, freeing myself up to enjoy family time at our house on the Cape. When I was done at the gym, I left. For the first time in my life, I felt like I had the best of both worlds. Because things were going so well, I always left the gym wanting more.

Very slowly, I began to build back the strength required to safely do high level gymnastics. Twelve weeks after I made the commitment to come back, I did my first back handspring on the floor. Then a few beam skills on the floor. Then I started doing them on the beam itself. That was absolutely terrifying— I had forgotten just how narrow a four-inch beam was! Mihai would have me do a series of ten beam routines on a line of tape on the floor, to build up muscle memory, endurance, and my confidence.

Mihai left me to work on my own during this time. As I conditioned, he would move around the gym, making corrections, and spotting other gymnasts on their skills. He just wanted to be sure I was serious about coming back, and I certainly didn't need to hear corrections on my push-ups! Once I proved that I was serious, I knew he would be watching me like a hawk. My dad would tell me to enjoy those moments, since he knew in a few months, Mihai would be glued to my side and I wouldn't be able to take two steps without Mihai giving me corrections!

All this gave me a newfound respect and appreciation for my body and what it could do. Gymnastics was all I had known for most of my life. It had taken stepping away from it and coming back to realize what incredible shape athletes are in! It's too easy to focus on how far away a goal is, but I learned that it's important to appreciate how far you've come. *We don't give ourselves enough credit*, I thought as I did backflip after backflip— ten in a row—sticking each one. I would lay on the floor seeing stars, dizzy from so many flips in a row.

No other coach but Mihai had been allowed to spot me since I had begun trying to go elite. That had always made me feel special and loved, knowing that he didn't trust any other coach to catch me. As I returned to harder skills, Mihai began stepping in to help me through my routines.

Folk music had become my signature on floor. Silvie thought it appealed to the international judges, who came from all over the world. Also, with so many gymnasts using modern pieces, she thought it helped me stand out. We selected the Russian folk song "Kalinka." Once Mihai had approval from Martha, Silvie began choreographing a routine she hoped would get me back onto the world stage—and hopefully back on the podium.

Slowly, I began to increase my hours. "Aly-lujiah, still no boyfriend?" Mihai teased as I sat on the floor sweating through box jumps one Friday night.

"Gymnastics is the only relationship I can handle," I said, in between jumps.

Now that I had been to the Olympics, I knew what it was like to win, as well as to come up just short. I could have retired after London, and on paper, my career probably would have seemed complete. But it wasn't—at least not to me. I still had enormous love for the sport, and a gut telling me I had more to accomplish.

I had yet to put on my grips and swing bars because I had needed to build up the muscle mass to prevent injuries before I could begin seriously training the event.

Bars and vault would be the hardest—and scariest—events for me to return to. Every gymnast has at least one event that's especially tough for them. Because I had such a rough time getting back onto those events, Mihai would spot me every time, joking that the older I got, the more chicken I became.

He patiently carried me through many bars skills. But in the fall of 2014, an old arm injury flared up and he had to have surgery! To lighten the mood while he was recovering, I joked to Silvie that he got surgery just to teach me to trust myself and not rely on his spotting! I felt terrible for him, but lucky to be his athlete. Not every coach would risk injury to themselves just to make sure their athlete stays safe. When he came back, I pushed my fears aside and did bars without his spotting, but he still spotted me on my floor routine due to the difficulty of my tumbling—using his non-dominant, non-injured arm. Silvie bragged that her husband was the only coach in the world who could spot perfectly with both arms.

For the first several months, nobody except Mihai, Silvie, and my family took my comeback seriously. History was not on my side. During the past decade, several Olympians had tried to come back after taking a break following the Games, only to fall short of a second Olympic team. In fact, it had been fifteen years since any American woman had done more than one Games (the last two were Magnificent Seven members Dominique Dawes and Amy Chow in Sydney in 2000).

Eventually, Mihai felt I was far enough along to talk to Martha about having me return to camp. But Martha said not to rush. She didn't want me to come back too soon and risk injury, which could kill my chances of an Olympic return. I was devastated that she didn't want me on the national team. Mihai and Silvie assured me that it was good news, though—if she wasn't thinking of me for the 2016 team, she wouldn't advise me to take it slow.

It wasn't long after I began doing double sessions again that I started feeling beyond tired after training. Training twice a day made a huge difference in my recovery and nutrition needs. Though I would drive myself to the gym, I often asked my dad to come and get me from practice because I was so exhausted I didn't feel safe being behind the wheel of a car. When my muscles began cramping again, like they had in 2012, I knew something needed to change. I had met with a nutritionist before who didn't end up being very helpful, so this time we found a sports dietitian who worked with elite athletes and understood our unique nutritional needs.

"Tell me about your diet," Ted Harper, my sports dietitian, said during our first session late in 2014. "Be very specific. What does your daily intake look like? I want to know what you eat, how much, where and what time you're eating these foods. The more you tell me, the better I can help optimize your nutrition regimen."

So I sketched it out for him: a lot of protein, small amounts of salad and fruit, a little bit of chocolate or candy if I wanted a treat—and I was back to eating almost nothing in the way of carbs from bread, cereal, pasta, potatoes, rice, and other grains and starches. "I try to adhere to what I read about," I explained. "It seems like a lot of people in Hollywood are going no-carb, and they're so fit. And I don't want to be puffy and bloated, so

I'm keeping my salt intake down. I need to make sure I can get my body back to how it looked in 2012 when I competed at the Olympics."

Ted put down his notepad and sighed. "There's a lot of nonsense out there about this diet and that diet," he said. "Many of those are fad diets that don't pertain to athletes. You need to disregard everything you read in magazines and trust me when I tell you that depriving yourself of things your body needs to function optimally is just not going to get you the results you want. Plus, you look like you're on death's doorstep and completely drained of energy." I could see he was very worried about me from the way I looked.

Ted explained that by cutting out carbs, I was actually depriving myself of a main energy source my body needed for training. Carbs were fuel for the muscles and the brain, he emphasized, and would help me maintain my peak power output and focus during routines. Instead of eating less of them, "they need to be a priority for you," he said. Eating carbs and protein together went hand in hand, he added. If I only ate protein, my body would convert a portion of it into a low-grade carbohydrate (essentially bad quality, poor efficiency fuel), which would have a negative impact on my training. Protein needs carbs to be able to fully do its job, strengthening my muscles and aiding in recovery between workouts.

"This is why it's imperative—absolutely imperative—that you eat carbs as well as protein in all your meals," he stressed.

He suggested that my pre-workout meal be heavier on carbs for fuel and my post-workout one be more stacked with protein for recovery, but insisted that both be consumed before and after workouts, a process he called "bookending" to help performance and recovery. He also thought I was going too long between meals and snacks and worked out a plan that had me eating roughly every three hours (or five to seven times a day) depending on when I woke up and when I went to sleep.

He also told me to stop obsessing over what I was or wasn't eating and start listening to my body. It wasn't about eating less or more, but providing my body with the nutrients it needed. "If you feel hungry before or after a workout, it means you need something more to eat," Ted said. "End of story."

As for my concerns about salt, Ted explained that while excessive intake can make a person *look* like they're retaining water, it was an important electrolyte that my body needed for hydration and to allow my muscles to work more efficiently. Not taking in enough sodium and carbs, and generally underfueling, had likely caused my cramping. He instructed me to begin sprinkling salt on my food and in my drinks during and after my workouts to stay hydrated, which would further optimize performance and recovery.

At the gym I had been feeling a drop in energy after an hour. Ted suggested eating or drinking a small amount of a slower digesting carbohydrate (like oatmeal, whole wheat bread, skim milk, or yogurt) combined with a simpler, fast digesting one (like bananas, all-natural fruit preserves, or no-sugar-added dried fruit) during rest periods while at workouts. These snacks wouldn't sit heavy or upset my stomach, he promised, but they would provide my body with the necessary energy so I could get the most out of my training. Finally, he recommended plenty of greens, like broccoli, spinach, and kale, as well as more antioxidants, like berries, watermelon, and pineapple to aid in recovery between workouts. Ted also introduced me to Cheribundi's tart cherry juice, which he told me to drink every day after workouts, as well as at night to allow my body to recover and bounce back faster for my next training session.

Incorporating all of Ted's suggestions into my routine made my body feel so much better in between workouts. All along I'd been convinced that there was a magic food formula that would make me lean and strong and quick, all the things I needed to excel in gymnastics. After years of trial and error, I was finally clued in to the secret: There is no one-size-fits-all diet. The real secret is having your own plan, tailored to you, based on the demands you place on your body, on your personal goals, and on your lifestyle.

How to listen to my body was a vital life lesson. Like with everything else, I got better at it with practice. I had been afraid to eat certain foods because I thought they would make me gain weight. To my surprise, I found it was the opposite: Once I increased my carb intake, I became leaner, had more energy for training, and recovered faster. In making the adjustments he recommended, I knew I would be better equipped for what lay ahead. The training demands were so intense that without Ted's plan for listening to my body and its nutritional needs, it would not have been possible for me to make a comeback.

As my training ramped up, I especially looked forward to Wednesday mornings, when I trained at the same time as the preschoolers. We quickly became friends. I found myself planning with the little girls which days we would wear pink or my patriotic "Aly" leotards from my GK Leotards line so we could match.

After watching me train for a while, a three-year-old named Anthony announced that he was going to marry me (later that year, he changed his mind and proclaimed that we had broken up, because I was "too busy and too old anyway"). No matter how stressed out I was feeling, the kids could always put a smile on my face.

They also kept me humble. One day, a four-year-old named Anna, whose family owns a house near ours on the Cape, walked into the gym and demanded to know what the deal was with all the photos of me on banners.

"You should take her photos down and put up some of me," she told Mihai.

"When you're an Olympic champion," Mihai said solemnly,

"I promise that your photos will be all over the gym." Satisfied, Anna nodded, and they shook on the deal.

Martha was ready for me to come back to camp so she could evaluate me for the following year's season. In addition to my leotards, sweats, and grips, I packed my fluffy blue bathrobe, a few tubes of my favorite skincare face creams, a box of mint tea, and a mug into my suitcase. I always overpack!

The younger national team members must have been surprised by the twenty-year-old who stood in front of the wooden cabins in her bathrobe and face mask, holding a steaming mug of tea.

It was Simone who came up with the nickname "Grandma Aly." After all, I did act like the little old lady of the group! It wasn't just my bathrobe and tea—while the younger girls stayed up late watching movies and chatting, I went straight to bed. If the others made too much noise, I would wake up and scold them via text. Ashton Locklear and Simone were really hyper at night, and they were the loudest. I loved those two during workouts and during the day, but at night I would get so annoyed with them, which Ashton and Simone thought was hilarious. When they ignored my texts, I'd sit up and bang on the wall for them to be quiet, and they'd shout back, "Go to sleep, Grandma!" The next morning at breakfast, we'd stare each other down until one of us would start laughing.

A few of the younger girls also shyly asked to take photos with me. Once they got to know me a little more, they sometimes asked for advice. I was always happy to oblige. I remembered my first camps at the ranch, and how I'd watched the Olympians in awe, trying to copy everything they did. Eventually I got a bunch of people hooked on facials.

Gymnastics-wise, Mihai and I agreed that going into the year 2015 I needed to show up at the national team camps to demonstrate to Martha the progress I'd made and how hard I was working. Timing a comeback was critical: If you do it too early, you risk injury or burnout. But if you show up too late in the process, you don't have enough time to build up the numbers and competitions to prove that you could handle an Olympics.

Martha seemed glad to see me, and happy about the example I set for the younger girls. "It is evident that Aly wants to be here and wants to be part of future teams," she told a reporter. "I love her attitude."

She didn't care for my new floor routine, though. "It's like white rice with no sauce," she complained, wrinkling her nose. "It needs something a little bit different." Mihai and I looked at each other in despair. My routine was already choreographed, and Martha was essentially telling us to start over.

It was a huge deal to have to start from scratch. Disappointed, Mihai pointed out to Martha that she had already approved the music. Martha replied that she didn't care because she didn't like it; she had changed her mind. Composer Barry Nease came up with the solution. He mixed the original piece with another Russian folk melody, giving the routine a more enchanted feel. Martha approved.

At the end of the camp, Martha announced that she was adding a couple of gymnasts to the national team. Gabby and I were missing from the list. After we left the gym, Gabby and I were so upset that despite our hard work, USA Gymnastics hadn't added us back to the team. They were making it clear that London was the past, and we had to prove ourselves all over again.

Eventually, they added us to the roster. Gabby and I were selected to go to Jesolo together. It was my first competition in two and a half years. I grabbed my bags, eager to prove I was back.

I stared down the floor exercise, concentrating hard on the work of the next six seconds. A lot was riding on my first tumbling pass. Not only did it set the tone for the routine, but it would also earn me bonus tenths for my start value from the judges—and a lot of respect from Martha.

I cast a brief look around the gym, reveling in the ambiance after my two-year absence from competition. The gym felt so familiar: the tiny snowflakes of chalk floating through the air, the hushed chatter of coaches and gymnasts, the *bang…bang!*

as gymnasts tumbled on the spring floor, shooting upward and absorbing the landings a few seconds later.

I hurdled into my tumbling pass and punched into the air. When I did my Arabian punch front, I did a tuck instead of the layout. I went so high that I hyperextended both knees. It was a miracle I was okay. Martha gasped. When she realized I wasn't injured, she turned to me. "That is why conditioning is so important! You're so lucky you didn't tear a ligament in your knee."

Martha then said that I was too hyper and excited to compete. That the excitement was good, but I needed to put less pressure on myself.

The Italian beach town was six thousand miles from Rio, but I might as well have been competing in the 2016 Olympic arena. The media, fans, other coaches, and especially Martha would be paying very close attention to how Gabby and I handled it.

Gabby and I roomed together. When we got to our room, I sat down on the bed and began stripping off my workout gear. Gabby turned to me. "Is your knee okay?"

"I'm fine," I replied. "I'm just so nervous for tomorrow's competition."

"Me too. We haven't competed in so long," she said.

"I know. But at least we have each other."

Feeling that I had to top what I'd done in London was driving me crazy, partly because I knew I wasn't there yet, and partly because I knew what a bad meet could mean.

Officially, the Olympic team is selected after the Olympic Trials. Unofficially, Trials begin months, even years before the Games, as gymnasts compete at home and abroad, proving over and over and over that they'll be able to deliver without mistakes in the big Olympic moment.

I lay down and pulled the covers up to my chin, feeling waves of jet lag wash over me. The pressure of competition was starting to creep in, but I did my best to think happy thoughts for the next day as I closed my eyes.

During the competition, I felt like my old self, and the meet went well. The team won the gold medal, and I finished third in the all-around and third on floor. Gabby and I finished in the same all-around rankings we had in Jesolo right before the 2012 Olympics, so we took it as a good omen.

CHAPTER 21

BODY POSITIVE

Needham, Massachusetts

Spring 2015

I was eating lunch at home, covered in chalk from training (as usual), when the phone rang.

"We've been in talks with ESPN to feature you in their Body Issue," a member of the Octagon team informed me.

The news threw me for a loop. The Body Issue was one of *ESPN The Magazine*'s most popular editions—and there was one big reason why.

"Naked, you mean?" I said nervously.

"That's the idea," he responded.

"Do I get approval of the photos?" I asked.

"No, you don't." That wasn't what I had hoped to hear. In my endorsement deals, there's always a line in my contract that says I have approval over the images. With magazines, that isn't the case. Not having control over the images was all the more nerve-wracking when we were talking about naked photos (even if they'd ensure that no private parts were visible).

"Can I think about it for a while?" I said.

When we hung up, I sat back, chewing thoughtfully. I was not at all sure I felt comfortable about posing naked. I pictured myself typing my name into Google, knowing that naked photos of me had been published—and there was nothing I could do if I didn't like what I saw. I also wondered how the people I knew would react. My coaches, for example. Or Martha. What would they think?

I thought about calling back immediately and saying no thanks, but something held me back. I had learned the importance of taking some time before making a big decision. Sometimes sitting back and reflecting for a while can make you see things in a whole new light.

I talked it over with my parents, who I was half expecting to quash the idea immediately. But to my surprise, they agreed with me that it was a great opportunity, and saw that it could be an empowering, confidence-building moment. After all, my parents had always taught me to love myself.

"We'll support you no matter what you decide," Mom said. "But you shouldn't say no just because you're afraid that some-one won't approve of it."

Brett was far less enthusiastic. "You're going to pose naked for a magazine?" he said, horrified. "Do you realize what my friends are going to say when they see this? I'll never hear the end of it!"

My sisters were divided. "If that's what you want to do, you should do it," Chloe said, shrugging.

"But why would you want to?" Maddie wanted to know.

I mulled Maddie's question over while driving to practice that evening. While chalking up for bars. While doing crunches. While stretching.

If I were a man, this would be no big deal, I told myself. Men pose for these things all the time. *Why is it different because I'm a woman?*

I'd come to realize that girls and women face lots of pressure from society about their bodies. Instead of feeling good about the wonderful things about them, they are taught to dislike what makes them stand out. I thought about my own experiences in school, when boys had made fun of me for being muscular (as if that was anything but rad!). Girls who had filled out early had teased me for not developing at the same rate. All along, others whom I'd thought were "perfect" confessed to feeling ashamed of their bodies. I shook my head. *Why do we all feel this way?* I wondered.

Even in sports, I realized the toughest female athletes are not always given the respect they deserve. On my beloved 1996 Olympic tape, the women who competed in Atlanta were referred to as "little girls" and their difficult floor routines characterized as "dancing."

I heard an actress who had been raped say that when she shared her story, people sometimes asked, "What were you wearing?" As though wearing a sexy outfit gave a man the right to disrespect her. As though it was her fault she had been attacked.

It made me mad. I realized that I wanted to tell people that everyone deserves respect, regardless of their body type or what they were (or weren't) wearing. We should all be able to express ourselves in any way we want, without judgment, no matter what our gender.

Sometimes, if you want to take a stand about something, you have to do something a bit controversial, I figured. If proudly displaying my muscular body helped one person feel good about theirs, I thought, it's worth it. And if seeing my photos and reading the accompanying interview could help teach the next generation to love themselves and their bodies—a task made difficult by social media—all the better.

Plus, I was tired of being afraid of what other people thought of me. I was used to being judged in competitions, which spilled over into worry that people were judging me in other ways, and now into concern that people would judge my naked body. As a result, there had been so many years when I had thought my body was too muscular, too this, not enough that. But I had worked my whole life to look the way I did, and I was through letting anyone make me ashamed of my body. I was now twenty years old, and training for a second Olympics had made me appreciate my body like never before. Everyone's body deserves to be celebrated. Everyone deserves to feel proud of who they are.

I had always weighed decisions by asking myself "What will everyone else think?" first and "What do I want to do?" second. It was time to listen to my voice above the others.

I called Octagon back the next day. When I spoke, my voice was firm.

"I'll do it," I said.

The crew had drawn two canvas curtains across the windows of a Newton studio and created a small alcove for hair and makeup. A white terrycloth bathrobe with the words "ESPN Body Issue" embroidered on the back in red was waiting for me. I slipped it on, along with ESPN slippers (so that my socks wouldn't leave imprints on my ankles) and sat in the makeup chair as the makeup artist dusted a light powder over my face, with straightened hair to add some drama.

We had a few phone calls with the ESPN team beforehand to discuss options that would make the shoot unique and the images artistic. Two giant light fixtures cast a soft white glow on the gymnastics equipment set up around the studio. From a distance, my mom and my aunt Jessica stood and took in the scene. Jessica had never been to one of my photo shoots before. "You really picked an interesting one to come to!" I said, laughing.

When the moment came to begin, I took a deep breath and dropped the robe, handing it off to an ESPN assistant. For five minutes I felt nervous, and then I forgot I was naked, just as the staff on the shoot had reassured me I would. Their support and professionalism made me feel completely confident.

I clicked with the photographer, Mark Seliger, right away. We were bouncing ideas off each other and I made the final decisions about the poses. Each was meant to highlight the beauty and power of the human form. Throughout the shoot, I felt empowered and strong.

A few months later, I was at July camp when I saw a tweet from *People* magazine and my heart started thudding in my chest. "Click here to see Aly Raisman naked," the tweet started. Being at the ranch where the cell and internet service was weak, of course the link took forever to load.

When it finally came up, I looked at the site for just a few seconds and closed it so I wouldn't be tempted to pick myself apart. Later, when I saw the photos in print, I felt proud. I was truly happy about the way I looked. And I hoped this would mark a new chapter for me, where I could move forward knowing that confidence has to come from within.

I was continuing to learn to appreciate the way my body looked, but I couldn't escape the way my body felt. Even during my time off, my back and hip problems never went away. The pain was hindering my progress, and on top of that, I needed a lot more time to recover from workouts than I had when I was fifteen or sixteen. If my body was going to do this a second time, I thought, I needed better medical support than I'd had the first time around.

I became my body's full-time manager, dedicated to making sure it was in the best possible condition. My training regimen grew to include a slew of activities outside the gym, from visits to the chiropractor to sessions in a flotation tank. Like triathletes, I also used NormaTec compression boots to reduce muscle soreness and improve circulation in my legs. Dr. Miller recommended a sports physical therapist he thought could really help me.

Joe Van Allen, the sports physical therapist, would have me lie down on my stomach and drape towels over my hips. He bustled around the room, stopping in front of a cardboard box from which he extracted a pair of gloves. He must have seen me watching as he stretched them over his fingers. "Is something the matter?" he asked.

"No," I said quickly. "I…it's just…you're wearing gloves," I said.

He laughed. "Of course," he said. "Sports physical therapists and doctors have to wear gloves at times."

Not everyone wears gloves.

CHAPTER 22

THE SURVIVORS

Needham, Massachusetts
Summer 2015

The call from USA Gymnastics president Steve Penny came in July 2015.

"A private investigator is going to fly to Boston and talk to you," he said. "I need you to be completely open with her and answer all of her questions. This is important."

"Now?" I asked. The US Championships were just around the corner, and I was in full training mode. When I was preparing for a meet, I preferred to shut out the world, because I knew that's what it took for me to succeed.

"Steve, I'm sorry, but I really don't have time," I told him. "I'm doing double sessions to get ready for Nationals."

He insisted. "You are the team captain, and I need you to do this for me."

"Why?" I asked. "What is this about?"

"I can't tell you," he said.

"What did Steve want?" Mom asked when I got off the phone.

I shrugged. "He wants me to meet with some investigator," I said.

"What? Why?" Mom asked.

I shrugged. "I don't know."

The private investigator's name was Fran. She drove up to my house in Needham one hot July afternoon. After we got settled on a bench in the front garden, Fran looked me straight in the eye.

"Do you know why I'm here?" she asked.

I looked around at the flowers blooming around the yard, gulped, and shook my head. I had come straight from practice, and was still wearing my workout clothes. I looked down at my shorts covered in chalk and took a deep, uneasy breath, thinking, *I hope this isn't about Larry Nassar.* But I dismissed the thought. I trusted him, because he was nice to me, and because he had tons of awards from USA Gymnastics and recognition from the US Olympic Committee. The whispers couldn't be true.

It wasn't until I started seeing other doctors and athletic trainers that I began to realize that their methods were far different from Larry's.

When I lay on my stomach to have my hamstrings worked on, towels were draped over my hips and buttocks for privacy and to ensure that there was no inappropriate skin-to-skin contact.

They never, ever crossed any lines in where they massaged. And there was never a moment when their methods made me uncomfortable.

It was different with Larry. I would lie on the table, my hands involuntarily balling themselves into fists as his ungloved hands worked their way under my clothing. "Treatment sessions" with him always made me feel tense and uncomfortable.

I dreaded being worked on. Larry had promised he could help ease the aches and pains that come with high-level gymnastics. He assured me that he knew just how to do it, too. The first time I met him, I was fifteen and in a foreign country without my parents. He was a doctor. All the adults loved him and were constantly singing his praises. Everyone said he was the very best, how lucky we were to have him around.

Who was I, a mere teenager with no medical training, to say any different, or to question his methods?

So I would grit my teeth, trying to convince myself that all this was part of the healing process. The truth was he never made my injuries feel any better, but I always obeyed because he had a reputation for being the best doctor.

Because I spent so much time training, traveling, and competing, I was very sheltered and innocent. That's probably why I didn't question why Larry would sometimes close his eyes or seem out of breath when he worked on me. More than once I would make excuses for his strange behavior. *He must be tired from a long day*, I would think, and wonder why he made me so uncomfortable. I felt guilty for thinking badly of someone everyone else liked.

I thought back to my first year on the national team in Australia, and to Larry knocking on the door of my hotel room at eight o'clock at night at the World Championships in Rotterdam.

I remembered how he had always brought us treats. We thought because he gave us little gifts that he was caring and kind. Larry would show up to our hotel room and surprise us with coffee, croissants, and candy. I figured he wanted us to be teenagers. He knew that we ate healthily, but he also encouraged us to splurge now and then.

He had seemed so supportive at first. We thought he understood us. When workouts were tough and I was stressed out, Larry's had seemed like a voice of rationality. When I was alone with him, even when he seemed to be crossing a line, he would often distract me by saying how great I was doing in training sessions.

He was full of kind words, sympathizing about hard workouts and the pressure of high expectations. Far away from my parents and family for weeks at a time, there were moments where he made me feel like he understood me, like he was my friend. Larry had my back. He had everybody's back.

Didn't he?

When Larry came to the ranch in March 2015 (as he some-times did), he seemed surprised to learn that I was making a comeback. He was negative about my chances of getting back to where I had been, which annoyed me. When I described my aches and pains, out of the blue, without any MRIs or tests, he announced that I likely needed surgery.

I came home and told my parents that the US team doctor thought I needed surgery.

"You need surgery?" Mom repeated, surprised.

"Of course I don't need surgery," I snapped irritably. "Larry just told me that because he's an idiot." Then I added, impul-sively: "I hate him. He's so irritating. I wish he'd just go away."

My mother looked at me, surprised. "That's not like you to say," she commented. "You've never said anything like that before about him. Where did this come from?"

"I just…never mind," I said peevishly. "He's just an idiot, that's all."

It turned out I wasn't the only one feeling uncomfortable. Over the years, among the girls who were invited to camps, there was some talk of Larry and his "treatment methods." Most of us thought the way he touched us was weird. But he did it to so many of us that we assumed, blindly, that he must know something we didn't.

He had been part of USA Gymnastics since before I was born, and the national team doctor since 1995. It didn't seem possible that he could be doing it to so many of us if it wasn't okay.

Over the years, we would discuss it amongst ourselves in the cabins. But we also talked about it openly in the gym. "He worked on me last night and it was so uncomfortable," one of the girls said to me as we sat stretching in a small circle one morning at a camp. "It's so weird," she continued, shaking her head. "How is what he does supposed to fix pain, anyway? That's what he keeps saying, but it makes no sense to me." She looked at me quizzically. "Are we *sure* this is allowed?"

"I'm not sure it is," another girl piped up. "A lot of us think it's weird, but I feel like if it wasn't okay he would've already been fired. Someone would have said something if it was wrong."

We didn't know it at the time, but our remarks were overheard by a female coach. Alarm bells went off in her head. And then she did the right thing: She spoke up. The conversation was reported to a USA Gymnastics official.

I didn't know it then, but that would be the last camp Larry Nassar attended, and the last time I saw him through USA Gymnastics. A few months later, he announced on his Facebook page that he was retiring from the national team. I didn't know what to think.

Had USA Gymnastics gone to the authorities? Would he go to jail? I wanted to be sure he would no longer be working as a doctor. My mom and I reached out to USA Gymnastics. They assured us that the situation was being handled, and said that we shouldn't interfere. Concerned we would jeopardize the case against him, we took USA Gymnastics at their word. We continued to reach out. Each time, we were told that they were handling it, but there was little that they could reveal.

In the yard, Fran was looking at me intently, waiting for me to say whether or not I knew why she was here.

There seemed to be so many reasons not to speak up. I ticked them off in my mind: First of all, what if I was wrong? Maybe what he did was a legitimate medical practice, just like he said all along. Maybe people wouldn't believe me, or would think I was exaggerating and being dramatic, or they'd hate me. Maybe they would think that I was doing it just to get attention. And then there was Larry's family to think of. What if I ruined their lives?

At this point, the Olympic Games were just over a year away. All of my thoughts were laser-focused on Rio. Making the team in 2012 had taken every ounce of strength and willpower that I'd possessed, and I knew the second time would be no easier. I was terrified that the media would find out, and bring it up at every turn, before I was ready to talk about it, before I had even begun to process it myself (I'm still processing it today). I worried, too, that facing everything that had happened would mess with me. I was overwhelmed with emotion.

Fran cleared her throat, interrupting my thoughts. *Did I feel safe?* she wanted to know. *Had anyone been making me feel uncomfortable?* I pictured myself opening the hotel room door to Larry at 8:00 PM, but I still said no. I wanted to say yes, but I was caught so off guard. *Is this actually happening?* I wondered. It didn't feel real.

Fran continued asking questions. They were all about Larry. What did he do, how, when, how many times, where were you, were other adults present, did you tell your parents, anyone at all? I answered as honestly as I could. Outside of a few girls at camp, I hadn't discussed it with anyone, not even my parents.

I was very uncomfortable—overwhelmed by the questions, and by all the thoughts, fears, and worries running through my head. I was embarrassed, and concerned what people at USA Gymnastics would think of me. I started to focus on all the adults around me who promised that Larry was the best, on all the times Larry was nice to me. So, as I later learned was not uncommon with those who have been abused, I began making excuses for him.

Yes, I did think Larry's methods were strange, I said. Yes, they made me uncomfortable. But I was sure he was just trying to help, I explained. I added that I didn't think Larry had done the things he had done on purpose. He was a doctor, you know? And he'd brought us little gifts a lot, which had been so nice....

When we were done, Fran stood up and thanked me for my time. From the front window I watched her get into her car and drive away. I went to find my mother. She was sitting in the living room, flipping through a magazine.

"Oh my God," I said, collapsing into the sofa. "That was what I worried it was about."

"But you told me you didn't know what it was about," she protested.

"I was scared it was about Larry, but I didn't want to tell you in case I was wrong." I took a deep breath and let the rest of the truth out. "Mom, the way he's worked on me for years made me really uncomfortable. I believed him when he said it was for medical reasons. Fran took me by surprise, but her questions got me thinking that wasn't the case."

I sat up thinking about it all night. It was like a stopper had been lifted in my mind, and the memories came flooding back clear as day: Larry. The hotel rooms. And afterward, the treats he would give us. Those little treats that planted the idea that he was looking out for us.

Oh my God.

I thought to call Fran, to tell her all these details that we hadn't discussed, but I realized she never asked me to follow up with her. So I called a USA Gymnastics official, and told her everything that I was remembering, the things I would have told Fran if I hadn't been in shock. Hours later, I got a text back from someone, saying that I needed to stop speaking about Larry. I was warned that there is a process in place and that staying clear of the process would protect me and others.

I barely slept. I kept rubbing my eyes, as if I could rub out those horrible memories. Maybe it had all been a terrible dream? By the time I got up the next morning, I felt completely betrayed.

We had been so manipulated. It had all been intentional. Of course he had known what he was doing. He had taken advantage of me. He had taken advantage of everyone he targeted; of our youth, of our innocence, of our trust in the adults there to help us, of our desire to excel in the sport—for years. He had seen how hard I worked, and understood how unlikely I was to complain or to question authority. I was a young girl with Olympic goals. I had been so horribly manipulated.

I wanted to throw up. Realizing that you've been a victim of sexual abuse is a horrible, sickening feeling. I didn't want to believe it, but it had all become clear. The facts now stared me in the face.

All through the years, there were so many distractions that kept me from analyzing his methods or my discomfort: another team to make, another competition to prepare for, another hurdle that required all my mental energy to surmount. Whatever was going on around me took a back seat to perfecting my routines, to making sure that nothing kept me from being able to perform well. Larry knew this, and that's what allowed him to get away with it for so long. I went from trusting him to hating him.

I am not going into specifics about what Larry did to me—that information is private—or what the many charges against him are. Frankly, I was planning to keep this part of my story private, as I continue to process it. I'm sharing my story publicly in hopes that it might help people who are going through something similar. Maybe reading this chapter has made you realize that the same thing is happening to you. If that's the case, I am truly sorry, and urge you to seek help.

According to RAINN (the Rape, Abuse & Incest National Network), every ninety-eight seconds another person experiences sexual assault, and sexual violence affects hundreds of thousands of Americans each year. *That is hundreds of thousands too many.* Too many abusers do horrible things and get away with it. Too many abusers are master manipulators, who act in ways that are 100 percent wrong and somehow make those they abuse feel guilty. It is completely twisted.

Everyone deals with trauma differently. Some, like me, push ugly things aside for years, allowing themselves to become numb to their own feelings. When you finally let yourself feel again, the emotions crash down on you like a waterfall.

Some survivors may have the same thought process I did. They think, *I must be reading into this. I'm sure he or she didn't mean to do that. If I tell someone, I'm going to get them in trouble.* Or even, *It's not so bad. This could be worse.* Or, *No one will believe me, anyway.*

To everyone reading this: Your story matters. *You* matter, and you should trust yourself. If something feels off, and you think you may be being manipulated or taken advantage of, speak up. You are strong and tough. You are not alone. You deserve to feel safe. It's as simple as that.

I wish someone had talked to me about the warning signs of a sexual predator: Do they make you uncomfortable? Do they touch you in ways you don't like? Do they give you gifts? Do they ask you not to tell other people about things they do? Do they seek to be alone with you when it's not necessary? Do they take advantage of their position of authority?

We have to keep the dialogue going to remove the stigma for those who survive abuse. Society is too afraid to talk and hear about it. There aren't enough people saying it's okay to speak up if you think something might be wrong. Take it from me: It is. There's no shame in asking questions and insisting on getting answers. People are *not* going to hate you for it.

In fact, you may be helping someone else, too. For all you know, other people could be being hurt, and those people might be feeling afraid to speak up, too.

You never think it can happen to you. In my case, I thought

I was safe with a doctor, that if a doctor is touching you, it's a valid medical treatment. But you should never, ever feel like they're crossing a line. When you're a child, you learn to watch out for "strangers," which is important. But it's equally important to recognize that when it comes to sexual abuse, most victims know their abusers. And if a sexual predator is committing assault, the unfortunate reality is that it might not be their first time, and probably isn't their last. That makes it even more scary, realizing it can happen to anyone.

I know that now, because it happened to me.

CHAPTER 23

HIGH ANXIETY

**Glasgow, United Kingdom
2015**

"On vault for the United States of America, Alexandra Raisman!"

I stared down the runway, hands on my hips, curling my toes beneath my feet as I tried to settle my mind. A red stop sign was flashing on the electronic screen, signaling that I didn't have the judges' okay to begin yet. I closed my eyes for a moment, picturing myself charging down that runway, flying into my most powerful Amanar vault.

Eighty feet in front of me, Mihai was standing off to the side of the podium. When he caught my eye, he gave me a nod and a smile, just like he always did. I was anxious and amped up after a mistake on floor exercise, determined to do better on this event.

I can do this.

I glanced at the screen again. A green light had replaced the stop sign. *Here we go*, I thought as I squared my shoulders, repeating my corrections one last time. *Strong straight arms and straight legs. Tight body, nothing loose, lots of power. Relax, you got this.* I shut my mind off and began to run. I knew the approach was good, the roundoff onto the board perfectly timed to give me the maximum amount of lift into the air as I pushed off the table. As my body twisted through the air I could feel that I was doing a good vault.

Too good, actually. *I can't control the landing*, I realized a second later as my feet hit the ground. Suddenly I was hurtling forward, taking giant steps to control my momentum. A single thought flashed through my mind: How did I do such a big vault? I didn't think I had that much power. Frankly, it was a much bigger, stronger vault than I usually pulled off—so big that I completely lost sense of where I was in the air.

Later, Mihai would ask me if I was running for the bathroom. It's a longstanding joke between us, because when I'm nervous I'm always running for the bathroom.

"Except for the landing, that was the best vault of your life," he added. "If that had been in practice, I would have said great."

Problem was, we weren't in practice. It was October 2015, we were at the 2015 World Championships in Glasgow, and I was having the worst meet of my life.

Somehow I had gotten through the summer. On paper, I did pretty well, especially after such a long time away. I even finished a respectable third—again!—at my first US Championships in three years, behind Simone and Maggie Nichols. By all accounts, I was back on track.

But I didn't feel right. In spite of the numbers I was doing in training and the vast improvement I'd made since returning to the gym, nothing was good enough for me. I put a lot of pressure on myself to stay on top, especially on floor. As the reigning Olympic champion on the event, I felt obligated to maintain my number one standing on floor—an ambitious goal, but there it was. To have a shot at winning, I added even more difficulty to my already extremely difficult routine.

Two months after the US Championships, I was named to the team for the World Championships in Glasgow, along with Simone, Maggie, Gabby, Madison Kocian, Brenna Dowell, and MyKayla Skinner (as usual, the alternate would be picked from our ranks just before the qualifying round). Being named to the world team in a pre-Olympic year is usually a good sign. If you do well, stay healthy, and maintain your difficulty, it generally means you have a decent shot at being on the Olympic team.

Being in Glasgow ramped up my anxiety, which had been building to an all-time high ever since my meeting with Fran.

I tried to block the whole unpleasant subject out of my mind, but I would often catch myself wondering how the investigation was going. I was very afraid that the press would get ahold of the story and that I'd be asked about it, so I began dreading doing interviews, too.

I had never been particularly calm before meets, but in Glasgow I started feeling nervous and psyched-out before every workout. My focus was on making the all-around final and getting redemption after the painful tiebreaker in London. As always, only the best two gymnasts per country advanced to the all-around final. Simone was almost guaranteed one of those spots. I was determined to win the other.

I developed a bunch of rituals in an attempt to feel like I was in control. When podium training went well, I became convinced that if I just repeated everything I had done there, things would be okay. I listened to Jason Derulo's "Try Me" and "Live It Up" by Colbie Caillat on repeat. I did my makeup exactly the same way every day.

Most neurotic of all, I had to sit in the same chair in the waiting room off the gym every day before practice. One day, when I found Gabby sitting in it, I asked her if she wouldn't mind moving. My teammates looked on, confused.

"You're going nuts, Grandma," Simone said bluntly. "Stop being so nervous! It's what you do in training that counts."

"Look, it helps," I said. "It makes me feel better."

Yet nothing was going my way. Practicing in front of

Martha was nerve-wracking as always, and now I was putting so much pressure on myself that I literally felt sick. My nerves were so intense that I could hardly eat anything, despite my best efforts to follow Ted's nutrition advice. And even though I was exhausted, I had trouble sleeping at night. Sometimes I had nightmares about being attacked. Other times I would lie in bed and stress about the next day's practice.

Every turn I do has to be exactly right, I would think, visualizing my routines for the umpteenth time. Then I would begin replaying the day's practice in my head, berating myself for each little mistake. The next day I would get up and go to practice more nervous than ever, and make even more mistakes. Somehow, I pulled everything together in podium training, enough to land an all-around spot in the qualifying round.

In training, bars was especially trying. I kept having fluke errors and falling on one of my release moves.

"No, Aly, that is not right!" Martha yelled as I hit the mat on a fall during a practice competition routine. Pulling myself onto my hands and knees, I hung my head in resignation. I could see the others standing on the other side of the bars, waiting to take their turns.

"Do the release again and continue the routine, like in competition," Martha commanded. "You have thirty seconds to get back up on the bar." After that, I knew I would have to repeat the routine all over again, from the beginning.

Sometimes when the first person has a mistake, it unsettles

the rest of the team. Sure enough, Maggie had a big form break. Then Simone fell on a pirouette. Even Madison, the most consistent barworker on the team, had problems. To cap it off, Brenna, the team anchor, fell on a transition from the low bar to the high bar.

Nothing annoys Martha more than this kind of domino effect. By the time I had picked myself up and went over to the chalk bowl, she was waiting.

"You are the veteran here," she snapped, looking displeased. "And in the competition, you will be first up on the event. It is up to you to set the example for the other girls. What you are doing is not acceptable. It's immature."

Do they think I'm messing up on purpose? I thought miserably. I tried as hard as I could, but I simply could not make things work. I was so worried about what everyone else was thinking about me, and I was letting that pressure get to my head.

The competition floor was white rather than the blue we were most used to, and I found it really disorienting. My heart started racing, and stars floated in front of my eyes. I felt like I was going to pass out. I knew I needed to rest, but there was no time. I went to the bathroom and hunched in front of the toilet, gagging and wishing the day were already over. All the stress I was feeling had caused me to lose weight in the days before the meet, which in turn threw all of my skills out of whack.

We sat on the floor for about twenty minutes, waiting to

be marched out to the competition. We were all taking deep breaths, rolling out on our foam rollers, and trying to make one another laugh. *It will be all right once we get underway*, I tried to tell myself. It's frustrating when you so badly want something to go right but have a gut feeling it's going to go wrong.

The Glasgow crowd was amped up. A giant LED screen stood just behind the field of play, and flamethrowers shot jets of fire into the air as we marched out. A digital image of each team's flag flashed in the background as teams were introduced.

The lights around the apparatus had been darkened for dramatic effect, and the judges had been seated to the sides of the apparatus instead of right around them, giving the field of play a theater-like appearance. When we looked up, we didn't see the crowd above us, only darkened stands and the occasional light from a cell phone. Being inside the arena felt like being at a concert or a club. It was much rowdier than I was used to, and the party atmosphere unsettled me.

Backstage, we were goofy and hyper. Our giggly behavior would have earned us a rebuke from Martha—who liked us to focus on our routines right before marching out—if she had been able to see us. But Martha was seated in the stands, and we felt like kids whose teacher has unexpectedly been called out of the classroom.

Our first event in prelims was floor. I was the last to perform. The crowd was cheering wildly for every competitor as they were announced. I paced back and forth, waiting my turn. My nerves ratcheted up with every step. It didn't help that I saw Brenna freeze when her music got messed up during her floor routine. My heart went out to her, and I worried something like that could go wrong for me, too. I looked at Mihai for one last-minute push of reassurance. He had been pleased with my warm-up and positive throughout the day. I hoped his energy would rub off on me.

As I assumed my opening pose on floor, time seemed to slow down. Then my music came on and I moved into the corner for my first pass, holding my breath.

One of the tricks to that pass was taking a very short first step into my roundoff, keeping my feet less than shoulder length apart. Brett, who watched all of my routines with an analytical eye, had noticed that if my first stride was too long, I would land out of bounds. It was something Mihai had taught me, and Brett's reminder kept it top of mind.

I got flustered and forgot to be in the moment—and to take that short step. Sure enough, I flew right out of bounds. When I saw that I was over the line, I knew that my chances of making the floor final were doomed. Standing there in the middle of my routine, I felt my confidence plummet. I still had to get through the rest of the routine. I hopped back in bounds and continued my routine.

My third run was equally challenging: a double layout to a split jump, which would earn some bonus if executed correctly. The double layout was good, but I bounced so high coming out of the double layout that I couldn't control the split jump. I windmilled my arms in the air coming down, a costly mistake.

Calm down, I told myself. *Breathe, just like you do in practice*. But the damage had been done.

Mihai said to turn the page and do a good vault, to calm down and use my head. "You are prepared, stop overthinking," he told me. *Just do normal*. In the middle of his speech, the bell rang and we had to march to vault.

When it was my turn, I took a number of steps forward on my landing and received the lowest score of any American.

We moved on to bars. I got off to a good start on my first sequence on the low bar. From the sideline, I heard Mihai yell "Yes!" as I swung cleanly out of my first pirouette. *This is going well*, I realized as I cast out and backward, letting go of the low bar and flying toward the high bar. *Let's keep this up*.

I grabbed the high bar and tapped upward for my Tkatchev, a release move in which a gymnast swings backward, lets go of the bar, and soars over it, straddling her legs and catching the bar on the other side. My hands reached out, and I felt them come into contact with the bar for a second. A moment later, the bar just slipped away.

The next thing I knew, I was on my knees below the bar.

This can't be happening, I thought. *Maybe this is all a dream and I'll wake up tomorrow and find out it never happened.*

Mechanically, I stood up and took a few steps backward. Madison's coach, Laurent, the team's spotter on bars, stood behind me, preparing to lift me back up to the bar. "Breathe," he said, and I realized I had been holding my breath. "You have thirty seconds. Take a breather, and when you get back up, finish strong." Feeling numb, I took a few deep breaths, and then Laurent lifted me to the bar. I don't remember the rest of the routine.

As we were getting ready to warm up on beam, Simone came over and gave me a hug. "Just be your normal self, Aly," she said. I hugged her back. I wanted to cry.

By the time I mounted the beam, I was gripped with fear that I wouldn't make the Olympic team. I was sure my life was over; the panic was so intense that I couldn't focus on anything. I went through the motions, reminding myself that it would be over soon. I felt like everyone was watching me, probably to see what mistake I'd make next. Just before my dismount, I felt my legs were shaking. That had never happened before. I gritted my teeth and hoped for the best on my dismount. To this day, I'm amazed that I landed it on my feet.

I made it through, though the routine could have been better.

The 2015 World prelims was one of the lowest days of my life. There is nothing worse than having an off day when the whole world seems to be watching you. I felt I had let everyone down.

The worst thing was that everyone seemed to feel bad for me. When Mihai looked at me, his eyes reflected sadness, not anger, like he just didn't know what to do with me. I felt even worse, knowing how badly he wanted me to do well. I swallowed and tried to hold back my tears. He gave me a big hug and told me that everything would be okay.

As we were gathering our things to leave the arena, I saw Martha standing alone, and knew I had to go up to her and face the music. A fresh wave of terror engulfed me. What would she say? I imagined a torrent of harsh words: Maybe she was going to tell me that my career was over, that this was it, that I was going home to Boston and I'd never be picked for another team. That this comeback business had been a terrible idea to begin with.

I met her eyes hesitantly. "I'm really sorry, Martha," I choked out before she could say anything. "I don't know what happened."

But once again, she surprised me. "You don't have to apologize to me," she said, opening her arms and hugging me to her chest. That shocked me even more than her words. Hugs from Martha are incredibly rare. They usually happen only after you've done something great. I had never seen her be so sensitive toward any gymnast.

"You just need to relax, to figure out what's happening

in your head, and figure it out for next year," she continued. "Sometimes not doing well isn't a bad thing, but you have to learn from it. Maybe this is a sign you're putting too much pressure on yourself, and you have to figure it out leading up to the Olympic year."

Her kindness in that moment made me feel even worse for letting her down, but it also gave me much-needed hope. The words "next year" stuck in my head. So there would be a next year. There would be another chance after all. She pulled me aside the next day and said they had taken me out of the vault lineup and put someone else in to give me a little mental break so I could just focus on beam and floor in the team final. She said when you get home, you need to fix your execution, and she told me she knew I could do it.

I ended fifth in the all-around prelim, behind both Simone and Gabby. For the first time at a World Championship, I had not qualified for any event finals. I felt like my life was over, because in that moment, I defined myself only as a gymnast. I forgot that there was more to life than my place on the podium.

Two days later, we won the Worlds team title, over Russia and Great Britain. Finals was another medal harvest: Simone and Gabby won gold and silver in the all-around, with US gymnasts winning everything but vault.

As part of the gold medal–winning team, I tried to be

satisfied. But it was so hard to watch the event finals from the stands. My emotions must have been written across my face— Mihai kept hugging me, and Martha looked at me during floor finals and said, "Don't worry, next year is your year."

But from up in the stands, "my year" felt very far away.

CHAPTER 24

DOUBT

Needham, Massachusetts, and New Waverly, Texas
November–December 2015

Balanced on one foot, I set myself up for the skill: a double turn with my free leg extended out at a ninety-degree angle. It shouldn't have been that challenging for someone at my level, but the day after we returned from Glasgow, I just couldn't get it right.

About three-quarters of the way through the turn, I would completely lose my balance and topple over.

"No," Mihai called from the edge of the floor. "You're dropping your leg too soon. It has to stay at ninety degrees or the skill will be devalued. Do it again." I did it again. The same thing happened. I did it five more times, and it still wasn't right.

I wanted to scream. *What is happening to me?*

The shadow of Glasgow loomed over me like a dark cloud. While things had never come easy in gymnastics, until 2015 I had never had problems of that magnitude during a major competition. I went to practice, trained hard, and achieved results.

All that went out the window with Glasgow. It was strange to have just won a world team gold medal and yet be wondering if my career was over—the national team was *so* strong, that one bad meet could make the difference between being in or out. In spite of Martha's kind words in Glasgow, I was consumed with worry that my name wouldn't be called for the Olympic team.

It didn't help that there were signs that other people seemed to share my fears. Four years earlier, I had been swept up in the pre-Olympic fever. This time around, I felt completely written off.

There were little examples of it all spring. Along with a few of my teammates, I went to the Olympic Media Summit in Los Angeles in March. I was looking forward to a day of photo shoots and meeting other athletes, and I had to swallow back an excited scream when I saw *Vanity Fair* magazine was there. However, they weren't on my schedule of magazine and TV station meetings. When I asked why, the USA Gymnastics official accompanying me said they hadn't wanted to interview me. I thought I'd go and say hi anyway and tell them how much I liked their publication, but the USA Gymnastics official yelled at me not to go into their room. Of course, I was too persistent to listen! I waited awhile and said I was going to use the restroom, and sneaked into the *Vanity Fair* area.

As soon as I walked in, one of the magazine's editors came rushing toward me. "Hi, Aly!" she exclaimed. "We're so happy to see you! We've been e-mailing USA Gymnastics about this photo spread for weeks, but they said you were too busy. Since you're here, would you have some time to do a quick shoot with us? The pages have already been confirmed, so I can't promise you'll be in the issue, but we'd love to try."

I couldn't contain my enthusiasm. "Yes!" I shouted. "I would love to do the shoot with you."

But her words replayed in my mind and my feelings were hurt. Obviously, Glasgow was still on everyone's mind.

I was well aware that my performance in Glasgow had put me in a hole that I would have to dig myself out of during the Olympic year. And now I couldn't even do a simple turn.

My frustration was written all over my face, but Mihai didn't want me to get in my head. "Listen, you cannot go back in time. I don't care if you feel sorry for yourself, I don't care if you are so tired you feel like you are dying—fix the skill. If you want to be an Olympic champion again, you'll work harder than ever before. Because we are behind. Got it?"

In the most challenging times of my life, I usually turned inward, toward my sport. So I squared my shoulders and tried the turn again.

No good. Again. I was holding back tears—and there were still three and a half hours of workout left. Standing in the middle of the freezing cold gym floor, in my leggings, leotard, and long-sleeved T-shirt, I wondered why I was putting myself through this.

Was going back to the Olympics really worth it if I felt so frustrated and inadequate all the time? Would I be happier if I stopped, became a full-time student, and tried to just stop worrying?

"Gymnasts, step away from the puppies!"

My mom and I were in LA for an Olympics promotion. There were puppies on set for one of our photo shoots. The handlers let us know that all the dogs were rescued and up for adoption. I got called over to pick out a dog to take pictures with. They were all so cute, but in that moment I recalled my dog Coco, who had recently passed. "Do you have any Maltese?" I asked.

"As a matter of fact, we do. You'll be the first one to work with him."

He brought out a little ball of white fur with big eyes. The moment I saw Gibson, I was in love. He was a sweet, loving ball of energy, and I instantly bonded with him. My mom and I agreed: We needed to make Gibson part of our family.

Throughout the day, whenever I wasn't with Gibson, I was racing over to see him. The organizers of the event were frustrated that I kept throwing them off schedule—not only by visiting Gibson, but by sending all my teammates over to meet him, as well! I remember Gabby, especially, getting in trouble, because she loved Gibson, too. But I made sure she knew that I saw him first!

As always, my persistence paid off—if only because it annoyed the organizers until they said what I wanted to hear. They promised me and my mom that Gibson would be waiting for us when I was done with the reporters and photographers— and that as soon as he was old enough to travel to Boston, he'd come home with us.

I rarely asked Mihai for time off, but that month I made an exception.

A professional athlete I'd been talking to for a while had invited me to visit him and watch one of his games—and after the debacle at Worlds, I figured I could use a distraction.

To my surprise, Mihai said I could skip practice on Saturday and Monday morning, as long as I'd be back in the gym on Monday evening.

"Go have fun," he said. "You deserve it." Although he took training very seriously, I appreciated that he understood I needed balance in my life and was supportive of me having a social life.

Saturday went well. The guy was attentive and fun, and we seemed to be having a good time. But when I met him

Sunday after his game, he had turned into a completely different person.

We were in his car when I made a move to change the radio station. "Don't touch the music," he snapped. I thought he was joking, so I continued to reach for the stereo buttons.

"I'm not kidding—don't touch it," he said sharply. "I just played a game, and you just sat and watched. You haven't done anything today. So we're going to listen to this sports radio station. I want to hear what they say about me." I sat silently for the rest of the car ride. I couldn't wait to get out. I felt embarrassed, but also angry that I had traveled to see someone who treated me so disrespectfully.

He was glued to his phone and ignored me as we sat and ate dinner. When I left for the airport, he hardly said good-bye.

I left confused. *Why did he ask me to miss my training to watch him if he was going to be so dismissive? How does someone go from being so nice and interested to so mean and rude?* I wondered. Clearly, the chemistry wasn't there, but there's no excuse for not being kind and respectful.

"I think you were lucky," Mom said when I told her about it later that evening. "That guy showed you his true colors right away. It's a blessing you won't have to deal with him anymore."

She was right. In any relationship, it's important for there to be mutual respect. And if someone shows you their true colors, don't make excuses for them or hope that they'll change—listen to your gut. You deserve to be treated well. Everyone does. A break from training turned into a valuable learning experience.

Workouts didn't get better. Mihai and Silvie knew I had lots to improve, and they wanted the best out of me. In between events, Silvie was a welcome distraction, talking to me about puppies, fashion, and anything that would make me laugh. For the next several weeks, I was a mess both in and out of the gym.

It was in this state of mind that I went to Texas that December for an extra national team camp. Normally camps weren't held in December to allow gymnasts to recover from the World Championships season, enjoy the holidays at home, and work on some new skills. But with the Olympics just over seven months away, there was no time to rest. Maybe Martha had just rewatched the video of the prelims at Worlds. Maybe she figured we needed a reminder that we always had to be 100 percent ready with our skills. Whatever it was, she decided we needed more practice. So off we went.

One good thing about the extra camp was that it gave me a chance to see my teammates. Alyssa Baumann was one of my closest friends on the national team. We would always room together, along with Madison, and I felt like we could talk for hours about anything. It didn't matter if we were upset about our workouts or happy about a new skill—we would spend hours laughing, dancing, and singing before bed, distracting ourselves from the stress of camp.

During the evening workout on the third day of camp, we practiced beam in front of Martha and two judges. I was one of the first to go, and though I made it through the routine without falling, Mihai wasn't happy with what he saw. When I got off, instead of saying, "Okay, learn from it," the way he usually did, he announced that I was going to stand and watch every other girl perform.

One by one, they mounted the beam, their features lighting up as they eagerly saluted the judges who had come to the ranch. The younger girls' routines were packed with style—in particular fifteen-year-old Laurie Hernandez, the reigning junior national champion, whose sparkle radiated in her every move. She had "it" factor, that extra special something that some people are just born with. When she performed, it was hard to take your eyes off her.

"Look at that," Mihai said, gesturing toward Laurie, who would turn senior in the new year. "Look at how hard she's working. She is showing the desire, the force. You can see how much she wants it. Do you want her to take your spot?"

And to that he added, "You need to clean up your execution, especially on beam. If you don't, you're not going to make the team."

His speech was meant to be motivating, I knew. But all the tough love did was hurt my feelings. "Mihai, I am working hard! I just need more recovery time." *Do you think I would be here if I didn't desperately, passionately want to go back to the Olympics?*

I thought. *Why would I put my whole life on hold to come here if I didn't care?*

By the end of the workout, I was crying. I was always taught not to show tears, especially to Martha, but I couldn't help it. I had reached the end of my rope. The other girls walked around the gym, quietly going about their business and trying not to look my way. I didn't care who saw me, though, I was exhausted and frustrated. That so much of my worth seemed to hinge on my routines made me feel terrible. My life revolved around gymnastics, and at that point I couldn't see anything outside of the sport. The Olympics had become life and death to me. Nothing else mattered.

Then a familiar voice broke into my stream of consciousness. "What is going on?" it asked.

Martha. Great. Just the person I wanted to see me fall apart.

She knelt down in front of me and put her hand on the back of my neck. Through my tears I could see her peering into my face, her features radiating—was that concern? She stood up and turned to Mihai. I thought she looked angry. "What is the matter?" she snapped at him. "Why is she crying?"

I barely processed Mihai's response. I was beyond controlling my emotions. The pressure was making me hate the sport I loved. I looked past her and couldn't utter a word. Eventually, she walked away.

That night, I called my mom, sobbing. On top of everything else, the cell service was so bad that every other word we said was breaking up, so neither of us could hear the other properly.

In my hour of need, I couldn't even have a phone conversation with my mother.

"That's it—I'm quitting," I finally said tearfully. "I can't do anything right. I'm not going to make the Olympic team. I don't know why I'm still doing this. I just can't take it anymore."

After we spoke for a while, my mom suggested it might also help to loop Silvie in. She hung up to call Silvie, and Silvie called me back a few minutes later. "Aly, what's wrong?"

"I don't know. I just can't do this anymore," I said.

"Aly, it's okay. Every athlete in the world has ups and downs. Don't give up. You'll be fine. Remember, you are an Olympic champion. You did it before, and you can do it again."

From then on, I'd call Silvie during training camps and competitions to remind me to believe in myself.

When morning came, I went back to the gym. Storming off wasn't my style. Besides, we were out in the middle of a national forest. There was literally nowhere to go. *I'll stay for the rest of the camp,* I told myself, *and then I'm done.*

I arrived thirty minutes early out of habit. I was putting my bag in a cubby when I saw Martha's reflection in the mirror in front of me. I straightened up and met her eye to eye. She seemed to have read my thoughts.

"Aly, listen to me," she said, putting her hands on my

shoulders. "You know this gets hard. Stick with it. You have just a few more months to go. Remember that gymnastics is hard and it is normal to have ups and downs. We have these camps and they are intense to prepare you for the big meets. We all want what's best for you."

I nodded robotically. But I didn't really believe that anything good was going to come from me continuing to do gymnastics anymore.

I felt the pop in my left foot as I landed an Arabian double pike during warm-up on floor the next morning. I collapsed to my knees and had to crawl off the mat. This time, the other gymnasts stared. Crying was rare, but crawling away from an event was even rarer. You didn't do that at camp unless something was very wrong.

Martha and Mihai got to me at the same time. Mihai gently picked up my foot, cradling the heel in his big palm. Both he and Martha were silent when they saw that it was already swelling.

When my foot was still swollen and painful the next day, Mihai asked Martha to let me leave camp early in order to seek much-needed medical attention. With plenty of competitions coming up in the spring of 2016, we were running against the clock, he said. Martha agreed. But when it came to changing my flight, a staff member said to call my mom and have her rebook the flight and pay the charges.

It wasn't about the money, but about the cold truth that came with it: I couldn't escape the feeling that after six years of training and competing at the international level, the organization had turned their back on me at the moment when I needed them the most. It seemed that if I wasn't in good enough health to perform, they didn't want anything to do with me.

As the plane climbed into the sky and away from Houston, I put my head against the headrest and let out a long, weary sigh. At least I was headed home.

In the calm of the airplane cabin, I considered just letting myself be done. I could stop now, and it would still be considered a great career. But when I asked myself what I really wanted to do, the answer was the same as it had always been.

I want to go to the Olympics. In spite of everything, it was still my dream.

By the time I reached Boston, all thoughts of quitting were gone. All I wanted to know was how long I would be out, and when I could start training again. There was an Olympic team to make.

Joe, my sports physical therapist, had just gotten off a red-eye and came straight from the airport to meet me. He was quiet as he examined my foot. Too quiet.

"What is it?" I asked, feeling more freaked out as the seconds ticked by without him saying anything. "What can you tell me?"

"I'm going to call someone I know—a foot specialist—to do some tests."

After doing an MRI and taking X-rays, the foot specialist, Dr. Theodore, was able to diagnose the problem: partially torn ligaments in the ankle. He put me in a boot and sent me home with strict instructions: no pressure on the ankle, and four weeks' rest.

Four weeks?!? "How about two?" I said jokingly.

He didn't laugh. "This isn't a negotiation," he said. "If you want a shot at competing in Rio this summer, I suggest you listen. If you take two weeks off and go back to training as hard as you were, you could very well tear the rest of it, and then you'll have no choice but to have surgery."

What he was really saying was: tear it and your career is over. There would be no time to recover from a surgery and get myself in good enough shape to make the Olympic team.

I went home and put my feet up.

CHAPTER 25

THE ROAD TO RIO

Needham, Massachusetts
Early 2016

Dressed in a pair of jeans, one olive green over-the-knee boot, and one black medical walking boot, I stepped out of my brother's car in front of Red Sox legend David Ortiz's house.

It was Christmas Eve, and we had been invited to the Ortiz home for a small gathering of friends and family. I first met Big Papi when I was invited to throw out the first pitch at a Red Sox game after London, and we'd stayed in touch. I was impressed by the remarkable kindness he always showed to everyone around him.

Brett munched on tapas as I chatted with people. David made the rounds, greeting everyone and making conversation. As we all sat down at his kitchen table an hour later to sample some wonderful homemade cuisine, David eyed my boot.

"How are you doing, Aly?" he said warmly.

I gave him a very brief summary of my injury, but explained that the partially torn ligaments weren't what was bothering me most.

"I just don't feel confident anymore," I confessed. "There are all these younger girls coming up, and they're all better than me."

David nodded understandingly and began talking about seizing the moment. "You have to use the moment and not let it use you," he said. My brother, who for the most part was just listening ("because who am I to give advice to an Olympic gymnast and future Hall of Fame baseball God for the Sox?" he recalled later), suddenly found his voice.

"Yeah," Brett said now, nodding at David and turning to me. "You need to control what you can control, Aly. No more and no less."

Big Papi's eyes lit up. "Exactly," he said in his warm Dominican accent, nodding his head enthusiastically. "You listen to him," he added with a smile, pointing a finger at Brett.

"I should have been the Olympian," Brett said with a grin.

Mihai and Silvie greeted me with big smiles and hugs when I walked into the gym with my big black boot the next day. For the next three weeks, I conditioned about two hours a day, wearing the boot as I climbed the rope or did pull-ups and leg lifts.

To compensate for the weight of the boot, Mihai strapped a five-pound ankle weight to my other leg and had me scale the rope with my legs held at a right angle to my torso. I would do it five times in a row, with a thirty-second pause between each climb. It was *so* hard, but I was working with a purpose: I didn't want to lose strength or endurance during the weeks I was sitting out.

Even though my training was limited, my family was making sure I worked on another aspect of the game: the mental one, which I'd been neglecting while stressing about scores. I consciously spent time doing things unrelated to gymnastics. I learned the value of taking time for myself. I spent time unwinding with my family, took hot baths and applied face masks to relax, and occasionally went outside to get some fresh air. I also enjoyed watching some of my favorite shows, like *Friends, Gossip Girl,* and *The Vampire Diaries.*

One day, my dad suggested that I go and watch my event finals routines from London on YouTube. "Remember who you are," he said. "You're the same Aly you were in London. You may be older, but you're wiser, too. Trust that."

I sat at the computer in the family room and Googled my name and "EF Floor London." As I watched the gymnast I had been—and hoped to be again—dancing to "Hava Nagila" and floating through her tumbling, I was blown away by how effortless it all looked. *How had I done that?* I wondered.

It was still on when Brett wandered in. "What are you watching?" he asked. When he saw I was watching my old routine, he nodded approvingly. "I read somewhere that when an NHL player was going through a big slump he used to watch old film of his best goals to get his confidence back up. I'm glad you're doing it, too. Because you are awesome."

"I was, wasn't I?" I joked.

"You still are. Your problem is that you're so wrapped up in winning an all-around medal that you've forgotten how special it is just to get to play," he said. "You're forgetting what an achievement it is just to be at the Olympics. Especially in gymnastics, where the US team is so deep. You should just enjoy it while you can."

"Thanks, Brett," I said.

"I'm the guy," he said proudly. "You know I'm the one who gives you the best advice." He grabbed an apple off the table and turned to go.

"No confidence issues there," I said, laughing.

Brett turned around. "If you don't believe in yourself, do you really think anybody else is going to?" he asked.

My injury had a silver lining: It gave me the extra time needed to clear my head for the challenges to come. When I got the green light from Dr. Theodore to return to full training that January, I felt more at ease.

Still, I knew I would need to prove myself at every competition that spring. To be considered for the Olympic team, where the selection committee is looking for the strongest scores on each event, I would need to start finishing in the top three among US gymnasts on vault, beam, and floor. At the moment, I was meeting that goal only on floor. That wouldn't be enough to get me to Rio.

The turnaround did not happen overnight, as nothing does.

In Jesolo in March, still stiff from the nine-hour flight, we went straight from the airport to the arena to work out. On one of my first double pikes I stuck the landing cold, but as my feet hit the mat I felt a sharp pain in my Achilles. I must have made a strange face, because Gabby giggled and asked, "What's wrong? You look so funny!" I giggled too—by this point, we giggled at everything—but the strain on my Achilles weighed on my mind. Every time I went up in the air, I wondered if it would tear when I landed. But I was afraid to speak up about it for fear of being benched, and I needed to prove that I was better than I had been in Glasgow. My confidence still wasn't where it needed to be, but it was getting closer.

In the competition, I fell on my Amanar vault and finished sixth in the all-around, fifth among the Americans. Mihai looked worried about the fall, and we both knew I was on thin ice and had to prove myself. I wasn't happy that I fell, but this time I didn't let it get me down. I remembered back to 2012, several months before the Olympic Games, when I was stressed and not at my best. I allowed myself to accept that it wasn't possible to be at my peak shape 24/7. It was a hard fact to accept, especially as a perfectionist athlete, but that's life—there are always ups and downs.

Like in 2012, having a good, consistent Amanar vault was essential to making the team. I also began paying special attention to beam, because that's where I saw I had the most competition from the likes of gymnasts like Laurie and up-and-comer Ragan Smith.

Since Glasgow, Mihai and Silvie had been recording my routines every day on Mihai's iPad for me to watch. Silvie, an international judge, would point out places where I could strengthen my score. They'd have me watch the recordings, often in slow motion, and I paid special attention to where I could improve. We spent hours and hours going over every detail, to build up my muscle memory so I would be able to feel confident and trust my training before competition. Silvie, who choreographed my beam routine, incorporated moments into my routines that would allow me to mentally prepare for the next skill.

In Jesolo, we went to a restaurant for dinner after the competition. I looked longingly at the pictures of pasta noodles and pizzas splashed across the menu, and primly ordered chicken with vegetables and potatoes. I wasn't trying to deprive myself anymore, but my sports dietitian had made it clear what was good fuel and what was not. At this point, I was texting him all the time to get advice on what to eat at certain points during the day. I would tell him if I was feeling more tired or sore than usual, and he would ask me what I'd already eaten that day and then make a recommendation.

The next generation was bolder than I was. A few seats over, in front of the entire coaching staff, Trinity, one of the juniors, lofted the dessert menu high over her head in open contemplation.

"Oooh, look at the strawberry cake," she exclaimed, pointing at a picture of a luscious pink dessert. "And there's chocolate cake, too! I wonder which one's better?" With a mischievous twinkle in her eye, she announced her verdict: "I guess I'll have to get both!"

I looked at Trinity and smiled into my chicken. I thought back to my first time in Jesolo, when I was yelled at for taking a slice of pizza at the banquet. I'd never found the confidence to eat pizza in front of the staff again after that experience. It gave me a great feeling to see a gymnast contemplating dessert without shame.

For my whole career, if I fell in a competition, I'd be sure to retire the "unlucky" leotard I had been wearing. But I didn't have that option today, since the leotard I wore in Glasgow was chosen as the team leotard once again. I sighed a bit as I pulled it on at the Pacific Rim Championships in Seattle.

That's when it hit me: I was wasting time worrying. I let go of my superstition. Pacific Rims was the beginning of a turning point for me. I finished second in the all-around to Simone, then won floor, and finished second to Ragan on beam. Things were finally coming together.

Mentally, I was making strides. But my body didn't get the memo.

I began feeling terrible pain in my left shin, and my Achilles continued to hurt. I would call Joe many times a week and ask for advice. He was very busy, but always made time for me. He would have me come in at least once a week and dry needle and massage my Achilles. He would also use a LightForce laser to help speed up the healing process, which helped a lot. He made me laugh during our sessions, and I knew I could go to him for anything.

When I told Ted about my aches and pains, he said I should come in and see him so we could figure out a plan. During our session, he asked me about my menstrual cycle. "I know it's a personal question, so bear with me, but are you getting your period every month? If you are not, then we need to adjust your nutrition regimen a little to tweak a few things so that we can try to fix the pain in your shins, help you recover better, and help get you more regular with your monthly period." I told him that I was getting my period every month, but it was very light.

"That's concerning. It's imperative to get your period back to where it should be, because that will greatly help your body recover faster every day and make you more prepared for competition." He told me to add more healthy fats to my diet, such as avocados, almonds, pistachios, and olive oil, and told me to slightly increase the amount of carbs I eat on a daily basis. Placing a lot of emphasis on his last recommendation, Ted instructed me to drink skim milk before workouts, mixed with the chocolate version of a powder drink he'd previously recommended.

As an athlete who stubbornly relies on routine, I was skeptical about all of these new adjustments. To my amazement, though, the pain in my shin disappeared after a few days and my recovery greatly improved throughout the following weeks. I couldn't believe it. Little did I know that Ted was specifically making nutrition recommendations to fight against and prevent me from fully developing the Female Athlete Triad while still trying to achieve an optimal fueling strategy for my training and more rapid daily recovery.

He was able to analyze my nutrition regimen in terms of my total daily calorie intake versus my total energy output from my basal metabolic rate (meaning how many calories I'm burning from my metabolism) and my intensive workouts. Because of that intensity, he recognized that I wasn't eating enough to meet the massive demands I was placing upon myself. I was dealing with low energy availability, which is one of the three prongs in the Female Athlete Triad, even though I was eating five to seven times a day based on the plan he developed with me. Nutrition isn't one size fits all—I needed to continuously adapt and alter my nutrition regimen. And in this case, the first plan he built for me that had worked well over the past year needed to be modified as my training intensified.

I stayed in constant contact with Ted so we could figure out what was working and what wasn't. He did the heavy nutrition lifting so I could keep my focus solely on gymnastics and how I could get better each and every day to compete at the Olympics.

Ted also introduced me to the float tank, a large Epsom saltwater tank with a domed lid that closes, leaving you floating quietly in a dark, restful world that allows your body to relax and recover. Once or twice a week, buoyed naturally by the Epsom salt water, I would think happy thoughts. Floating is a form of sensory deprivation that deprives you of the senses of touch, smell (since you only smell salt), sight, and sound (if you don't listen to music in the tank), which allows you to more deeply rest and relax for better mental recovery. The Epsom salt helped relieve some of my soreness and pain in areas of my body, so once I got out of the tank, I was very relaxed and refreshed. It felt like I slept for two to three hours even though I was only in the tank for forty-five to sixty minutes.

My new nutrition routine included chicken, salmon, or steak with a bigger portion of whole wheat pasta or brown rice after every workout. I also made sure to eat plenty of vegetables. Ted recommended drinking smoothies as an efficient way to add more calories into my diet while also getting in a lot of different nutrients my body needed. My metabolism was so fast at this point, that this new way of drinking my calories was really beneficial.

I'd always had a sweet tooth, and during one of our sessions, I popped a mint candy into my mouth as Ted came into the room.

"Tink," his nickname for me, short for Tinker Bell, "why in the world are you eating that? Spit it out."

"What? Why?" I protested. "I had a long day of training. It's just one. It's not going to make me gain weight."

"That's not the point," he said. "The problem is that your body doesn't recover as well if you're eating a lot of processed sugar because it can be pro-inflammatory and delay the recovery process. With the Olympics just five months away, I suggest you cut out candy until after they're over so that we can streamline your recovery and make it as rapid as possible to keep you ready. You are getting plenty of healthy natural sugars from whole grains, starches, and fruit within your nutrition plan that help you perform optimally and recover faster. These healthy natural sugars are very different from the processed simple sugar you currently are hiding in your mouth."

My jaw dropped, and the mint nearly fell out of my mouth. *No sweets until after Rio!?*

On the other hand, no one had ever told me that processed sugar from candy and sweets impairs recovery. There is a time and a place to incorporate all foods into your diet, even sweets, but I was determined to do whatever it took to reduce my pain. I was amazed that these changes really did help my inflammation. My Achilles pain began to fade once my body adjusted to the new routine. It wasn't perfect, but thanks to the great support and help around me, I was on the right track.

I was up on the beam on the first night of the US Championships, and preparing for my dismount. The routine had been good: I had done so many numbers in the gym in the past few months that once I mounted the beam in competition, muscle memory took over—all those days of refining my routines with Mihai and Silvie were worth it. My tumbling was more stretched out, the extension through my arms and legs longer.

But my dismount proved to be the best part. When I landed that Arabian double front, I was right where I needed to be: standing up, chest up, hips squared. My feet didn't move. *Bam*.

I put my hand to my collarbone as I went down the steps of the podium and let out a sigh of relief. I felt like the new me was here.

I had approached every event with a new mindset: I didn't need to be the very best, I reminded myself. I just needed to be in the top two or three. That took a little bit of the pressure off, and I think it actually helped me perform better. I had the second-highest scores on floor, beam, vault, and in the all-around, all behind the unstoppable Simone.

It wasn't a first place finish. But it was *my* best, and that's what mattered.

The scene in San Jose was familiar: The Olympic Trials were being held in the same city and same arena as in 2012. "This is good luck for us," I remarked to Gabby.

"Yes it is!" she said. "I know we can do this."

"That's right," I said, and we hugged.

I had a huge cheering section for Trials: In addition to my parents, Brett, Chloe, and Maddie, my cousins Brooke, Mikayla, and Tyler, and my aunts Lauren and Jessica, and uncles Michael and Eric all flew out to support me. Uncle Eric had printed up hundreds of rubber bracelets stamped with the words "Team USA 2016 Team Aly," which he handed out proudly to whoever wanted one.

Joe, Ted, and their families were also in San Jose. I had flown them and their families out for Trials to help me—at this point, they were like part of my extended family. I could go to them for anything, and I really enjoyed their company. They were always so kind and helpful, and even knew how to crack the enormous pressure I was under and make me laugh. It made such a difference to have strong medical support.

Sadly, one person who had worked so hard to be at the Olympic Trials wasn't there: My friend and teammate Alyssa, who had called me in tears a few days before, explaining that she had dislocated her elbow. My heart broke as I listened to her sobs, and I felt sick to my stomach at the awful thought of getting injured right before a big meet. I tried to calm her down, but what do you say to someone who is in so much pain, their dreams in tatters? Alyssa was like a sister to me, and I knew how hard she worked for her chance to be part of the Olympic Trials. A true friend, she texted me her support every day of the Trials.

A national team staff member stood by each piece of equipment in the training gym, watching every girl and taking notes on everything she did to be reported back to Martha. I felt like we would get critiqued for breathing the wrong way!

Fortunately, Martha herself could only watch one person at a time. When training bars, I'd look around to see where she was looking as I chalked my grips. If her attention was diverted elsewhere, I would jump up quickly and do my routine. I still got nervous when she watched me!

The arena buzzed with the same electricity that I remembered from four years earlier, the sort that's unique to the Olympic Trials. I was proud to be there, proud to be showing off what I had accomplished, both mentally and physically. Finishing second at Nationals proved once and for all that I was ready.

As the Olympics approached, I finally felt close to peak form. Just in time: Like in 2012, the American team was so deep that I knew that Trials would likely be more nerve-wracking than the Olympics—if I made it to Rio.

In San Jose, I would call or FaceTime with my parents every day, even though they were just a few miles away. USA

Adventures with Bubbie were always fun, and I guess they could also be exhausting! Me, between my cousins Brooke (left) and Mikayla, fast asleep in the back of Bubbie's car

At age seven, practicing my best Britney Spears moves for the camera!

The Raisman women: me, Chloe, newborn Maddie, and our mom

At the Exxcel end-of-the-year
gym show in 2002

Mom and Dad brought me flowers to
congratulate me following the show.

Casco 3
Session 2- Bunk 5L

In 20 years I will be . . .
Taylor - A mom, counselor & actress
Jennie- A mom, singer & actress
Mikayla- A dancer, soccer player & actress
Aly- An Olympic gymnast
Olivia- A teacher, vet & singer
Amanda- Still at Wico
Ruth- A retail manager
Kristyn- A camp counselor

Remember when . . . ?
Talent shows
"Toilet Time"
Sleepover in the gym
Dancing with Brennan

In 20 years I will be . . .
Taylor - A mom, counselor & actress
Jennie- A mom, singer & actress
Mikayla- A dancer, soccer player & actress
Aly- An Olympic gymnast
Olivia- A teacher, vet & singer
Amanda- Still at Wico
Ruth- A retail manager
Kristyn- A camp counselor

45

As a nine-year-old, I was determined
to make it to the Olympics someday!

One of my early journals.
I always loved to write....

A family portrait:
Brett, Dad, Maddie, me, Mom, and Chloe

Rett Ware

With Bela Karolyi in 2003.
I was so happy to meet him,
I had to ask for a photo!

Penelope Capozzi

During my level 8 floor
routine at the Massachusetts
state championships in 2005

At the 2005 US Classic in Virginia Beach,
where I competed in the pre-elite meet.
Mihai introduced me to Martha, who I was
excited to meet.

Floor at the 2006 Massachusetts
level 9 state championships

Mihai and me at the US
Challenge, a pre-elite meet, in
2006. I still have that medal!

All smiles with Mihai and Silvie at
Brett's bar mitzvah

Mom took this photo from the stands during the 2012 London floor medal ceremony.

The pins my family and I collected (my parents and siblings traded pins during the Games as well). We had them framed when we got back, and this hangs in our house in Needham.

Uncle Michael, Auntie Lauren, Maddie, Mom, Chloe, Brett, Dad, Tyler, Mikayla, and Uncle Eric in London for the 2012 Olympics

Eric Raisman

One of my text exchanges with
Simone when I was just trying to get
some sleep at training camp! ☺

My parents and me just
after I was selected for the
2016 Olympic team

Mid-vault during the
individual all-around final
in the 2016 Olympics in Rio

Mihai and me after
podium training in Rio

Simone and me hugging after the floor
exercise final at the 2016 Olympics.
We ended up going one-two in the event!

Gymnastics had a rule that we weren't allowed to see our families in national team competitions, unless they gave permission (which they rarely did). The call we had before competition was very brief and always the same. "Hi, Mom, hi, Dad," I would say. "I'm getting ready to leave soon to go to the venue."

"Okay, Lala, we love you," they'd say. "Be confident, but remember that we love you no matter what. Whatever is meant to be will happen. You are certainly prepared enough. Now go show that equipment who's boss!"

"Thanks," I'd reply. "I love you guys, too." And then Brett would chime in, "Go, Lala, remember the small step!" I'd roll my eyes. "I'll try to remember," I'd tell him with a smile.

At the Olympic Trials, when I would be facing down the vault or standing by the floor and waiting for the judges, I would calm myself by repeating another piece of advice from my mom. "It's not whether you win the competition that's important," she said. "People will always remember you for the kind of person you are, not just what you do on the floor."

I repeated that to myself during every hard moment of that tension-filled meet. When I was wading in uncertainty in regards to my gymnastics—*Did that wobble on beam affect my chances? Were my execution scores good enough? Was I doing enough to prove that I could hit these routines in Rio?*—I told myself that I was a good person, no matter where I ranked. Measuring myself by the person I was and not my results helped get me through.

My teammates and I also helped each other through the

Trials. We enjoyed each other's company, and also were the only ones who understood what we were each going through.

When the second day of competition was over, we huddled in the little room off the arena. The coaches broke the tension with jokes, and a lot of us passed the time on our phones, but we couldn't escape the reality that five of us were about to be elated—the rest of us, crushed. After a long wait that reminded me of 2012's, Martha and the selection committee joined us.

The 2016 Olympic team—me, Gabby, Laurie, Madison, and Simone—was one of the most diverse ever selected. Each of us had a unique story, a unique identity that helped us bond as a team from the very beginning.

Gabby and I, the London veterans, had proven that it was possible to take time off and come back to make a second Olympic team. Madison was the defending world champion on uneven bars. People were excited to see Laurie, the talented newcomer, compete. And Simone was so dominant that she was expected to win multiple golds.

That didn't mean I didn't want to win. "Let's make a deal," I kidded her after Trials were over. "You're obviously going to win the all-around gold in Rio. Won't you just let me win floor?"

"Um, no," she said, and we laughed.

The next morning, I jumped out of bed, and ran over to my roommate Madison's bed. She was fast asleep, but this was a moment that was worth waking up for.

"We did it!" I shouted.

From the moment we arrived at the Olympic training camp, we were told that Simone and Gabby would be competing all-around in the qualifying round. With one remaining spot, that left Laurie and me in direct competition for the third all-around spot. At the pre-Olympic camp after Trials, both of us trained all four events, knowing only one of us would compete all-around in the prelims.

The battle was fought at every practice from the time we arrived at camp. Routine by routine, we both strived and struggled to prove that we deserved that coveted place. People might think that there's no competition between the Olympic Trials and the beginning of qualifications in Rio. Not true. Not in our case. We always had to prove ourselves—every skill, every routine, every practice, every day.

After one of our first practices at camp, I went up to Laurie. "We can't let this ruin our friendship," I said. "Let's make a pact that no matter what, whoever wins the spot, the other will be happy for her. Okay?"

"Okay," she said, a big grin spreading across her face. I hugged her, happy with our deal. Our friendship was so valuable to me that I wanted to make sure gymnastics did not get in the way.

CHAPTER 26

ALL-AROUND CONFIDENT

Rio de Janeiro, Brazil
July–August 2016

Gazing at her reflection in the mirror of our Olympic Village apartment, Laurie opened her mouth and began singing a spot-on rendition of the Zulu lyrics from the opening scene of *The Lion King.*

"*Naaaaaaaaaants ingonyaaaaaaaamaaaaaaaaaaa bagithi Baba,*" she chanted, pausing for dramatic effect while Simone, Gabby, Madison, and I burst out laughing. Simone began dancing around and waving her arms like she was conducting an orchestra, while Laurie resumed the chant.

*"Naaaaaaaaaaaaaaants ingonyaaaaaama bagithi Babaaaa-
aaaa...."*

We sat around on green beanbag chairs and goofed off, having contests to see who could sing the most obnoxiously. When
we met other athletes who lived near us, they asked us if we were
the ones they'd heard singing. We would blush and admit it,
and they would laugh and tell us we should stick to gymnastics.

The Village in Rio was a brand-new high-rise apartment
complex just outside the Olympic Park. As the buses left the
complex to go to the venues each morning, we would pass the
other buildings, where teams had hung national flags or other
decorations from their balconies. A vertical banner with the
words "Time Brasil" ("Team Brazil" in Portuguese) cascaded
down the side of one. "I sLOVEnia" was pasted on the top balcony of another. Hanging over railings were flags from every
nation, displays of national pride and friendliness.

In the Village, I roomed with Madison. We knew each other
well by this point, having shared a room at the 2015 Worlds
and most of the camps leading up to the Games. Madison was
as organized as I was messy, and she would help me keep my
clothes in order. Most importantly, our nap schedules aligned!
Simone and Laurie, the most energetic of the group, shared
another room, while Gabby had her own room.

At night, Madison and I just couldn't get Laurie and Simone out of our room! It would be 11:00 PM, and they'd be

there dancing and singing around our beds, while Madison and I would laugh at their antics until we were gasping for breath. When I'd finally insist that we all go to sleep, Laurie would tuck me in. "Good night, Mama Aly," she'd say. Simone would echo, "Night, Grams." Madison would laugh until she fell asleep.

They made us giggle so much that our abs would hurt the next morning. Martha, who had a room across the hall from us, definitely heard our racket. But as long as our workouts were good, she never questioned us.

"All right, girls, does everyone have everything they need?" Martha asked as we stood in the elevator on the day of team prelims, tracksuits on and ready to go. "Did everyone remember their brains?" she teased.

"Yes, but I forgot my grips," Simone joked back. We all gaped, wide-eyed. Only Simone would have the guts to say that to Martha!

The boisterous crowd hummed with enthusiasm as we moved through the Rio Olympic Arena, heading for our first event. In the random draw that determined which event teams would start on, the US had drawn to start on floor exercise, the same event I started with at Glasgow the year before.

Nervous as I was, the years of training for this very moment took over once we were in the arena. I felt like I was exactly where I needed to be.

Still walking in our line, we circled the cream-white floor before mounting the podium to begin our one-touch warm-up as the noise climbed to a fever pitch. Listening to the crowd explode as we were announced gave me a little extra energy boost.

In the stands my parents, Brett, Chloe, and Maddie were on their feet, screaming my name. My mom had coins she found in Rio in her pocket—a good-luck ritual from the last Olympics. My dad and Brett were wearing the exact same clothes they'd worn in London. "The same underwear, too," Brett later joked. "Kick some butt and be confident. Small first step," he'd said, referring to my first pass, when I'd called my parents right before leaving for the arena.

In living rooms all over America, I knew people of all ages were glued to their TVs and portable devices. That's the beauty of the Olympics—the whole world comes together, united in their love for sports. I let myself have a moment to think about how momentous this was. I thought of all the different people who would see us compete: Men like my grandfather, who had taped the competition for my mom twenty years before; women like my mother, the high school gymnast; guys like my brother, who enjoyed the sheer athleticism of sports.

And maybe, I let myself think, kids who would watch our performances over and over again, dreaming of competing in their own Olympics someday.

All the athletes got into place, and we were introduced one by one. I felt a thrill as my name was called.

As we waited to compete, we milled around the floor, shaking out our arms and legs to stay warm and giving each other encouraging comments, supporting each other through every flip, every leap, every landing. Throughout the one-touch warm-up we could hear Martha cheering from the stands, yelling, "Good job, girls!" No matter where Martha was in an arena, we could always make out her voice.

While Gabby, Laurie, and Simone were performing, I paced around nervously, trying to keep warm. Mentally, I went through my routine, focusing on taking a short stride into my first tumbling pass. Today I was in control. I was going to be confident. And I was going to do this for myself.

Finally, it was my turn. I'd done everything in my power to be ready. *You owe it to yourself to do well. You deserve to have a good day.* The nerves were not going to get in my way.

As soon as Simone saluted the judges at the end of her routine, I took one look back at Mihai. He nodded. I ran up the stairs to the podium, bent down to get some chalk, and bounced up and down as I waited for Simone's score to come up. I knew that soon after it did, I'd have the green light from the judges to begin my routine. I focused only on positives, not permitting myself to think about anything else. Mihai made a calming gesture. *You are prepared*, his eyes told me. *Be calm.*

You're a good person, I told myself again as I saluted the judges and stepped out onto the white carpet. *Remember that. That's what matters most.*

As soon as I stepped into my first tumbling pass—a little step, less than shoulder-width apart—I could feel that it was going to be a good day.

I did my normal, and as I stepped off the floor, I breathed a huge sigh of relief. I knew my routine was strong enough to get me to the floor final. I had a spot in an event final, for my favorite event. Some of the stress I was carrying dissolved. *Good start.*

With that first page of our Olympic story in the books, we moved to vault. In practice, I had been doing the strongest vaults of my life. The Amanar still scared me, but I had trained it well, so many times. I hoped my muscle memory would allow me to stick the vault like I had in practice. Eighty feet from the vault, I took a deep breath, standing tall. I locked my arms like I always did, to remind myself to have straight arms and straight legs. Racing down the runway, I was composed and cool, trying to ignore the big camera that shadowed me. These cameras were only around at Worlds and the Olympics, so we never got used to them. It was always disorienting to see a big unmanned camera running next to me! That Amanar was one of the best of my life, powerful and well-controlled. I stuck the landing and held it there for a moment, proud of how far I had come. Glasgow was a distant memory.

"Does Aly Raisman look even *better* than she did in London?" NBC commentator Al Trautwig asked his colleagues.

There was shock in his voice—because I was twenty-two, because I was at my second Games. Because history says that in gymnastics, you typically get one crack at the Olympics. Maybe because they had made the mistake of writing me off.

I was first up on bars. After a quick warm-up, I was still out of breath, but didn't have time to rest. I quickly stretched my calves and forearms off the edge of the bar mats. Out of the corner of my eye, I saw my teammates warming up and silently wished them good luck. Madison was wrapping up her warm-up, and her coach, Laurent, signaled to me to start chalking up for my routine. Because only one male and one female coach are allowed on the floor at any given time at the Olympics, the coaches tagged in and tagged out, passing their floor accreditations from one to the next, depending on whose athlete was about to perform. For bars, Laurent remained on the podium.

I snuck a look at Mihai, watching this event from outside the field of play. When I looked at him, Mihai was smiling. Mihai trusted Laurent to give me just the right words of advice. "Take a deep breath. One skill at a time. You can do it." I nodded and took my place under the bar. I stared at the event screen, waiting for my green light. My last thought before grabbing the low bar and swinging into the routine was about how many hours my coaches and I spent together in the gym working on this routine, and how much I wanted to make them proud.

The momentum held: The judges awarded me 14.7 points,

the highest bars score of my elite career. My mouth dropped open when I saw it, and I looked back at Mihai and he mouthed "wow." He was jumping up and down, with tears of pride glistening in his eyes. The next time I glanced over at him, he had pulled out his phone and was taking a photo of the screen that showed the bars score. I laughed and ran over to hug him. "Great job," he said. "Silvie will be so proud!" It was her dream, she told me once, to see me get a 14.7 on bars.

"Focus on beam now," Mihai reminded me. "Just one more." I had to stay in the moment, I knew, because there was still more to do. In any sport, it's never over until it's really over.

As usual my heart was racing as I waited for the green light on beam. I thought of Mihai and Silvie, who had helped me finesse every little detail, making sure that the movements were clean and polished. And of Silvie's advice to never show the judges that you're nervous. I was beginning to let myself think that I had a real chance at the all-around final. Still, I didn't want to know the score that I needed to ensure my spot, so I didn't look up at the standings.

Competing on beam is so nerve-wracking because the beam is so terrifyingly narrow that it feels like the whole world stops. For me, competition always makes the beam feel even narrower than it does in practice. In training, I would do routine after routine, building great momentum. But in a meet, you only have one chance, and that doesn't leave any room for overthinking. It's vital to find a way to calm your mind and your thoughts. I imagined Mihai and Silvie standing alongside the beam, filming my every move. It made me relax, just a little bit, picturing myself at my home gym rather than here.

It worked—I started off strong. Midway through the routine, I made my only mistake, nearly coming off on a side aerial. *Uh-oh.* My heart jumped into my throat as I wobbled, desperately trying to keep my balance. I momentarily flashed back to the 2012 Olympics, where I almost came off the beam in the all-around final. I collected myself. *Not today. Today I'm in control.* I could see Mihai out of the corner of my eye, having a minor heart attack. Martha gasped, yelling for me to save it and stay on. It took only a second for me to straighten up and move on. I took a deep breath. No more room for errors.

I knew that slip would cost me the beam final. My mind jumped to my all-around chances. There was no doubt that Simone would qualify. But the second place was up for grabs.

Or had I just blown it?

The rest of the routine was clean, but I wasn't sure it had been enough. Mihai looked horrified. "Now it's a waiting game," he told me. "Let's see what the judges say."

Time seemed to stop as the arena hung in suspense. I could only hope my score would be enough. High above us, my parents and my brother couldn't bring themselves to watch. The camera zoomed in on the three of them, all consciously looking in different directions to avoid the scoreboard.

It took minutes for the judges to determine my score. Each second seemed to last an hour. I didn't sit down. *I can't until I know*, I thought. When a number flashed on the screen at the edge of the podium, I could hardly look. When I did, I broke into a smile: I was once again in first place in the all-around, with Simone still to come.

The goal was accomplished. Regardless of what Simone did, I was guaranteed to advance to the all-around final. I was one step closer to accomplishing what I almost had four years ago in London: an all-around medal. The dream was coming true.

Mihai was standing just off the floor. I went to hug him. In full view of the cameras, he playfully tapped me on the forehead with his open palm. "You almost let your chance slip away," he scolded me jokingly as he hugged me. "Good job!"

Gabby and I had hugged when I came down from the beam podium, and now I'd be the one advancing. I felt for her, and the unfairness of the two-per-country rule hit me once again. Had Simone, Gabby, and I all been allowed to compete, we would have stood a good chance at sweeping the all-around medals.

In the mixed zone with the media later, I didn't hold back. "I think the two-per-country rule is the dumbest thing ever," I told the journalists. "Who cares if there's five Chinese girls in the finals? If they're the best, they should compete."

The United States was ahead of every other team by nearly ten full points, meaning we could have fallen nine times and still been in the lead. It was the equivalent of being ahead in the Super Bowl by seven or eight touchdowns, as one writer put it.

"That means you girls better win by ten points in the team final!" Martha said with a big smile when she met us in the mixed zone with a hug for each girl, only half joking.

We laughed. "Isn't gold enough?" I asked.

"Well, yes," said Martha happily. "But winning by ten points is even better!"

CHAPTER 27

THE FINAL FIVE

Rio de Janeiro, Brazil
July–August 2016

We were in the dining hall one evening when I saw an athlete in a Team Canada tracksuit eating at a nearby table. We had run into him a few times, so I nudged Simone.

"See that guy over there?" She nodded. "He's my boyfriend," I joked. She giggled.

Just my luck, Martha overheard. "Oh, Aly, which one is he?" she asked, looking around with interest.

I gestured vaguely toward the table where the cute Canadian was sitting. "He's the Canadian over there, but I don't know his name," I said.

"He's your boyfriend, but you don't know his name?" Martha looked confused. I looked at Simone for help.

"Martha, she was just joking," Simone explained. "We have lots of options here—we're just picking them out."

"*Simone*," I whispered, horrified, as we walked away to grab some food. "Do we really want to discuss this with *Martha*?" I looked pointedly toward our national team coordinator, who was eating her croissant. As we piled our plates with chicken, brown rice, veggies, and slices of fruit, Simone just looked at me and laughed.

"Girls, there will be plenty of time for boys later," Martha had said firmly. "For now, you need to focus on the competition."

Doing the Olympics with Simone was truly a unique experience. She had so much energy in and out of the gym. She also roused my "motherly" instincts—with good reason.

We were making oatmeal one afternoon in the Team USA common room when Simone grabbed my mug and began filling it with tap water from the sink. I stared. "Simone, what are you doing?"

"I'm making your oatmeal," she replied. "What does it look like I'm doing?"

"With tap water?" I asked, incredulous.

"Well, yeah, once we heat it up, it's not dangerous anymore. You always worry so much!"

"Simone! You know everyone has told us a million times that we have to use bottled water. We'll get sick."

"What's the big deal? You ate it like this yesterday," she protested.

My eyes widened. "You mean when you made me oatmeal yesterday, you made it with tap water?"

"Yup," she said.

"*Simone!*" I said, horrified. "I get that I worry too much, but maybe you should worry a little more... at least until we're done competing."

When I opened my eyes on the morning of the team final, Madison was already awake. We looked at each other and smiled, feeling good about the test to come. As we sat doing our makeup and getting ready, she said, "I can feel that I'm going to do my best bar routine today."

I loved seeing how the hard work Madison put in during practices translated into positive thoughts before the competition. "You've been so consistent in practice," I said. "Today is definitely going to be your best day yet."

By the time we got to the team final, we were beginning to enjoy ourselves. We dominated the prelims, and there was a lot of talk about us being the favorites to win it all. We felt confident in our preparation and thrilled to be living our dreams at the Olympics. At the same time, we wanted to live up to Martha's expectations. She didn't just want to win—she wanted us to obliterate the competition on every event, to cap off a career that launched with Nadia's perfect tens forty years before. We never stopped being aware of those expectations. We never stopped worrying about whether we were doing enough to live up to them. Mihai once told me that it's hard to be number one in the world—but it's even harder to stay there.

As we waited in the tunnel to march out and begin, I looked around at our American flag leotards, heavily studded with crystals. They reminded me of the leotards I admired as I sat in my living room and rewatched my tape of the 1996 Olympics. We stood together, holding hands and hugging each other, making sure each one of us was in the moment together. Gabby and I smiled at each other, savoring being back at the Olympics, thinking about how special it was to be able to experience a moment like this not just once, but twice. This was our night. Twelve routines and we would be Olympic champions again.

Laurie led off on vault with an excellent double-twisting Yurchenko, setting up Simone's and my Amanars. Clockwork. We both nailed them. Just as the vault had energized the team four years ago, again we knew the night was ours.

We sat on the green carpet off the podium and waited for the Russian team to perform their vaults. We faced the crowd so we wouldn't be watching the competition, trying to sit in a circle to stay with one another. We did splits and used foam rollers to keep our muscles warm. We joked about how we'd corner Martha, eager for hard-won compliments. We knew she'd be happy with our vaults.

Both teams moved to bars, where the Russians would perform before us. Laurie's eyes wandered through the audience, and at one point she grabbed my arm. "Oh my gosh!" she exclaimed, her eyes wide. "I see a YouTuber over there!" Laurie's face lit up.

"Laurie," I said, laughing, "you can fangirl over him after the meet. Right now we need to get ready to do beam!" On our way to winning an Olympic gold medal in the team final, I thought, only Laurie would be excited about spotting a celebrity in the audience!

Simone, Gabby, and Madison each delivered on bars. We maintained our lead.

The momentum continued on balance beam. I led off with a strong routine, Laurie followed with another excellent set, and Simone remained solid to keep the United States ahead. By the time we went to floor, we knew that if we did our normal, we would end up on top by a wide margin. These last routines almost became more about putting on a great show for the people back home than about the scores.

When I stepped up after Laurie, I didn't dare look at the scoreboard, but I thought it was safe to assume that we were accomplishing our goal. The coaches seemed relaxed, and there was a lot of excitement in the air. However, I knew I still had to deliver a good routine—nothing is ever guaranteed and you have to stay in the moment and not get ahead of yourself.

I was fired up. I felt confident and in control. I saluted the judges and then forgot about them as I stepped onto the floor. As I struck my opening pose, I couldn't wait to get started. I shut my brain off and did what I had trained so hard to do that it came like second nature: a routine for myself, my teammates, my coaches, my family, and everyone who had helped me get to this point. Performing that floor routine gave me the best feeling ever.

Mihai greeted me as I came down the steps with a hug and a grin. Simone was the last to go. We practically lost our voices cheering and jumping up and down during her routine! She came down from the podium and we stood around hugging one another while Mihai and Simone's coach, Aimee, engaged in their own victory dance.

When Simone's score came up and made our gold medal official, we jumped onto one of the podiums and spent a couple of minutes waving to the crowd. We each tried to find our parents in the stands. The whole crowd was up on their feet, cheering and chanting "U-S-A, U-S-A," and with all the commotion, I couldn't spot my family. Then we huddled up, well aware of the camera in front of us. Putting our hands into a circle, we whooped and raised them in unison, shouting, "We are the Final Five!"

We had been going back and forth before the Games in our group text debating names for the team. The media had suggested that we call ourselves the "GLAMSquad." They landed on it because it incorporated the first letter of each of our names, but it felt sexist to me. (No one would ever suggest naming a men's team "Glam"!) Laurie suggested Slay Squad, which made us all laugh, but eventually we decided to do something more meaningful. Since we would be the last team Martha would coach at the Olympic Games, we landed on the Final Five. It was also a reference to the rule that is set to go into place for the 2020 Olympic Games, where team members in gymnastics will drop from five to four.

We ran backstage to put on our Team USA warm-ups and get lined up for the medal ceremony. We saw our fellow medalists from Russia and China. Although we didn't all speak the same language, we did our best to congratulate each other with hugs and hand gestures! Before we knew it, an Olympic official was ushering us to the medal podium.

Walking with our heads held high to receive our gold medals, I was trying to do a million things at once. I wanted to take in this moment, a moment I knew I'd cherish forever. At the same time, I wanted to share it with the people who made it possible. As I walked with my teammates, we exchanged proud looks, satisfied with what we had accomplished together. Nothing can compare to the feeling of standing on a podium, hearing that the United States team is the Olympic champion, listening to the national anthem, knowing that your dream came true. I turned the medal over in my hands, thinking I never wanted to take off this marker of everything we had accomplished.

Martha came down from the stands, and we met her at the entrance to the mixed zone. I explained to Martha that we were calling ourselves the Final Five in her honor, since we were her final team. Martha cried. She pulled us into a group hug so tight we feared she might suffocate us.

Just as in 2012, I knew Mihai deserved to share the medal. When I found him, we hugged, and I put the gold medal around his neck. We did it: back-to-back.

CHAPTER 28

A SILVER LINING

Rio de Janeiro, Brazil
August 2016

There are Olympic goals, like giving your best performance
and hopefully earning a medal. Then there are Olympic *goals*:
things you do at the Games because you know you'll never get
to do them anywhere else.

One of my Olympic *goals* was meeting superstar sprinter
Usain Bolt, who had been too fast for us in London. So when
Gabby and I spotted him in the cafeteria, we nearly overturned
the table as we jumped out of our seats and ran up to say hi.

Usain was seated at a table way in the back of the cafeteria,
eating two big plates full of pasta. When he was finished, we
introduced ourselves to him. "We're gymnasts," we said.

"I can tell!" he exclaimed, flashing a big smile at us. We

returned to our table, practically shrieking with glee. *Usain Bolt!* Other Olympians in the cafeteria swarmed us, jealous that we had the confidence to go talk to him, and asking us for details about meeting Usain!

Another day, Mihai pointed out tennis player Novak Djokovic across the cafeteria. "Go ask Djokovic if he has any pins to trade you." Simone and I, who were eating after finishing our workout before all-around finals the next day, went up to him.

"Excuse me, but when you're done eating, may we have a photo with you?" I asked.

"Sure," he said. "Where are you sitting?" We showed him, and he promised to come over when he was finished. He kept his word, and thanked us for being so respectful and sweet in letting him finish his meal. I asked him if he had any pins (I still loved collecting them!), and he laughed and said, "No, I don't," then, "Say, do you do gymnastics?"

"Yes," we laughed.

"Are you good?" he asked, all curiosity.

"We're okay," we responded.

"Actually, they won the team gold last night," Simone's coach, Aimee, chimed in from behind us. (So much for modesty.)

Novak's eyes widened. "Wow!" he exclaimed. "I think I'd better get a photo with *you*."

"Yeah, and you should watch us tomorrow in the all-around final, too!"

"I definitely will. Good luck!"

The day in between team finals and all-around finals, Simone and I had one workout. It was our last opportunity to refine any small details in our routines. I was so exhausted from the exertion of the previous two competitions and the pressure building ahead of the all-around final. I struggled on beam in practice, as I kept replaying the mistake I had made in the qualifying round a few days earlier, and the 2012 mistake that still haunted me.

Simone had already finished and was stretching on the side, but I was still practicing, hoping to end on a strong note. Simone cheered for me and shouted encouraging words. Mihai and Martha told me that I was prepared and to stop worrying.

I took a couple of minutes to collect myself, feeling overtired and letting some of my old anxieties creep back in. I told Mihai that I needed rest more than I needed to keep practicing. Mihai agreed, but told me to do one more routine, to take my time, to make it a good one, so I could go to sleep calm that night. I nodded, went back, and did it.

Simone came bouncing into my room the next day. It was the morning of the all-around final, the day I had pictured during every hard day of training I'd had for the past three years.

"Today's the day," Simone said, taking a seat on my bed.

"Yup," I said, and we hugged.

"Are you ready?" I asked.

"Yeah," she said. "Are you?"

"Yes. Today is going to be a good day," I said, smiling.

"One-two today?" she said, grinning herself.

"Yes, duh," I returned.

We took it easy that morning. We sat on our green beanbag chairs, listening to our favorite songs, like "Final Song" by MØ, "Lush Life" by Zara Larsson, "Once In a While" by Timeflies, and "Try Me" by Jason Derulo. We took our time with our hair and makeup, which we always found therapeutic, before putting on the leotards each of us had selected for the all-around final. Initially, Martha had picked another crystal-embellished American flag number as the all-around leotard for whoever qualified for the final, which Simone did end up wearing. But I preferred a long-sleeved red leotard. Red was one of my favorite colors to compete in. When I put it on, it just felt right.

"I'd rather wear the red one for all-around finals," I told Martha.

"All right, wear whatever you feel good in," she responded. I read between the lines: Martha knew I was nervous and was telling me I could do whatever I needed to in order to be at my best. I loved that Simone and I each got to wear a leotard that we felt the best in.

I put it on, added some matching red lipstick, then snapped a photo and sent it to Silvie. "Love the leotard!" she texted back. "Good luck today!"

Simone and I got to the arena a few hours before the competition to stretch and warm up. We repeated positive things to each other, assuring ourselves that we had worked so hard and owed it to ourselves to compete well. I couldn't keep some nerves from creeping in, but I trusted Mihai, Silvie, and Martha when they said I was ready.

And maybe this is the difference: I trusted myself, too.

It wasn't lack of hard work that cost me in London—it was lack of belief in myself. That was the missing piece. Yes, I was still nervous, but I wasn't going to let this chance get away. *Aly, you've worked so hard, you deserve to compete well*, I told myself over and over. *You owe it to yourself to do your best.*

In the back gym, Simone and I looked at each other. I could tell that we were both nervous, but also excited and feeling prepared. We could see in each other's eyes that we each needed support. We exchanged looks that said it all: *We can do this. Normal.*

In the dark hallway, waiting to be led into the arena, we jumped up and down. I was filled with both extreme nerves and slivers of excitement, trying to strike a balance between not letting the pressure get to me and being in the moment. Each minute felt like an hour, but at the same time, the wait was over quickly. As we shook our arms and legs, we took deep breaths as if we could exhale the nerves.

After we marched into the arena, the all-around finalists were introduced one by one as we stood facing the crowd on our respective events. The top six from the preliminaries—including Simone and me, as well as Aliya—stood beside the vault, stepping forward to wave to the crowd as our names were called.

Vault was first. The screen read "Alexandra Raisman, USA," but the light was red. I jumped up and down, wishing I could just go. I looked at Mihai, eighty feet down the runway, next to the vault, and he smiled. I could see in his face that he believed tonight would be my night. I realized that it was my turn to believe it, too.

Just like practice. I can do this. Tight arms, tight legs.

The light changed to green. I heard Simone cheering for me, I tuned out the camera, and I broke into my run. My vault was high and clean, just as it had been all week in Rio. When my feet hit the mat, I knew it was a good one—I was right where I needed to be in the air, and had enough time to complete the twist and anticipate the landing. The crowd let out a roar as I turned to salute the judges, did a brisk half turn, and ran off the mat. I received a 15.633, the highest of all scores from the rotation, except for Simone's 15.866. Mihai and Aimee congratulated both of us, and we hugged each other. Simone and I joked to our coaches that we just needed to get bars and beam over with, and then we could have some fun on floor.

As we walked over to bars, it hit me that my competition order for each event was the same as it had been in the London all-around final. I was first up in bars, which I liked since it didn't give me time to get into my head. The only problem with going first is that my body didn't have as much time to recover from the warm-up. I made sure to stretch and sip water on the side as the rest of the gymnasts warmed up. I did my bar routine. It definitely wasn't my best, but I survived it without any major errors. For me, that was a win.

Mihai was frustrated that I didn't match my score from qualifying. He kept mentioning it, which was not helping my nerves! I turned to him and said, "Mihai, not now. Let's worry about beam." NBC caught the moment on camera and thought it was funny, so it ended up in their Olympic coverage.

Going first on bars meant I was last in the beam rotation. Which meant I had a very long wait. As I waited for all my competitors to finish on bars, and then to go through their beam routines, I couldn't help thinking back to London and wondering, *What if I mess up on beam again? What if this lineup is bad luck?* I kept pacing back and forth to try to pass the minutes. I closed my eyes and took a deep breath, imagining myself doing the best routine possible.

Brazil's Rebeca Andrade had gone up just before me, and the Brazilian crowd had not liked her score. As they jeered and booed, it took all of my control to block everything out and focus on the task at hand. It's not often in life that we get a redo on past errors. This was the minute and a half that would decide if I could finally do it for myself. I stared at the red stop sign on the illuminated screen. I looked back at Mihai again, as the booing started to get to me. "It's okay," he said. "They're booing the score, not you." I nodded.

Do what you know how to do, I thought. *Nothing more and nothing less. One skill at a time.*

During the routine, I paid special attention to my side aerial on beam, making sure to lift my chest enough on the takeoff and really plant my feet on the beam. In the moment, I didn't think, I just launched myself into the air. Just before the takeoff, I heard Martha yell encouragement from the stands. I also made sure to pay special attention to the skill that was my undoing in 2012: the front pike. My routine was clean. When my feet hit the mat on The Patterson dismount, I breathed an audible sigh of relief. I knew my performance would keep me in the running for a medal. Floor would decide the color.

I ran off the event podium and into Mihai's arms. I breathed another sigh of relief, which Mihai echoed. Then I ran and gave Simone a big hug.

Simone and I allowed ourselves a little peek at the scoreboard before we went to floor. I was in third place, behind Simone and Aliya. Our eyes went from the scoreboard to each other, and we smiled, each thinking the same thing: If we just do a normal routine, we'll go one-two in the all-around, just like we'd dreamed. We grabbed each other's hands and squeezed as we walked toward floor together. We competed with each other, not against each other.

One more, I kept repeating to myself during the one touch on floor. *One more*. Adrenaline kicked in as I stepped up onto the mat. I felt present, fully in the moment. I stood there, right arm extended forward, left hand over my right shoulder, head held high, and a smile on my face.

My first pass was dead on, and the double turn that came after it—the skill that had given me so many problems the year before—was the best I'd ever done it. When I came out of the turn, I registered Mihai in my line of sight, clapping and yelling "yes!" in excitement. He knew that after the first pass and the double turn, the rest of the routine would be okay for me.

In that moment, I didn't feel like I was at the Olympic Games. I had found that inner eight-year-old, the one who danced in front of the TV, trying to copy the moves of the world's best gymnasts, dreaming of a moment like this some- day. That floor routine was one of my favorite of all time.

When I struck my final pose, I realized that the specta- tors, many of them on their feet, were chanting "Al-ly! Al-ly!" I put my hand to my heart, absolutely overcome. Like in the team final in London four years before, the tears started to flow before I stepped off the mat. I'd never been overcome with that much emotion before. All the struggle of the past four years, all that uncertainty, it all came out in that moment. I had achieved my goal. I had an all-around medal. I cried even harder as the crowd's support grew—to be in another country and hear that kind of cheering for the United States was something incredibly special. I couldn't believe that the moment I had dreamed of—but didn't always believe was within reach—was better than I had imagined. I couldn't see them at the time, but in the stands Mom, Dad, and Brett were sobbing as hard as I was. My brother and dad high-fived, thinking that their "lucky clothing" contributed to my success. Chloe and Maddie cheered and hugged, and were somewhat amused to see us all in tears.

As time passes, you understand and learn to appreciate yourself and everything you've been through. For the first time in an all-around final, I had competed without any major mistakes, and no matter what the medal color, it was a huge moment for me. I hugged Mihai, and we celebrated my silver as if it was gold. We stood side by side, ready to watch Simone seal her Olympic gold.

Simone ran over to me and we hugged while waiting for her score. Aimee, Mihai, Simone, and I couldn't stop smiling and hugging each other. We congratulated each other and savored the moment. When her score flashed and her gold medal win was official, she climbed up to the podium to wave to the cheering crowd. A moment later, she beckoned to me.

"Go up there," Mihai whispered in my ear. So I hopped up onto the floor and joined her. The crowd became even more frenzied as we stood together and waved and waved, smiling with the overwhelming joy of it all. Later, Simone would say that she was more pleased with me earning silver than with herself for taking gold. "I've seen how hard she's worked for it," she said.

In her own interviews with the media, Martha concurred. "In all the years, and it's been many years, one time I could not say 'Aly, try harder' because she always tried her best," she said. "It doesn't always turn out the best, but you could not blame her, because she always gave what she had."

After the press conference, we were whisked off to the studios of NBC Rio, where we were interviewed by Olympic host Bob Costas. They had us watch our vaults on a big screen in the studio. Martha laughed when she saw them. "Vault wasn't good there, girls," she chided.

"Martha, get over it, they're one-two in the world!" Aimee protested, and Martha smiled and leaned over to hug us. She never, ever, ever stopped searching for improvement.

On the other hand, that's what had made us great.

When we finally got back to our apartment, Laurie and Madison were already in bed. A special surprise was waiting for me on my bed—a sweet note from the two of them:

Aly,

We couldn't be any happier for you! All your hard work is paying off, and now you're an Olympic AA silver medalist!! We've looked up to you from the beginning of our elite careers & you've inspired us in so many ways! We're so thankful to have you cheering us on, and helping us through this Olympic journey!

We love you, Mama Aly ♥

> Love,
> Maddie & Laurie
> ♥   ♥

Their words and thoughtfulness meant so much to me, especially since Laurie and I had been competing for the all-around opportunity. My teammates understood my journey differently than anyone else in the world since they lived it alongside me. I got into bed thinking how lucky I was—not only to have won an Olympic silver medal, but also to have such loving and supportive teammates. That love and support was what had gotten us through the intense workouts, and allowed us to rise above the pressure of the Olympic Games to be the best versions of ourselves as we competed. Hard work was a huge component to what we had accomplished, but our camaraderie was the secret ingredient to our success.

The floor final was held on August 16, and while my lucky number is seven, Mihai and I told ourselves that sixteen was lucky because 1 + 6 = 7. We were always able to find an excuse for why the day it counted would be a good day, though deep down I was aware that it was my work in the gym that really mattered. Thinking it was my day didn't hurt, though.

Doing the floor final was a push, because I felt sick from exhaustion, but then again, how often do you go out to compete in an Olympic final? Here was my chance to close the book on this amazing Olympic experience—and I wanted to go out with one last medal.

The Final Five had continued to round out its medal collection in event finals: Simone won gold on vault and bronze on beam; Madison got silver on bars; and Laurie got silver on beam.

Floor was my Olympic encore performance. In addition to being my favorite event, it was the one where I felt the most confidence. I already had two team gold medals, a gold medal on floor, a silver in all-around, and a bronze on beam. I felt proud of my Olympic career, and Simone and I were favored to go one-two again. I felt empowered. It felt amazing not to worry what the judges might think, because I knew I was doing it for myself.

Before stepping onto the mat, I focused on the routine ahead, but also on the sights and sounds of the Olympic arena, the special magical ambiance that comes around only once every four years. How lucky I was to have been able to live it twice.

I joked with Simone that I wasn't sure if it was nerves or her oatmeal, but I had a stomachache throughout the day. But it didn't impact my performance. I won silver, the sixth Olympic medal of my career. Among American gymnasts, only Shannon Miller, with seven, has more. Crazy. I often wonder: Will it ever sink in?

CHAPTER 29

BALANCE

Rio de Janeiro, Brazil
August 2016

After the floor final, my teammates and I were in NBC's Rio studios. Before we went on air, we were sitting in the green room staring at platters of grilled chicken and vegetables. An assistant was standing nearby.

My teammates looked at me to say something. We'd had enough grilled chicken to last awhile. "Excuse me, but could we get some pizza?" I asked. "And, if you have any, maybe some cupcakes for dessert?" The assistant went off and returned a few minutes later holding a paper plate with one slice of pizza on it.

We stared at the single slice and started laughing. "Thanks, but there are five of us! We all want pizza." The assistant came back a few minutes later, loaded down with pizza and cupcakes. We smiled at one another. And then we dug in.

Simone's crush Zac Efron flew down to surprise us in Rio as we filmed *The Today Show*. I had been feeling sick before (maybe pizza and cupcakes weren't the best idea after my floor final stomachache, not to mention the stress and exertion of competing) and wanted to lie down for a few minutes. I asked, if this one time, I could sit out an interview to take care of myself. But people who were in on the surprise were like, "No, you *really* need to go." They were right—I would have hated to miss Zac!

The next day, Simone, Madison, and I were relaxing on the beach. My mom was with us, and she noticed there was a paparazzo taking photos of us in our bathing suits. I put my sweatshirt on and crossed my arms. It felt so uncomfortable to have someone invading our private moment, with no consideration to the fact that we wanted time to ourselves, and weren't consenting to a photo shoot. That was just a small taste of what was to come. At the airport, there were so many cameras and reporters that they were knocking one another over trying to get to us. It was early in the morning and we were exhausted from the stress and excitement of the Games, and having all those flashes in our faces didn't help us relax before our international flight.

We flew to New York City. Our schedules were packed, but we made sure to make time to see *Hamilton* on Broadway.

We presented at the MTV VMAs and at the Country Music Association Awards, and played "Hungry Hungry Humans" on *The Tonight Show* with Jimmy Fallon. I got to go on *The Ellen DeGeneres Show* with my parents. Simone and I performed on *Lip Sync Battle*, and we flew on a private plane in order to get to our next commitment, at a Fashion Week event, on time. It was an overnight flight, but it was such a cool experience that we didn't sleep. We danced, sang, and walked up and down the plane aisle as if it was a Fashion Week runway! We collapsed in laughter, eventually taking quick naps before we landed.

In the fall, we met with the Obamas. The president did splits with us and joked he'd go as the Final Five for Halloween. We also participated in another Tour of Champions. As we went from city to city, I met so many people. Talking to them reminded me that everyone has a unique story that deserves to be heard. At one of the hotels, I ran into Audrey Nethery, a six-year-old with a rare bone marrow disorder, and she was so happy and full of life. We danced together in the hotel lobby. She ended up coming to one of our shows, and I've been watching her on YouTube ever since.

In interviews, I was talking more and more about my early struggles with confidence and spreading my message about body positivity. I had no idea how much my words were being heard and resonating until people started stopping me on the street and sharing their own stories with me. People would tell me that they could relate—and sometimes that they were recovering from eating disorders—and that hearing from an athlete who competed on a world stage in a leotard while projecting confidence, that I struggled with body image, made them feel less alone. These interactions were gratifying, but they always surprised me. Hearing that my experience and words were helping people motivated me to be even more outspoken about body positivity.

Living in the social media age gave me great platforms to connect directly with fans, and to share details of my life. Social media definitely has its benefits, as well as its downsides. Oftentimes social media posts can make someone's life seem "perfect," but the reality is that no matter how many followers someone has or how great their life looks, we're all human. Sometimes I find myself looking at other people's photos and comparing myself to them, and when I step back to think about it, it hits me how backward it is that we spend so much time obsessing about other people's lives. Don't get me wrong, I love social media and being able to connect with people and hear their stories, but I think we could use a healthier balance. Our generation is always on their phones, and I often wish that we could be more in the moment!

One way that I think social media can be great is to speak up for yourself. For example, I started calling out double standards. When I was going through security before a flight one day, a security agent recognized me as a gymnast. Her male coworker replied, "I don't see any muscles there. It can't be her." Little did he know that my arms were a source of personal insecurity for many years. His words made me angry—who was this man to be judging my body and commenting on it? I posted the experience on social media, and was shocked that it went viral! Clearly the moment touched a lot of nerves.

It reminded me of another experience, when I was eating breakfast in a restaurant with my dad. A stranger came up to us, and she asked me how much weight I had gained since the Olympics. I posted about that interaction, too, incredulous that this woman felt it was okay to comment on my body like that. Her words stirred my insecurities and made me think that everyone else was judging me the same way. It's so important to think before we speak, and to be sensitive to other people's feelings. Because I've spent a good chunk of my life in front of cameras, it's easy to forget that I'm a person with feelings, too.

My work with Reebok gave me another platform to talk about body image. Their "perfect never" campaign aims to remind people that there's no such thing as "perfect," and that everyone should just be true to themselves and celebrate the imperfections. It doesn't matter if you're an Olympic gymnast, a model, a UFC fighter, a single mom, a high school student—we are all badass and unique! I love this message, and the way that Reebok brought it to life with so many different strong women coming together.

When I was younger, I felt like there were rules to femininity— that boys wouldn't like me if I was stronger, more successful, a better athlete, or smarter than they were. As I got older, I learned to love my imperfections and be confident and comfortable in my own skin. It's still a learning process and sure, there are definitely days when I don't feel confident, but every morning, I look in the mirror and try to focus on something that I like about myself to start the day on a positive note. For years, *Sports Illustrated* has been moving toward breaking the perception of the "perfect body type" by featuring more athletes and diverse bodies in their Swimsuit edition. I met with the editors of the Swimsuit issue following Rio, and we sat and talked for three hours about the pressures put on girls and boys to have a certain body type, my own personal struggles with being confident and learning to love my body, and my goal to help kids, and anyone really, to just feel comfortable in their own skin. I sat in their offices in jeans and a T-shirt, and was blown away by their passion for breaking stereotypes. I was asked to be part of the 2017 issue and flew to Texas for the shoot.

The mood on set was relaxed and empowering, and it was liberating not to worry about what other people were thinking of me. I loved how the photographer, James Macari, captured the strength and power I worked so hard for. "There is no perfect body type—it's 2017!" I declared in an interview afterward. I knew that there would be mixed reactions to my involvement— I feel that people like to put me in a "gymnastics" box, and every time I step outside of it, it ruffles some feathers. But for me, the photo shoot was about doing something for myself. You can't please everyone. You have to follow your own heart, and make the decision that feels right for you.

I think there's a lot of pressure for women to dress a certain way, look a certain way, act a certain way, and I think everyone is entitled to wear and do whatever makes them feel confident and happy. It's not for other people to judge! We've come a long way, but there is still a long way to go.

I'm lucky to be in a position where I can align myself with partners that share my values, in hopes of making a real difference in people's lives. In addition to Reebok, I started working with Leesa, a company that donates one mattress to a homeless shelter for every ten that they sell. I visited a homeless shelter in Boston, where I met a lot of single mothers. I got to help a four-year-old named Pearl unpack her mom's new mattress. As soon as it was in place, she jumped up onto the bed to show me her gymnastics moves! It was a special moment to get to see her joy, and an important reminder that it's easy to take things for granted.

My family always taught me the importance of giving back. Several years before she died, Bubbie took up the cause of fundraising for lung cancer research. In her honor, I've continued that work, and seized on additional opportunities to work with the community.

I'm passionate about helping the younger generation to grow up and be confident and independent. I've always loved spending time with the youngest kids at my gym, because they still have their natural confidence and are so pure of heart. I feel like I really connect with the younger generation, so I enjoy speaking to and meeting with groups of kids. You never know what someone else is going through and sometimes we get so caught up in our own problems and forget that small acts of kindness can really make a difference to someone.

On a visit to the Boston Boys & Girls Club with Life is Good, I asked the kids to show me their strength. One girl was embarrassed, saying she didn't have muscles to show. "Strength doesn't always mean muscles, or what you look like on the outside. It's about feeling strong on the inside. Part of that is being confident. Can you show me how you're confident?" It broke my heart to see a young girl who was so insecure and couldn't see her own potential. We need to do a better job of teaching kids the importance of believing in themselves and that with hard work and support, they can be whatever they want to be when they grow up. Life is Good worked with me to create a line of T-shirts with empowering messages. The shirts celebrate courage, authenticity, kindness, and optimism, values inspired by my parents' long-ago advice: that it's more important to be kind than to be on a podium.

The Olympics changed my life in so many ways. I'm so grateful for all the opportunities the Games have led to. At the same time, I've learned how important it is to have a balance.

My family and I spend vacation weekends in Cape Cod, in a warm, relaxed community. It's the kind of place where we can dash over to a neighbor's house uninvited, and everyone lends a hand—it reminds my parents of a simpler time. We've been going there for so many years, and everyone is so friendly, that all the neighbors treat me like family.

We spent the Fourth of July weekend this year at the Cape. I was playing with a group of kids on the beach: Anna from Brestyan's, Brian, Gabriella, baby James, Julianna, Lauren, baby Lawler, Lyla, and Max. Gabriella told me that it was just okay to see me on TV at the Olympics, but it was cooler to see Maddie and Chloe in the stands!

Behind us, a little girl's voice called out, "Is that Aly Raisman?!"

"Did she just ask if you were Aly Raisman?" Anna said, confused.

"Yes," I said simply.

She looked at me inquisitively, furrowing her brow. "My mom says you're famous, but I don't get why," she told me. "I don't really think the Olympics are that big of a deal. My friend and I already did the Olympics," she added, referring to Brestyan's Olympic-themed end-of-the-year gym show, "and we're only six. C'mon, let's go swim."

As we walked toward the water, laughing, I thought to myself: *I'm so lucky.*

THE FIERCE GUIDE TO LIFE

* Find something that makes you happy, and go with it.

* Look for silver linings. Things may not always work out as planned, but sometimes they lead you places that are even better than you hoped.

* Find people you can trust. Quality over quantity!

* Don't be afraid to speak up, even if you're not entirely sure something's wrong. Trust your instincts, ask questions, and don't settle until you're satisfied with the answers.

* Make time for yourself and appreciate your own worth. Because you're worth a lot!

* Realize that you're allowed to show emotion. We're all humans, not robots. We all get scared, sad, or frustrated now and then. It's completely normal!

* Strive to make the world a kinder place. The impact of your kindness can be bigger than you think.

* Go outside and get some fresh air. Appreciate nature and the world around you. Being outdoors can help you start the day off right, or unwind and unplug from a long day.

★ Don't let anyone tell you what's best for you. Listen to advice, and weigh it carefully, but remember that you should be the one making the decisions. Most of the time, you know what's best for you.

★ Give it your all—and then take a breather. Resting and recharging your batteries is one of the keys to living a happy, healthy life.

★ Forgive. Forgive yourself for making mistakes and forgive others. Nobody's perfect.

★ Apologize if you need to—and then move on. Turn the page and try not to hold grudges.

★ Take time to pat yourself on the back for your achievements. You've worked hard for them! Enjoy the destination—but don't forget to appreciate the journey as well.

★ Never be afraid to dream big! Channel your inner child, who believes that no dream is too big.

★ Think about the characteristics that make you unique— and embrace them!

★ Set goals for yourself and don't be afraid to follow them as far as they'll take you. Accept the fact that if you don't accomplish your goals, that's okay. Focus on the hard work you put into it and be proud of that.

★ Focus on what you love about yourself. Don't fall into the trap of picking your body apart.

★ Make a point of looking in the mirror and identifying three things you love about yourself.

★ Don't sell yourself short. You are smarter and stronger than you think!

★ Make sure to create "me" time. Don't forget it's okay to put yourself and self-care first sometimes.

★ Put your phone down, and go enjoy your life!

AUTHOR'S NOTE

Most people watch women's gymnastics every four years. In those televised moments, you see girls competing and smiling on the podium. What you don't see are the behind-the-scenes moments—the highs and the lows that go along with it.

I've been through a lot at a young age and have learned so much. Remember that I'm human like you, and I come from a sport where it's ingrained in us from an early age that perfection is the only standard, so I guess it's natural that I still sometimes worry people are judging me (even though I try not to!). As a result, I debated how personal I wanted to get in this book. But the hard moments are part of the fabric of my life, so I wanted to share them alongside the good times because they have shaped the person that I am today. I feel so lucky to have the opportunity to share my story. Thank you for reading it.

Please know that your story deserves to be heard. I know a lot of people *don't* feel heard. And if you're one of those people reading this right now, I am sorry, and please know that you matter. When I was younger, I sometimes doubted my instincts. I was afraid of what people would think of me, and I was so manipulated into trusting an unworthy person that I tried to make excuses. I came to realize, though, that it's not right and not fair. No one should ever be abused. Ever. *It is never okay.*

Getting professional help and leaning on my support system showed me that sharing your thoughts is crucial to recovery and finding ways to cope with whatever life throws at you. The truth is, I'm still coping with it. Not everyone realizes that abuse goes beyond suffering in the moment—most deal with it for the rest of their lives. Some days are better than others. When I focus on how far I've come, it helps me feel so empowered and strong.

I worry that we live in a culture that puts too much pressure on today's kids, and where people get away with abuse and bullying too easily. Far too many of my friends have their own personal stories of sexual abuse. How can I help if I don't share my own story and do my best to support others through their difficult times?

If you feel alone or recognize that someone is mistreating you, I hope reading my story helps you find your voice. I know it's not easy. In fact, it may be the hardest thing you'll ever do. But I promise it is what you deserve. Your story is important.

Revisiting my high school years for this book, and thinking about the importance of being heard, has made me think a lot about another major moment in my life. I was in the kitchen when my parents sat me down and shared terrible news: My classmate Jake Borson had taken his own life. I was so confused, upset, and angry. *Why would Jake do this? Didn't he know we would all miss him so much? Didn't he know how much his family and friends loved him?* Jake had a twin brother, Zack, and

I couldn't even begin to imagine how he and his family felt. It was a total shock to our school, and I remember a lot of my friends had no idea he was depressed. The school administration opened up a room for Jake's classmates to go and talk to one another, but they didn't talk to us about what happened and how we could cope with the loss of our friend. I wish they had checked in to make sure no one else among us was feeling suicidal and had provided resources for people struggling with depression.

Jake's family went on to do a lot of good in Jake's name, from honoring Jake's wish to be an organ donor and save others' lives to giving out scholarships in Jake's name to creating a foundation for helping those less fortunate. But nothing can bring Jake back, or take away the pain of his absence. If you feel alone or depressed, know that it's okay to not be okay and to ask for help. Suicide is never an answer. In fact, if you or someone you know is suicidal, asking for help could save a life that very much deserves to be saved. Don't ever sell yourself short—you are stronger than you think. It is amazing what we can do when we put our minds to something. I never thought I'd have the courage to be so open about what I've learned about myself, but here I am, pouring my heart out onto these pages.

Thank you to all who took the time out of their busy schedules to read my story. Remember *your* story matters and you deserve to be heard. I appreciate all the support more than you can ever imagine. I feel so lucky to be in the position that

I am in today, which is why I want to give back. I'm passionate about working with the younger generation to encourage kids to be confident, independent, and kind. I want them to grow up with a desire to be the best versions of themselves and chase after their passions—not because a parent or an adult is pushing them too hard, but because they love what they do so much and they don't want to live without it. In my opinion, we are all put on this earth for a reason. We can find our reason by going through the ups and downs, not being afraid to make mistakes, and helping others who are lost along the way.

I hope you find your reason, and I hope you'll help others find theirs, too. Finally, I hope you'll be kind, be determined, be loving, be humble, hold your head up high, and above all...

Be fierce,

Ally

RESOURCES FOR SURVIVORS

RAINN (Rape, Abuse & Incest National Network) is the nation's largest anti-sexual violence organization. RAINN created and operates the National Sexual Assault Hotline (800-656-HOPE, online.rainn.org) in partnership with more than 1,000 local sexual assault service providers across the country and operates the Safe Helpline for the Department of Defense. RAINN also carries out programs to prevent sexual violence, help victims, and ensure that perpetrators are brought to justice.

ACKNOWLEDGMENTS

Mom and Dad: These few sentences don't do justice to everything that I would want to write, and words could never express how much you both mean to me. Thank you for always trusting me to make my own decisions and helping me become the person I am today. You are both kind, unconditionally loving, and completely selfless when it comes to your kids. I am so lucky to have parents who always put their kids first, no matter what. Thank you for not putting pressure on me and allowing me to do gymnastics for myself. I would have never gotten through the pressure of competing on a world stage if I thought you would both be disappointed in me if I didn't perform well. Thank you for teaching me that being a kind person is far more valuable than any place on the podium. And thank you for constantly reminding me that I should be confident and strong.

Brett: Thank you for always supporting me and always being someone I can call for advice. You have always been the best brother I could ask for. You always support me no matter what and never lose faith in me. You always believe in me and encourage me to believe in myself. Thank you for constantly reminding me and our sisters to be confident and find things that make us happy. I love how we both share a love for sports, and I love watching you continue to make steps closer to your dream job. You know wherever life takes you, I will always be there to support you.

Chloe: Thank you for being fun, spontaneous, kind, and loving. You always seem to know how to make me laugh when I need it most. Thank you for allowing me to vicariously live through your social life. When people meet you, they are instantly amazed by your incredible personality. You always seem to find ways to make sure everyone is having a good time.

Madison: Thank you for being the sassiest younger sister I could ever ask for. You are the oldest soul of a younger sister I have ever met in my life! I am so proud of your independence and your confidence to be your own person. I can't wait to watch you grow up and see where your incredible creativity takes you. You may be young, but your maturity amazes me when I need someone to talk to and to go to for advice.

Mihai and Silvie: Thank you both for being the best coaches. At times I spent more time with you both than my parents. Thank you for always believing in me through injuries, tough times, and life. I would never ever have become the gymnast I am if I didn't have you as coaches. Thank you, Mihai, for spotting me every day. You always would catch me to prevent me from getting injured, even if it put you at risk. Silvie, thank you for letting me call you whenever I needed to talk; you always made sure to help me when I was having a hard day. Thank you, Mihai and Silvie, for always welcoming me to talk to you about being nervous or scared, and thank you, for teaching me both what it means to be a hard worker and how valuable it is to be confident and strong.

Bubbie and Papa: Thank you, both, for creating so many memories from my childhood that I will cherish forever. Thank you for taking such good care of us and for always having your door open any time. Bubbie, the whole family wishes you were still here with us. I think about you all the time. I still can't believe you aren't here to witness your grandkids' lives. I know you would be so proud of all of us. Thank you for creating so many memories so that during family holidays we never run out of funny moments to share about you. We still fight over who was your favorite!

Grandma and Grandpa: Thank you for taking such good care of me when I was little. I used to love going over to your house and watching Grandpa work on his computer. Grandma, thank you for taking me to the park and to the Cookie Lady next door. Thank you, both, for loving me and supporting me throughout my life. I wish you were still here to see all your grandkids and how grown up everyone is!

Uncle Eric and Auntie Jessica, Uncle Michael and Auntie Lauren, Mikayla, Brooke, Tyler, and Drew: Thank you for always being so supportive. I always look forward to spending holidays with you all. Thanksgiving is always my favorite because we spend the whole evening hysterically laughing and reminiscing on special memories. Thank you for always making me feel loved. I feel so grateful for being a part of such a special family.

Joe Van Allen: I don't even know where to start! Through your tireless efforts to manage my injuries, I was able to come back successfully. Thank you for always helping me by keeping me healthy enough to be able to compete. You not only help my body, but you quickly became a person who I could come to for anything. Our dry needling sessions became therapy sessions for me as well. You always make me laugh no matter how tired or upset I am. Thank you for being someone who I could trust and for being like a second dad to me and for inviting me to spend time with your wonderful family. Jodi, Emma, and Andrew, you guys are the best!

Ted Harper: Thank you for helping me become less stubborn when it comes to my preparation and recovery. As an athlete, I always wanted to stick to what I was comfortable with. Thank you for reminding me the importance of having a good balance with food and telling me to constantly fuel my body in the best way possible. Thanks for always looking out for me and taking such good care of me. I always enjoy our time together because I know I can go to you for advice in all aspects of life!

Dr. Miller: Thank you for being the best chiropractor ever. Every time I see you, I feel like I leave with a new body. You always make me laugh and have so many stories to tell. You are always so kind and supportive of me and my family. Thank you for always caring for me and doing anything to help me stay healthy.

Mike Boyle: Thank you for taking time out of your busy schedule to work with me, for helping me during my training, and for teaching me how important it is to rest my body. You helped me realize I don't have to push myself to the point of exhaustion every single workout. Your exercises have been crucial to my recovery after Rio because you simplify the movements so that my body can learn to strengthen the weaker muscles, which ultimately leads to healing the bigger injuries.

Emily Hejlik: Thank you for being an incredible manager. Thank you for putting up with my persistent ways! I am so grateful to have someone who has become such a close friend to me. I know I can go to you for anything! You always make me laugh when we travel. I can't thank you enough for all the crazy opportunities I am not sure will ever sink in. I am so excited to see what we will do next together!

Octagon: Thank you to Peter, Emily, Drew, Ben, Harry, Janey, and the rest of the team. I remember at the end of 2011 when we sat for a meeting and you quickly realized I had a very clear vision for my future. I totally knew what I wanted! Thank you for helping me find such exciting new ventures and new journeys for me to embark on. I constantly have to pinch myself to remind myself that this isn't a dream. I can't thank you all enough for all your hard work. I can't wait to see where the next journey takes us!

2012 and 2016 teammates: I will always cherish the moments we had together. We are all so close because we have experienced the best and hardest moments together. Thank you, girls, for helping me through all the moments; no matter what life threw at me you always seemed to keep me laughing. I love you girls and will always have a special place in my heart for each one of you. I will always be cheering each and every one of you on. Can't wait to see where life takes you!

Little, Brown: Ever since I was young, I kept a journal because it was therapeutic, but also because deep down I always dreamed I would write a book one day. Thank you to everyone who has been involved in helping me share my story. Especially a big thank-you to Lisa, who has been on the phone with me and my mom, and edited every detail of this book. Lisa, you have helped so much, and I can't thank you enough for helping me make this book so special and so honest. Lisa, you have gone above and beyond. You are seriously the best!

Blythe: Thank you for helping me organize my ideas onto paper. You really helped give shape to my story. It was great to work with someone who knows gymnastics so well and has watched my career for years.

Magic, Coco, Gibson: Thanks for being the best dogs. Love you so much and we miss you, Coco!

Needham: I love my hometown! Thank you for all your support over the years, from the parade in 2012 to the rally in 2016, and all the encouraging signs posted around the city.

Boston: I am proud to be a part of such a great city. Boston Strong!

DISCUSSION GUIDE

1. Aly starts *Fierce* at the 2016 Olympics, then flashes back to her childhood. What connects those moments?

2. From a young age, Aly was convinced that she would make it to the Olympics. Why do you think Aly was able to make this dream a reality?

3. In chapter two, we see that Aly's mom decided not to tell Aly about pre-team tryouts, or when Aly was falling behind her teammates. How do you think knowing the truth would have affected Aly's confidence and enjoyment of the sport?

4. Why did Aly choose to change gyms from Exxcel to Brestyan's? How do you think that decision impacted her life?

5. Once Aly started training at Brestyan's, Mihai explained that the best athletes are completely dedicated and adhere to a strict regimen, with no vacations. What would you have done in Aly's shoes? Have you made tough choices to pursue a dream?

6. Why do you think Aly's classmates made fun of her muscles? How would you have reacted in that situation? What do you think you can do to combat bullying?

7. Aly's teammates became her lifelong friends. What are your impressions of them, and why do you think Aly grew so close with these young women?

8. On page 93, we see Aly criticized for falling, and how deeply those words stung. Have you ever been criticized by a parent or teacher? How did you react? Do you think another approach would have been more effective?

9. Aly saw many of her teammates get injured, and she dealt with injuries and excruciating physical pain herself. What do you think motivated her to keep going in the face of these risks?

10. In chapter ten, Aly begins to realize that her teammates see her as a leader. Why do you think her teammates started coming to Aly for advice and encouragement?

11. Throughout the book, Aly writes about fun and goofy moments shared with her teammates. How can humor and friendship help take the edge off stressful situations?

12. On page 123, Aly imagines being judged by her peers in the same way she's judged in competition. How does Aly combat those fears? When you feel like others are being critical of you, what strategies can you try to feel more confident?

13. How did Aly's description of the Olympics and the experience of competing differ from what you see on TV? Were you surprised by any of the behind-the-scenes details from the competition?

14. Gymnastics is one of the few sports where you compete individually and also as a team. How do you think that affects the dynamic between teammates?

15. Aly has won medals in individual and team events. If you could only win a medal as an individual *or* part of a team, which would you choose and why?

16. How did Aly defy expectations at the London Olympics? Have you ever been in a situation where people doubted you? How did you react?

17. After the Olympics, Aly and her teammates were thrust into the spotlight. What were the highs and lows of the post-Olympic whirlwind? How do you think it would feel to suddenly become so recognizable?

18. How is Aly's training for *Dancing with the Stars*, in chapter eighteen, different from her gymnastics training? How is it similar?

19. What made Aly decide to return to training and give the 2016 Olympics a shot? Do you think you would have made the same choice? Why or why not?

20. Why do you think Simone Biles and Aly clicked so instantly? Have you ever met someone you immediately knew you'd get along with?

21. What did Aly learn from her sports dietitian? What does that tell you about the importance of healthy eating and avoiding fad diets?

22. In chapter twenty-two, Aly reveals that she is a survivor of abuse. How is being a "survivor" different than being a "victim"?

23. What steps can adults take to keep young people, and athletes, safe?

24. Aly continued to train for the Olympics under tremendous physical and emotional pressure. What kept her going? How was she able to accomplish so much while facing so many obstacles?

25. *Fierce* introduces us to the family and friends who have been there to support Aly, and whom Aly is always there to support. Why is having a support system important? Whom do you trust most in your life?

26. Why do Aly's teammates call her "Mama Aly"? How does Aly grow as a leader throughout the book?

27. Even with her busy schedule, Aly has learned to take time to do things she loves and that make her happy. Write down three things that make you happy, and think about how you can incorporate them into your daily life.

28. Aly closes her book by reflecting on how lucky she is. Why does she feel this way? Can luckiness and hard work go hand in hand? How do you think Aly stays humble even while living in the spotlight?

29. Aly recommends taking time away from phone screens. In what ways—negative and positive—do social media and the internet impact your life? How can you make it a force for good?

30. What did this book teach you about the importance of self-care? What can you do to be kinder to yourself and others?

ALY RAISMAN

is a three-time gold medal–winning Olympic gymnast and the team captain of the 2012 and 2016 US Olympic gymnastics teams. Aly was the most decorated US gymnast at the 2012 Games and first American gymnast to win gold in the floor exercise. She went on to steal the hearts of millions during her silver medal performance in the all-around competition at the 2016 Games. She is the second most decorated American gymnast of all-time with six total Olympic medals. Aly was also a member of two gold-winning American teams in the World Artistic Gymnastic Championships.

A native of Massachusetts, Aly started gymnastics as an eighteen-month-old during Mommy and Me classes and fell in love with the sport after watching a VHS tape of the gold medal–winning 1996 US women's gymnastics team. Like many kids, Aly dreamed of going to the Olympics someday, but she had no idea at the time how hard it would be to achieve that dream.

The oldest of four children, and "Grandma" or "Mama" Aly to her Rio teammates, Aly is a leader on and off the floor. She is a devoted advocate for body positivity and empowering everyone to be comfortable and confident in their own skin.

Aly invites you to visit her online on Instagram (@alyraisman), Twitter (@Aly_Raisman), and Facebook (facebook.com/AlyRaisman).